W9-APR-294

PowerPoint® 2013

2013

ABSOLUTE
BEGINNER'S
GUIDE

Patrice-Anne Rutledge

800 East 96th Street,
Indianapolis, Indiana 46240

PowerPoint® 2013 Absolute Beginner's Guide

Copyright © 2013 by Pearson Education, Inc.

All rights reserved. No part of this book shall be reproduced, stored in a retrieval system, or transmitted by any means, electronic, mechanical, photocopying, recording, or otherwise, without written permission from the publisher. No patent liability is assumed with respect to the use of the information contained herein. Although every precaution has been taken in the preparation of this book, the publisher and author assume no responsibility for errors or omissions. Nor is any liability assumed for damages resulting from the use of the information contained herein.

ISBN-13: 978-0-7897-5063-1
ISBN-10: 0-7897-5063-5

Library of Congress Cataloging-in-Publication Data is on file.

Printed in the United States of America

First Printing: February 2013

Trademarks

All terms mentioned in this book that are known to be trademarks or service marks have been appropriately capitalized. Que Publishing cannot attest to the accuracy of this information. Use of a term in this book should not be regarded as affecting the validity of any trademark or service mark.

Warning and Disclaimer

Every effort has been made to make this book as complete and as accurate as possible, but no warranty or fitness is implied. The information provided is on an "as is" basis. The author and the publisher shall have neither liability nor responsibility to any person or entity with respect to any loss or damages arising from the information contained in this book.

Bulk Sales

Que Publishing offers excellent discounts on this book when ordered in quantity for bulk purchases or special sales. For more information, please contact

U.S. Corporate and Government Sales
1-800-382-3419
corpsales@pearsontechgroup.com

For sales outside of the U.S., please contact

International Sales
international@pearsoned.com

Editor-in-Chief
Greg Wiegand

Acquisitions Editor
Michelle Newcomb

Development Editor
Charlotte Kughen

Managing Editor
Sandra Schroeder

Project Editor
Mandie Frank

Copy Editor
Bart Reed

Indexer
Tim Wright

Proofreader
Jess DeGabriele

Technical Editors
Geetesh Bajaj
Vince Averello

Editorial Assistant
Cindy Teeters

Designer
Anne Jones

Compositor
TnT Design, Inc.

Contents at a Glance

Table of Contents

About the Author

Patrice-Anne Rutledge is a business technology author and consultant who specializes in teaching others to maximize the power of new technologies. Patrice has used—and has trained others to use—PowerPoint for many years, designing presentations for meetings, seminars, trade shows, and worldwide audiences. She is also the author of five previous books about PowerPoint for Pearson Education. She can be reached through her website at www.patricerutledge.com.

Dedication

To my family, with thanks for their ongoing support and encouragement.

Acknowledgments

Special thanks to Michelle Newcomb, Geetesh Bajaj, Charlotte Kughen, Vince Averello, Mandie Frank, and Bart Reed for their feedback, suggestions, and attention to detail.

We Want to Hear from You!

As the reader of this book, *you* are our most important critic and commentator. We value your opinion and want to know what we're doing right, what we could do better, what areas you'd like to see us publish in, and any other words of wisdom you're willing to pass our way.

We welcome your comments. You can email or write to let us know what you did or didn't like about this book—as well as what we can do to make our books better.

Please note that we cannot help you with technical problems related to the topic of this book.

When you write, please be sure to include this book's title and author as well as your name and email address. We will carefully review your comments and share them with the author and editors who worked on the book.

Email: feedback@quepublishing.com

Mail: Que Publishing
        ATTN: Reader Feedback
        800 East 96th Street
        Indianapolis, IN 46240 USA

Reader Services

Visit our website and register this book at quepublishing.com/register for convenient access to any updates, downloads, or errata that might be available for this book.

INTRODUCTION

Microsoft PowerPoint 2013 is part of Microsoft's latest suite of business software applications, Microsoft Office 2013. Using PowerPoint, you can quickly create a basic slide show or delve into sophisticated features to create a customized presentation. Because PowerPoint is part of the Microsoft Office suite of products, you'll find it to be very familiar and intuitive to use if you already work with any other Office application such as Word or Excel.

Microsoft PowerPoint 2013 Absolute Beginner's Guide is designed to get you up and running on PowerPoint as quickly as possible. This book starts with presentation basics and then introduces you to the many new features of PowerPoint 2013. These features can give your presentations the wow factor, enable you to collaborate with colleagues around the world, and extend the power of PowerPoint with third-party applications. Because knowing how to use the software is just part of creating a successful presentation, *Microsoft PowerPoint 2013 Absolute Beginner's Guide* also provides tips on presentation design, content, rehearsal, and delivery. For now, turn to Chapter 1, "Introducing PowerPoint 2013," to get started with this powerful presentation tool.

Who This Book Is For

This book is for you if...

- You want to become productive with the latest version of PowerPoint as quickly as possible and are short on time.

- You're new to PowerPoint and need to learn the basics in an easy-to-understand format.

- You want to move beyond a basic bulleted list presentation and make the most of PowerPoint's many design features.

How This Book Is Organized

PowerPoint 2013 Absolute Beginner's Guide is divided into five parts.

Part I, "PowerPoint 2013 Basics," introduces the fundamentals of using PowerPoint, such as navigating, using views, getting help, creating a basic presentation, and saving and opening files. If you're an experienced computer user, but are new to PowerPoint, these chapters will get you up and running quickly. If you've used PowerPoint extensively in the past, they can serve as a quick review and introduce you to the new, exciting features of PowerPoint 2013.

In Part II, "Editing and Formatting Presentations," you continue on to the most essential, and universally used, features of PowerPoint—formatting, organizing, and adding content to your slides. You find out how to work with text and tables, organize with Outline view, and customize and format your presentation.

Next, you can start exploring some of PowerPoint's more advanced capabilities. Part III, "Working with Pictures, Illustrations, and Media," introduces you to techniques you can use to make your presentations more creative. For example, you can add charts—including organizational charts—to provide additional information in a presentation. Or you can add photos, videos, audio, and animation for a complete multimedia effect. For a finishing touch, you can format, customize, and add a variety of special effects to these media objects.

Part IV, "Making Presentations," takes you to the logical next step—the actual delivery of a presentation. You discover how to easily set up a slide show, create timings and narrations, preview your work, present online, and even create portable PowerPoint presentations to display from another computer. Finally, you find out how to create a variety of printed material, such as notes and handouts, to go with your show.

Part V, "Maximizing the Power of PowerPoint," shows you how to customize PowerPoint, access PowerPoint on the Web and from mobile devices, as well as use Microsoft add-ins and third-party tools that enhance your PowerPoint experience.

Conventions Used in This Book

Microsoft PowerPoint 2013 Absolute Beginner's Guide uses a number of conventions to provide you with special information. These include the following elements.

 TIP   Tips offer suggestions for making things easier or provide alternative ways to perform a particular task.

 NOTE   Notes provide additional, more detailed information about a specific PowerPoint feature.

 CAUTION   Cautions warn you about potential problems that might occur and offer advice on how to avoid these problems.

1

INTRODUCING POWERPOINT 2013

PowerPoint is a powerful, easy-to-use presentation design application that is part of the Microsoft Office suite of products. You can use PowerPoint to create presentations for a variety of audiences and for a variety of purposes. A presentation communicates information, and a good presentation can truly convince, motivate, inspire, and educate its audience. PowerPoint offers the tools to both create a basic presentation and enhance and customize your presentation slides to meet your goals. In this chapter, you explore the many features and benefits of using PowerPoint, including the new features introduced in PowerPoint 2013.

Understanding What PowerPoint Can Do

One of PowerPoint's strengths is its flexibility. Using themes, templates, and other presentation building blocks, you can quickly create a basic presentation even if you have little or no design skills. If you are a designer, PowerPoint's advanced features and customization options give you complete creative control. With PowerPoint, you can do the following:

- Create a presentation using a color-coordinated theme or a template, or you can create a blank presentation. You can also import a presentation outline from another application such as Microsoft Word.

- Add text and tables to your presentation slides to convey basic information.

- Add visual content with charts, pictures, clip art, SmartArt graphics, and other shapes or objects.

- Bring multimedia into the picture using sound, video, and animation.

- Add interactivity with hyperlinks and action buttons.

- Create and print notes and handouts for you and your audience.

- Share and collaborate on presentations with others in your organization.

- Access PowerPoint using the PowerPoint web app or a mobile device.

- Deliver a presentation onscreen using a computer, broadcast it online, or create a presentation video that you can post on the Web.

Exploring New PowerPoint 2013 Features

PowerPoint 2013 includes many new features that users of previous versions will enjoy, including the following:

- **Start screen**—Get started with PowerPoint by opening a recent presentation or selecting a theme to create a new presentation.

- **Theme variants**—Apply a variant to a theme. This feature is useful if you like a particular theme, but your branding requires different colors or design elements.

- **Alignment guides**—Align objects and text automatically.

- **Merge shapes**—Combine two or more selected shapes by using a union, fragment, intersect, or other effect.

- **Enhanced Presenter view**—Enhance the Presenter view with slide zoom and a navigation grid.

- **Reply comments**—Enrich the collaborative process by adding replies to presentation comments.

- **Full screen mode**—Click the Full Screen Mode button in the upper-right corner of the PowerPoint screen to display Normal view in full screen.

- **Online video**—Search for and insert videos from YouTube or your SkyDrive account. Also search Bing for relevant videos or use a video embed code to insert online videos.

- **Online audio**—Search for and insert royalty-free audio clips from Office.com.

- **Online pictures**—Search for and insert pictures from Office.com, your SkyDrive account, and Flickr. Also search Bing for relevant pictures licensed under Creative Commons.

- **Enhanced Sharing**—Share your presentations online on SharePoint or SkyDrive by default.

- **MP4 video creation**—Create MP4 videos from your PowerPoint presentations.

- **Account window**—Update your user information and connect to other accounts.

- **Widescreen support**—Provide built-in widescreen (16:9) support. Optionally, switch to standard slide size (4:3).

Getting Started with PowerPoint

Before you start creating presentations, you should set up your Microsoft account and familiarize yourself with basic PowerPoint components such as the start screen, Ribbon, Backstage view, toolbars, task panes, and PowerPoint views.

Exploring the Start Screen

When you first open PowerPoint, the new start screen greets you (see Figure 1.1).

From here, you can perform any of the following tasks:

- Open a recent presentation.

- Open other presentations. (PowerPoint opens the Open window where you can search for and select another presentation on your computer or on SkyDrive.)

- Create a new presentation by clicking a theme.

- Search online for themes and templates.

- Switch to another account.

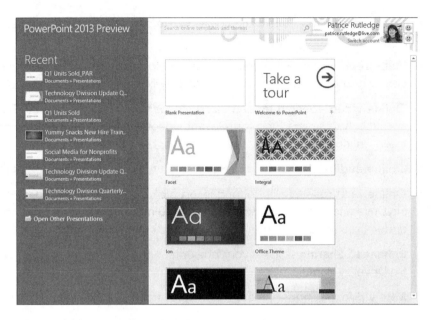

FIGURE 1.1

Getting started with PowerPoint is easy.

 NOTE If this is your first time using PowerPoint 2013, no recent presentations display.

Setting Up Your PowerPoint Account

The *Account window* is where you set up your Microsoft account and connected services, which are both important for taking full advantage of PowerPoint 2013. When you first open this new version of PowerPoint, be sure to take a few minutes to handle this important task.

To open the Account window, click the File tab and select Account (see Figure 1.2).

Here's what you can do in this window:

- **Specify the Microsoft account to use with PowerPoint**. PowerPoint 2013 connects you to the Web with your Microsoft account—an email and password you use to access all Microsoft services such as SkyDrive, Messenger, Hotmail, and Outlook.com. Formerly, this was called a Windows Live ID.

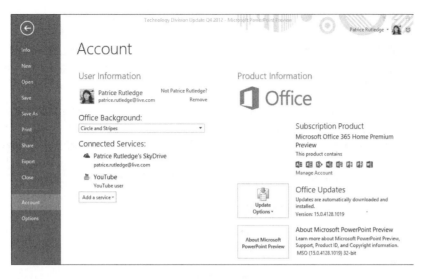

FIGURE 1.2

Set up your Microsoft account and connected services in the Account window.

 TIP   If you don't have a Microsoft account, you can sign up for one at https://signup.live.com.

- **Select the Office background you prefer**. The default background is Circle and Stripes, but you can also select from a variety of other options, including Clouds, Straws, or no background.

- **Specify the services you want to connect with**. The Account window displays the services you've already connected with (Office finds some services automatically based on your Microsoft account email address). Click the Add a Service button to add more services, including Flickr, YouTube, Office 365 SharePoint, SkyDrive, Facebook, LinkedIn, and Twitter.

- **Manage your Office account**. Click the Manage Account link to sign in to your Microsoft account.

- **Specify how you want to update Office**. By default, Office updates happen automatically, but you can disable this if you prefer.

Using the Ribbon Tabs

Although the *Ribbon* isn't a new PowerPoint feature (it was introduced in PowerPoint 2007), it does represent a new experience for anyone upgrading from version 2003 or earlier.

The *Ribbon*, which replaces the menu structure found in previous versions of PowerPoint, provides an easy way to access common commands and buttons using the least amount of space possible. The Ribbon is divided into tabs: Home, Insert, Design, Transitions, Animations, Slide Show, Review, and View. Each Ribbon tab includes groups and buttons of related features.

Figure 1.3 shows the Home tab.

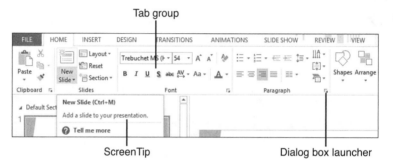

FIGURE 1.3

Ribbon tabs are where you find all your PowerPoint commands.

To quickly determine the function of tab buttons and commands, pause your mouse over each option to display a basic description in a ScreenTip. If a hotkey is available (such as pressing Ctrl+C for Copy), it also displays in the ScreenTip.

Common Ribbon features include the following:

- **Galleries**—Galleries offer a menu of visual choices that pertain to a selected button or command. For example, when you click the down arrow next to the Themes group on the Design tab, a visual gallery of theme images displays (see Figure 1.4).

- **Live Preview**—Most, but not all, PowerPoint galleries provide a live preview of each option before you actually apply it to your slide. As an example, the Themes gallery enables you to see how each theme appears on your presentation when you pause your mouse over it. That way, you can quickly try out several options before making any changes to your actual presentation.

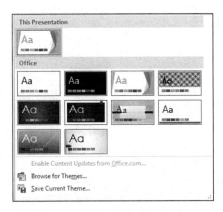

FIGURE 1.4

Galleries offer a quick overview of potential visual effects.

- **Dialog box launcher**—Clicking one of these small diagonal arrows in the lower-right corner of a group opens a dialog box of related options. For example, the Home tab includes dialog box launchers in the Clipboard, Font, Paragraph, and Drawing groups. The Clipboard dialog box launcher, interestingly enough, doesn't launch a dialog box, but rather a task pane. All the other launchers launch a traditional dialog box. See the section, "Using Task Panes," later in this chapter, for more information about task panes.

- **Contextual tabs**—Although the main tabs always display on the Ribbon, PowerPoint also includes several contextual Ribbon tabs that appear only when you're performing specific tasks. For example, when you select a chart on a PowerPoint slide, the Chart Tools tab displays, which includes two subtabs: Design and Format (see Figure 1.5). They remain as long as you work on your chart. When you click elsewhere on your slide, they disappear.

FIGURE 1.5

PowerPoint opens additional contextual tabs depending on the task you perform.

See Chapter 19, "Customizing PowerPoint," for more information about customizing the Ribbon tabs.

NOTE A few buttons include two sections: The upper portion performs a default action, and the lower portion (with a down arrow) opens a drop-down menu or gallery of options. For example, clicking the upper portion of the New Slide button on the Home tab automatically inserts a new slide using the default Title Slide layout. Clicking the lower portion opens a gallery of options.

Using Backstage View

PowerPoint's *Backstage view* enables you to perform PowerPoint's most common file-related tasks in one place. For example, Backstage view is the place where you create, open, save, share, and print presentations.

To access Backstage view, click the File tab. Figure 1.6 shows Backstage view.

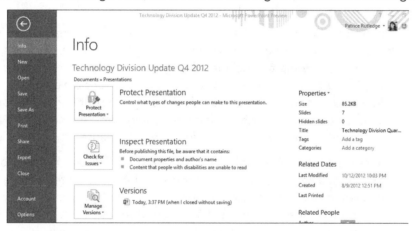

FIGURE 1.6

Perform all your file-related tasks in one place: Backstage view.

On the left side of the screen, you see a list of buttons and tabs. Clicking one of the tabs (Info, New, Open, Save, Save As, Print, Share, Export, or Close) displays related content on the right side of the screen. Future chapters, including Chapter 2, "Creating a Basic Presentation," cover all the features available in Backstage view.

Using Toolbars

Although PowerPoint 2013 uses far fewer toolbars than earlier versions of PowerPoint, you need to know about two types of toolbars: the Quick Access Toolbar and mini toolbar.

Using the Quick Access Toolbar

The *Quick Access Toolbar* is a small toolbar that displays in the upper-left corner of your screen (see Figure 1.7) and is available no matter which Ribbon tab you select.

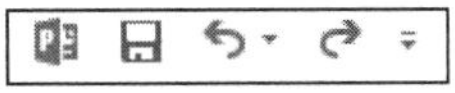

FIGURE 1.7

Common commands are at your fingertips no matter what you're doing in PowerPoint.

By default, this toolbar contains three buttons: Save, Undo, and Repeat, but you can customize it to include almost any PowerPoint command. See Chapter 19 for more information about customizing the buttons on this toolbar and moving it to another location.

Using Mini Toolbar

The mini toolbar is a small contextual toolbar that appears when you perform specific tasks. For example, when you select text, a mini toolbar appears with options related to text formatting (see Figure 1.8).

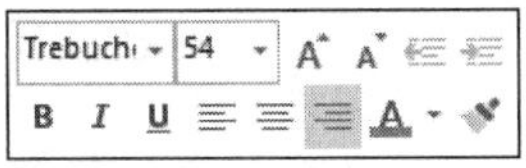

FIGURE 1.8

When you edit text, the mini toolbar appears with common text-editing commands.

Although you can perform the same tasks using the commands on the main Ribbon tab, using the mini toolbar makes these commands available in a more convenient location.

Using Task Panes

A *task pane* is a window inside PowerPoint that enables you to perform common PowerPoint tasks without covering your slide area. You can keep more than one pane open at time, but keep in mind that too many open task panes can clutter your screen. Many dialog boxes are now panes in PowerPoint 2013. Here's a sampling of PowerPoint's task panes:

- **Format Shape**—Apply a wide variety of formatting options, fills, and special effects to PowerPoint shapes. Right-click a shape and select Format Shape from the menu to open this pane, as shown in Figure 1.9.

- **Clipboard**—Collect and paste up to 24 different items. Click the dialog box launcher in the Clipboard group on the Home tab to open this task pane.

- **Animation pane**—Apply sophisticated animations to your slides or objects on your slides. Click the Animation Pane button on the Animations tab to open this pane.

FIGURE 1.9

The Format Shape pane is one of many time-saving panes in PowerPoint.

You can make the task pane wider or narrower if you prefer. To do so, pause the mouse pointer over the left edge of the pane until the pointer becomes a two-headed arrow. Click the mouse and drag the left edge to either the left or right until the task pane is the width you want.

To close a task pane, click the Close (x) button in the upper-right corner.

Understanding PowerPoint Views

PowerPoint includes several different *views*, which are arrangements of slides and tools on the screen that you use to work with and look at your presentation. Which view you use depends on what you're doing. The View tab, shown in Figure 1.10, includes numerous view buttons in the Presentation Views group and the Master Views group.

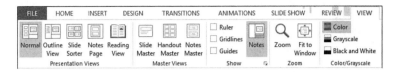

FIGURE 1.10

Select a view option on the View tab.

 TIP   You can also click one of the view buttons in the lower-right portion of the PowerPoint window to display the Normal, Slide Sorter, Reading, and Slide Show views.

PowerPoint's views include the following:

- **Normal view**—This is the default view, as shown in Figure 1.11. Normal view displays your current slide in the middle of the page, a Slides pane that displays thumbnails of all the slides in your presentation, and a Notes pane that includes space for you to write speaker's notes or notes to yourself about your presentation.

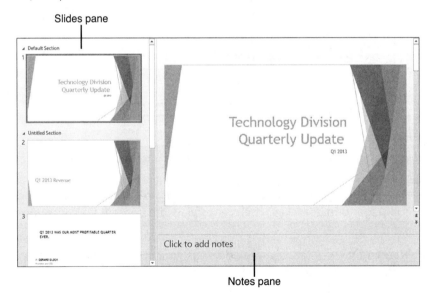

FIGURE 1.11

Normal view is PowerPoint's default viewing option.

 TIP   Use the scrollbar on the right side of the Slides pane to navigate between presentation slides. You can also use the Page Up and Page Down keys to move among slides.

NOTE PowerPoint's default view for a new presentation is Normal view. If you want to change this, click the File tab, select Options, and go to the Advanced tab in the Options dialog box, where you can specify your default view in the Display section.

- **Outline view**—This view displays an outline of your presentation, including the text in the title and text placeholders.

- **Slide Sorter view**—This view, as shown in Figure 1.12, displays miniature previews of all the slides in your presentation, making it easier for you to organize them. See Chapter 7, "Outlining Presentations," for more information.

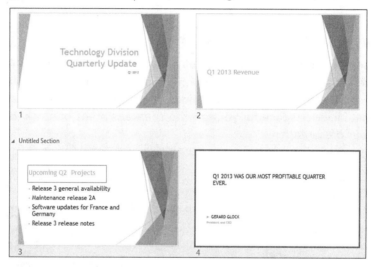

FIGURE 1.12

Seeing miniature versions of your slides can help you rearrange them.

- **Notes page view**—This view, shown in Figure 1.13, displays your notes in a full-page format, making it easier to view the content you enter on the Notes pane.

- **Reading view**—Reading view displays your slides as they would appear in a slide show, full screen, but with navigation buttons and menus in the lower-right corner.

- **Master views**—PowerPoint's three master views include the Slide Master, Handout Master, and Notes Master views. You use these views only when you customize your masters, including the placeholders, backgrounds, and colors that appear on your slide layouts. See Chapter 19 for more information.

FIGURE 1.13

Add and view notes, full screen.

Getting Help

Although PowerPoint is an intuitive program, there are times when you might need additional help in completing an in-progress task or figuring out how to do something. Fortunately, help is just a click away. Microsoft continuously updates its help system, so if you're connected to the Web while you search for PowerPoint help, you always get the latest help content.

To search for help on a specific topic, follow these steps:

1. Click the Help button in the upper-right corner of the screen (a small question mark) or in the upper-right corner of a dialog box to open the PowerPoint Help window (see Figure 1.14). Pressing F1 is another way to access help.

2. To search for help on a specific topic, enter keywords in the text box. For example, if you want to search for help on creating sections, you could enter **sections**.

3. Click the Search button to initiate the search. The Help window displays a list of search result articles.

4. Click the article title that best matches your search to view the help content.

The top of the PowerPoint Help window includes the following buttons:

- **Back**—Return to the previous help screen.
- **Forward**—Continue to the next help screen.
- **Home**—Return to the main PowerPoint Help screen.
- **Print**—Print the open help article.
- **Use Large Text**—Make the help text larger.

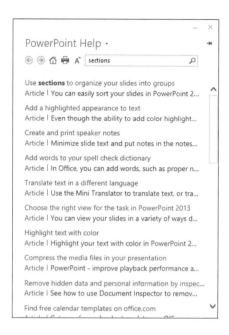

FIGURE 1.14

The PowerPoint Help window displays detailed help on your selected topic.

Office.com (http://office.microsoft.com) also offers searchable help, tutorials, and downloads.

THE ABSOLUTE MINIMUM

Here are the key points to remember from this chapter:

- PowerPoint is a powerful, easy-to-use presentation design application that is part of the Microsoft Office suite of products.

- PowerPoint's many new features include the start screen, theme color variants, alignment guides, reply comments, full screen mode, widescreen support, and the capability to insert online videos, pictures, and audio files.

- Before you start creating presentations, you should set up your account and familiarize yourself with basic PowerPoint components, such as the start screen, Ribbon, and Backstage view as well as the various toolbars, task panes, and views.

2

CREATING A BASIC PRESENTATION

After you learn—or refresh your memory—about how to navigate PowerPoint, you can create a basic presentation. This chapter gets you up and running on presentation basics so that you can quickly move forward to more advanced and sophisticated PowerPoint techniques.

Understanding PowerPoint Presentations

Before you start creating your first PowerPoint presentation, you need to understand **themes**, **templates,** and **slide layouts,** which are the presentation building blocks.

A theme and a template are not too different. Whereas a theme has built-in styles for fonts, colors, effects, backgrounds, and layouts, a template may have a collection of sample slides that you can use to create your slide content rather than starting from scratch. All themes and templates contain one or more Slide Master, which you can access within the Slide Master view. Finally, each Slide Master has a set of child layouts that cater to different slide uses, such as a title slide, a title and content slide, a picture slide, and so on. The individual location of different placeholders on these slides is controlled by Slide Layouts. In the next few paragraphs, you discover more about how these individual building blocks work together.

Understanding Themes

A *theme* is a standalone file with colors, fonts, and effects to use in a single presentation. Other Microsoft Office 2013 applications, such as Word and Excel, also support themes. This enables you to create a consistent look and feel between your Office documents. A theme also stores information about backgrounds and layouts other than colors, fonts, and effects.

Each theme contains the following:

- **Fonts**—A theme contains two fonts: one for headings and one for body text.

- **Colors**—PowerPoint color schemes include a set of coordinated colors for text, backgrounds, accents, and hyperlinks. Each theme provides multiple color *variants* that give you more options for customizing a theme you like with the colors you require.

- **Effects**—Office themes apply graphic effects to tables, text, charts, diagrams, shapes, and pictures.

Every presentation has a theme—even a blank presentation, which uses the Office theme. You can apply a theme when you first create your presentation or apply one at any time to an existing presentation. See Chapter 3, "Customizing Themes and Backgrounds," for more information about themes.

Understanding Templates

A *template* is a starter document that you apply when you create a new presentation. Templates can include slide layouts; theme colors, fonts, and effects; background styles; and content for a specific type of presentation, such as for a project status meeting or training seminar.

Understanding Slide Layouts

In addition to themes and templates, the other important design feature you need to consider is the **slide layout**. A *slide layout* helps you add specific types of content to your slides, such as text, tables, charts, and pictures.

By default, PowerPoint offers multiple choices of layout (see Figure 2.1), but you can create your own layouts as well. If the predefined layouts don't suit your needs, you can modify a blank slide or modify one of the existing layouts by adding, moving, or deleting objects.

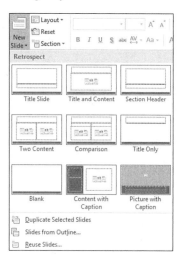

FIGURE 2.1

Choose an existing layout or start from scratch.

The default layouts are as follows:

- **Title Slide**—Include placeholders for a title and subtitle.

- **Title and Content**—Include placeholders for a title and one content item, such as a table, chart, SmartArt graphic, picture, or media file.

- **Section Header**—Introduce a new presentation section. See the section, "Adding Sections to Your Presentation," later in this chapter for more information.

- **Two Content**—Include placeholders for a title and two content items.

- **Comparison**—Include placeholders for a title and two content items, each with a text heading.

- **Title Only**—Include a placeholder for a title only.

- **Blank**—Include a completely blank slide.

- **Content with Caption**—Include placeholders for a brief title, text, and content item.

- **Picture with Caption**—Include placeholders for a large picture, title, and text.

Depending on the theme you apply, some or all of the following additional slide layouts might also be available (for example, the Facets and Slice themes both include additional slide layouts):

- Panoramic Picture with Caption

- Title and Caption

- Quote with Caption

- Name Card

- Quote Name Card

- True or False

- 3 Column

- 3 Picture Column

 NOTE If you enabled support for Far East Asian languages, additional layout options are available.

The Title and Content, Two Content, Comparison, and Content with Caption layouts include a content palette as a placeholder. This content palette includes six buttons, as shown in Figure 2.2:

- Insert Table

- Insert Chart

- Insert a SmartArt Graphic

- Pictures

- Online Pictures

- Insert Video

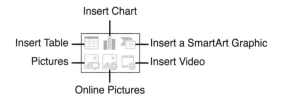

FIGURE 2.2

The content palette makes it easy to add tables, charts, pictures, and more.

 NOTE See Chapter 4, "Working with Text," for more information about inserting text in placeholders.

On any slide that contains the content palette, you can also enter a bullet list using the starter bullet that displays in the upper-left corner of the slide area. If you click one of the buttons on the palette, this bullet disappears. Future chapters cover each of these options in more detail.

Creating a Presentation

You can create a presentation in several different ways, depending on the amount of content and design assistance you need. You can create the following:

- **Presentation using a theme**—Creating a new presentation using a PowerPoint theme provides an initial design with coordinated colors, fonts, and effects.

- **Presentation using a template**—Use one of PowerPoint's existing templates, a template you create yourself, or a template from Office.com's collection of templates.

- **Blank presentation**—A blank presentation contains black text on a white background with no content suggestions. Create a blank presentation only when you are experienced with PowerPoint and want to create a custom design. Even if you want to create a custom presentation, it often saves you time to start with a similar existing design and then customize it.

 TIP If you're going to create a complex presentation, it's often beneficial to create a storyboard before actually working in PowerPoint. A *storyboard* is a visual roadmap for your presentation. Begin by mapping out your complete presentation flow. By determining up front the order of your content and the best way to communicate your message (text, tables, charts, audio, video, or pictures), you can design your presentation faster and more effectively.

Creating a Presentation with a Theme

Using a coordinated PowerPoint theme as a starting point is a good way to create a presentation.

To create a presentation with a theme, follow these steps:

1. Click the File tab and then click New to open the New window in Backstage view (see Figure 2.3).

FIGURE 2.3

Create a coordinated design using a theme.

NOTE Step 1 assumes you already have PowerPoint open and the Ribbon is available. If you're just opening PowerPoint, you don't need to click the File tab to view the theme thumbnails.

2. Review the theme thumbnails that display on the New window and select the theme you want to apply to your presentation. PowerPoint opens a dialog box with more options (see Figure 2.4).

View sample slide layouts for this theme   Click to apply a variant

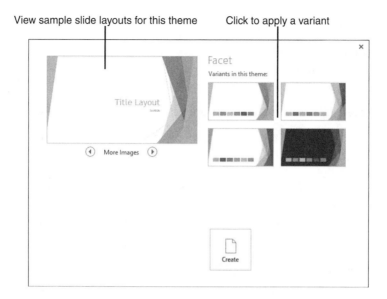

FIGURE 2.4

Customize your selected theme with a variant.

3. Select a color variant to apply to your theme.

4. Click the Create button. PowerPoint opens a new presentation with a Title Slide layout. Figure 2.5 shows a sample new presentation.

FIGURE 2.5

Get started with your new presentation by adding slides and content.

Creating a Presentation from an Online Template or Theme

In addition to the default themes that come with PowerPoint, you can search an online collection of thousands of templates and themes, one of which is sure to be a great match for your presentation.

To create a presentation from an online template or theme, follow these steps:

1. Click the File tab and then click New to open the New window in Backstage view (refer to Figure 2.3).

 NOTE Step 1 assumes you already have PowerPoint open and the Ribbon is available. If you're just opening PowerPoint, you don't need to click the File tab to view the Search Online Templates and Themes box.

2. In the Search Online Templates and Themes box, enter keywords related to the type of template or theme you're looking for, and then click the Search button. PowerPoint offers a few suggestions below the search box that you can click. PowerPoint displays options that match your search criteria (see Figure 2.6).

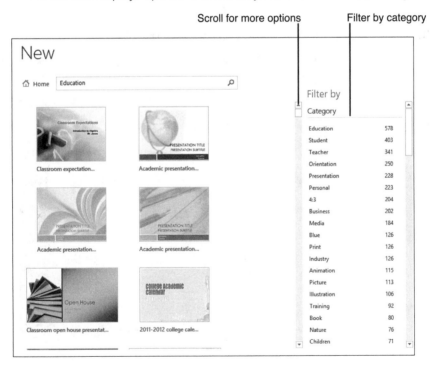

FIGURE 2.6

PowerPoint offers a vast collection of online templates and themes from which to choose.

TIP Optionally, you can further filter your results by selecting one of the categories that display on the right side of the window.

3. Select the template or theme that you want to apply to your presentation. PowerPoint opens a dialog box with more information about your choice (see Figure 2.7).

FIGURE 2.7

Learn more about your selected template.

4. Click the Create button. PowerPoint opens a new presentation based on your selected template or theme.

Creating a Presentation from Scratch

If you have your own vision for your presentation and want to start with a blank slate, you can create a presentation from scratch.

To create a blank presentation, follow these steps:

1. Click the File tab, and then click New to open the New window (refer to Figure 2.3).

2. Click the Blank Presentation thumbnail to open a blank slide in Title Slide layout. Figure 2.8 illustrates a sample blank presentation.

FIGURE 2.8

To have complete design control, start with a blank presentation.

3. From here, you can adjust the design and formatting to suit your needs.

Adding Slides to Your Presentation

To add a new slide to an open presentation, on the Home tab, click the lower portion of the New Slide button. From here, you can take one of the following actions:

- Select a layout from the gallery that appears (refer to Figure 2.2). Refer to section, "Understanding Slide Layouts," earlier in this chapter, for more information about layout options.

- Select Duplicate Selected Slides to insert duplicates of the slides selected on the Slides tab.

- Select Slides from Outline to create slides from an outline you created in another application, such as Microsoft Word. See Chapter 7, "Outlining Presentations," for more information.

- Select Reuse Slides to open the Reuse Slides pane, as shown in Figure 2.9. You can reuse slides from another PowerPoint presentation or from a slide library. See Chapter 17, "Sharing Presentations," for more information about slide libraries.

FIGURE 2.9

Reuse slides from a presentation on your computer or in a slide library.

TIP Alternatively, click the top portion of the New Slide button to add a slide using the layout of the active slide automatically without opening the gallery. Pressing Ctrl+M also performs this same task.

Adding Sections to Your Presentation

PowerPoint enables you to add sections to your presentations. These are particularly useful for large presentations where it's easy to get lost in a sea of slides. You can use sections to define presentation topics or distinguish between speakers, for example.

You can also use the Section Header slide layout to further define presentation sections. Refer to section, "Understanding Slide Layouts," earlier in this chapter, for more information.

To add a section to your presentation, follow these steps:

1. In either Normal view or Slide Sorter view, select the slide that starts the section you want to insert.

2. On the Home tab, click the Section button and then select Add Section from the menu (see Figure 2.10). PowerPoint inserts an untitled section.

TIP Alternatively, right-click between two slides on the Slides pane where you want to insert a section and from the menu that displays click Add Section.

Section button

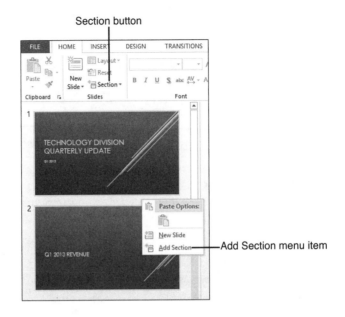

—Add Section menu item

FIGURE 2.10

Add sections to better manage large presentations.

3. Select the untitled section, click the Section button again, and select Rename Section (see Figure 2.11). The Rename Section dialog box displays. You can also right-click the section to open this dialog box.

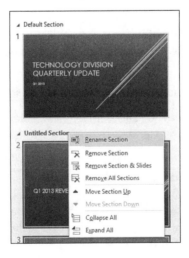

FIGURE 2.11

Select Rename Section to give each section a meaningful name.

4. Enter a Section Name setting and then click the Rename button.

You can follow this procedure to enter as many sections as you need in your presentation.

Collapsing and Expanding Sections

If you have a lot of slides and sections, you might want to collapse them for easier viewing on the Slides tab. To do so, click the Section button on the Home tab, and then select Collapse All from the menu. You can also collapse sections by right-clicking a section and selecting Collapse All from the menu. Expand collapsed sections by selecting Expand All from these same menus.

Removing Sections

To remove a section, select it, click the Section button on the Home tab, and select Remove Section from the menu. To remove all sections, select Remove All Sections. You can also remove a section by right-clicking it and selecting Remove Section from the menu that appears.

When you remove a section, PowerPoint deletes the section marker but not the slides in that section. If you want to remove a section and its slides, right-click the section and select Remove Sections & Slides from the menu.

 CAUTION   PowerPoint doesn't ask for confirmation when you delete sections, so think carefully before proceeding.

Managing Presentations

Saving, opening, renaming, closing, and deleting presentations are common PowerPoint tasks. This section shows you how to handle these basic functions quickly and easily.

Exploring PowerPoint File Formats

PowerPoint enables you to save your presentation in a variety of file formats. Table 2.1 lists the available options.

TABLE 2.1 PowerPoint File Types

File Type	Extension	Result
PowerPoint Presentation	PPTX	Save as a PowerPoint presentation (an XML-enabled format).
PowerPoint Macro-Enabled Presentation	PPTM	Save as a presentation with macros enabled.
PowerPoint 97–2003 Presentation	PPT	Save as a presentation you can open in PowerPoint 97 to 2003.
PDF	PDF	Save as a PDF (Portable Document Format) file.
XPS Document	XPS	Save as an XPS (XML Paper Specification) file.
PowerPoint Template	POTX	Save as a template that you can use as a starter for future presentations.
PowerPoint Macro-Enabled Template	POTM	Save as a template with macros enabled.
PowerPoint 97–2003 Template	POT	Save as a template you can open in PowerPoint 97 to 2003.
Office Theme	THMX	Save as a theme that includes colors, fonts, and effects.
PowerPoint Show	PPSX	Save as a slide show.
PowerPoint Macro-Enabled Show	PPSM	Save as a slide show with macros enabled. .
PowerPoint 97–2003 Show	PPS	Save as a slide show you can view in PowerPoint 97 to 2003.
PowerPoint Add-In	PPAM	Save as an add-in that includes custom commands or VBA code.
PowerPoint 97–2003 Add-In	PPA	Save as an add-in that you can open in PowerPoint 97 to 2003.
PowerPoint XML Presentation	XML	Save in XML format for use in an XML information storage system.
MPEG-4 Video	MP4	Save as an MPEG-4 video.
Windows Media Video	WMV	Save as a video in Windows Media Video format.
GIF Graphics Interchange Format	GIF	Save as a graphic for use on the Web.
JPEG File Interchange Format	JPG	Save as a graphic for use on the Web.
PNG Portable Network Graphics Format	PNG	Save as a graphic for use on the Web.

File Type	Extension	Result
TIFF Tag Image File Format	TIF	Save as a TIFF graphic image. .
Device Independent Bitmap	BMP	Save as a bitmap graphic image.
Windows Metafile	WMF	Save as a 16-bit vector graphic image.
Enhanced Windows Metafile	EMF	Save as a 32-bit vector graphic image.
Outline/RTF	RTF	Save as an outline in Rich Text Format, which you can open in Microsoft Word.
PowerPoint Picture Presentation	PPTX	Save as a PowerPoint presentation in which each slide is converted to a picture.
Strict Open XML Presentation	XML	Save in Strict Open XML format.
OpenDocument Presentation	ODP	Save in a format that you can open using applications that support ODP files, such as Google Docs or OpenOffice. .

 CAUTION Be aware that if you save a PowerPoint 2013 presentation in an older format, you could lose some presentation features if they aren't compatible with the older version.

Saving a Presentation to Your Computer

To save an open PowerPoint presentation to your computer, follow these steps:

1. On the Quick Access Toolbar, click the Save button. Alternatively, press Ctrl+S. If this is the first time you've saved the presentation, the Save As window opens, as shown in Figure 2.12.

2. On the left side of the window, select Computer.

3. Click the Browse button to open the Save As dialog box (see Figure 2.13).

 TIP Optionally, you can save time by selecting one of the options in the Recent Folders list. If you often save your presentations to the same folder, pause your mouse over that folder name and click the Pin This Item to the List icon to ensure that this folder is always at the top of the list for easy convenience.

4. Select the folder in which to save your presentation. PowerPoint automatically selects your default folder, but you can change this if you want. You can customize the default folder on the Save tab in the PowerPoint Options dialog box (choose Tools, Save Options from the Save As dialog box).

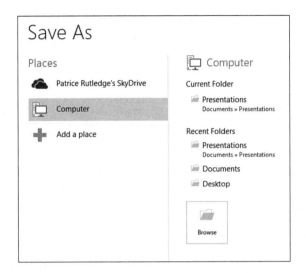

FIGURE 2.12

Choose between several save options in the Save As window.

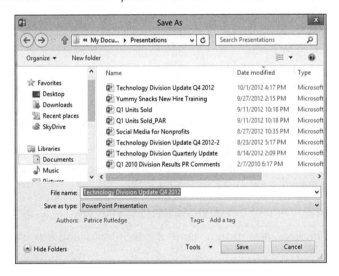

FIGURE 2.13

Specify save parameters in this dialog box.

TIP To set and modify save options such as default formats, file locations, embedded fonts, and AutoRecovery, choose Tools, Save Options from the Save As dialog box.

5. In the File Name field, type a name for the presentation. The drop-down list in the File Name field includes previously saved presentations. Even if you choose one of these filenames, PowerPoint warns you so that you don't accidentally overwrite an existing presentation.

6. Choose the file format from the Save as Type drop-down list. Refer to Table 2.1 for a list of available file types. If you want to save as a PDF or XPS document, see "Saving as a PDF or XPS Document," later in this section.

7. Click the Save button to save the file.

TIP After you save a presentation for the first time, press Ctrl+S or click the Save button to save new changes without opening the Save As dialog box. If you want to save an existing presentation to a new location or change its name, click the File tab and select Save As.

You can also save your presentation to SkyDrive (Microsoft's online storage and file-sharing solution) from the Save As window. On the left side of the window, select SkyDrive, click the Browse button, and select a folder to store your presentation.

Saving as a PDF or XPS Document

PowerPoint enables you to save directly as a PDF or XPS document without requiring an add-in.

TIP Be sure to save your presentation in PowerPoint before you save as a PDF or XPS documents.

To save as a PDF or XPS, follow these steps:

1. Click the File tab, and then click Export to open the Export window (see Figure 2.14).

2. On the left side of the window, select Create PDF/XPS Document.

3. Click the Create PDF/XPS button to open the Publish as PDF or XPS dialog box (see Figure 2.15).

4. Select the folder in which to save your document.

5. In the File Name field, type a name for the presentation.

6. In the Save as Type drop-down list, select either PDF or XPS Document.

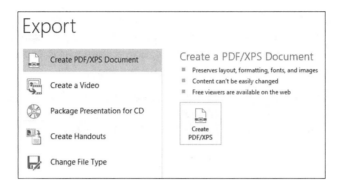

FIGURE 2.14

The Export window lets you export your presentation to different formats.

FIGURE 2.15

Save your presentation as a PDF or XPS document in this dialog box.

7. Select the Open File After Publishing check box if you want to open your presentation after saving. This option is available only for XPS documents.

8. If you want to create a document that's suitable for both online viewing and printing, select the Standard option button. If you just want people to view it online, select the Minimum Size option button.

9. Click the Options button for more options. Figure 2.16 shows the Options dialog box that opens.

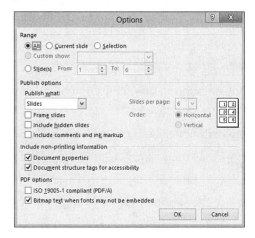

FIGURE 2.16

PowerPoint offers many options for customizing PDF or XPS documents.

10. Select any of the advanced options you want to use in this dialog box. Options include the following:

- **Range**—Choose whether to include all slides, the current slide only, the slides you've selected (on the Slides tab, for example), a specific range of slides, or the slides in a custom show.

- **Publish What**—Publish slides, handouts, notes pages, or the Outline view. If you select handouts, you can specify how many slides to include on each page (up to nine) and the orientation (horizontal or vertical). See Chapter 16, "Creating and Printing Presentation Materials," for more information about these options.

- **Frame Slides**—Place a border around the slides.

- **Include Hidden Slides**—Include slides you chose to hide on the Slide Show tab.

- **Include Comments and Ink Markup**—Print comment pages and any ink markups you made onscreen with your presentation. This option is available only if your presentation contains comments or ink markups.

 NOTE   You can also include nonprinting information such as document properties, make your document ISO-compliant, or convert text to bitmaps if PowerPoint can't embed the applied fonts.

11. Click the OK button to return to the Save As dialog box.

12. Click the Publish button to publish your document based on your specifications.

Changing to Another File Type

If you save your presentation in one file format and want to convert it to another, you can easily do so.

To change your presentation's file type, follow these steps:

1. Click the File tab, and then click Export to open the Export window (refer to Figure 2.14).

2. On the left side of the window, select Change File Type.

3. On the right side of the window, select one of the following file types (see Figure 2.17). Refer to section, " Saving a Presentation to Your Computer," earlier in this chapter, for more information about each of these file types:

- Presentation
- PowerPoint 97–2003 Presentation
- OpenDocument Presentation
- Template
- PowerPoint Show
- PowerPoint Picture Presentation
- PNG Portable Network Graphics
- JPEG File Interchange Format
- Save as Another File Type

4. Scroll down to the bottom of the list and click the Save As button to open the Save As dialog box (refer to Figure 2.13).

5. Enter a new filename for your presentation, if desired.

6. Click the Save button. PowerPoint saves your presentation in the format you specified.

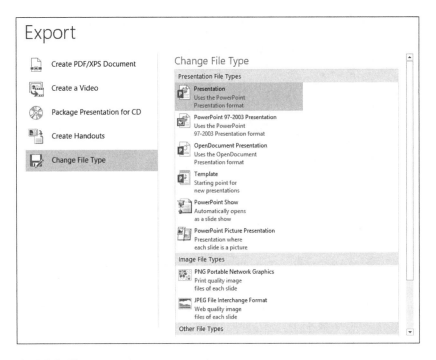

FIGURE 2.17

Quickly change a PowerPoint file type.

Opening a Presentation

PowerPoint offers a variety of ways to open a presentation, including the following:

- In the window that displays when you first open PowerPoint, select one of the presentations in the Recent list or click Open Other Presentations to open the Open dialog box (see Figure 2.18).

- Press Ctrl+O to open the Open dialog box.

- Click the File tab, click Open, and choose one of the following options for finding the file you want: Recent Presentations, SkyDrive, or Computer (click the Browse button on the right side of the window to open the Open dialog box).

- Double-click the name of a PowerPoint presentation in Windows Explorer.

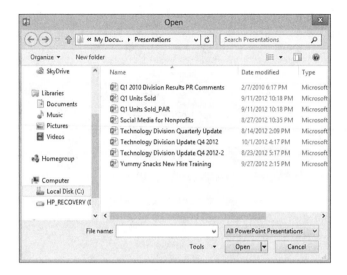

FIGURE 2.18

The Open dialog box includes many additional features, including file management and search capabilities.

If you choose a method that displays the Open dialog box, select the file you want and then click the Open button.

Although opening a presentation directly is the most common action you'll take in the Open dialog box, clicking the down arrow to the right of the Open button provides several other options:

- **Open Read-Only**—Open the file as read-only. For example, if you've applied a password to the presentation, others can open it only as read-only. To change and save this file, click the File tab, choose Save As from the menu, and save with another name.

- **Open as Copy**—Open the presentation as a copy of the original. You might do this if you want to keep your original and create another presentation based on it.

- **Open in Browser**—Open a presentation in your default browser that was saved in a web page format (.HTM, .HTML, .HTX, or .ASP) from PowerPoint 2007 or earlier.

- **Open in Protected View**—Open the file with restrictions to protect damage to your computer. Protected view is advisable for opening potentially dangerous files, such as those you download from an unknown source on the Internet.

- **Open and Repair**—Open and attempt to repair a corrupted presentation.

TIP   If you need help finding the right file, you can enter related keywords in the Search Presentations box and click the Search button. You can also click the Show the Preview Pane button to preview presentations before opening them or click the down arrow to the right of the Change Your View button to specify how you want to view files in the Open dialog box: Extra Large Icons, Large Icons, Medium Icons, Small Icons, List, Details, Tiles, or Content.

Renaming a Presentation

To rename a PowerPoint presentation, select it in the Open dialog box and perform one of the following actions:

- Press F2.

- Right-click and select Rename from the shortcut menu.

- Click the Organize button and select Rename from the shortcut menu.

- Click the filename, wait a second, and then click it again.

PowerPoint converts the filename to an edit box in which you can overwrite the existing name.

Closing a Presentation

At times, you might want to close a presentation without exiting PowerPoint. This is particularly useful if you have many files open and want to save memory.

To close an open presentation, you can do one of the following:

- Click the File tab and select Close from the menu. If you haven't saved your file, PowerPoint prompts you to do so. If your presentation has been saved, PowerPoint closes it immediately.

- Click the Close (x) button in the upper-right corner of the screen to close an open presentation. Note, however, that if this is the only presentation you have open, this action also closes PowerPoint itself.

- Use the shortcut key, Ctrl+W.

Deleting a Presentation

If you no longer need a PowerPoint presentation, you can delete it. To delete a PowerPoint presentation you no longer want, select it in the Open dialog box and press the Delete key on your keyboard. A warning dialog box appears, verifying that you want to delete the file and send it to the Recycle Bin. Click Yes to confirm the deletion.

 TIP Another option is to click the Organize button and select Delete from the shortcut menu. You can also delete a PowerPoint presentation in Windows Explorer. To do so, click the presentation file in Explorer and press the Delete key.

THE ABSOLUTE MINIMUM

Here are the key points to remember from this chapter:

- Before you start creating your first PowerPoint presentation, you need to understand themes, templates, and slide layouts, which are the presentation building blocks.

- You can create a presentation using a theme or template, or create your own design from scratch.

- Adding slides to you presentation is easy with PowerPoint's collection of ready-made slide layouts.

- Using sections is a great way to break up large presentations where it's easy to get lost in a sea of slides.

- PowerPoint offers numerous—and easy—options for handling common tasks such as saving, opening, renaming, closing, and deleting presentations.

CUSTOMIZING THEMES AND BACKGROUNDS

PowerPoint offers numerous tools to help you create presentations quickly and easily. There are times, however, when you might not like your initial choices or need to go beyond existing designs to create a truly unique presentation. Fortunately, PowerPoint makes it easy to switch to a new theme, apply multiple themes, change your theme's color variant, or format a presentation background.

Applying a New Theme to Your Presentation

When you create a presentation, PowerPoint prompts you to choose a theme, which is a coordinated set of colors, fonts, and effects. However, you can easily change the theme originally applied to your presentation in a matter of seconds.

 NOTE   See Chapter 2, "Creating a Basic Presentation," for a reminder about the components of a theme.

To apply a new theme to your existing presentation, follow these steps:

1. Click the Design tab to view the Themes group (see Figure 3.1), which displays several potential themes. Your presentation's current theme displays to the far left.

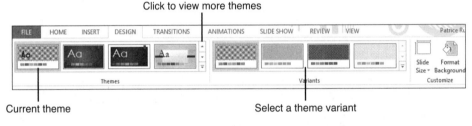

FIGURE 3.1

Select a new theme in the Themes group.

2. If none of these themes suits your needs, click the down arrow on the right side of the Themes box to display a gallery of additional themes, as shown in Figure 3.2.

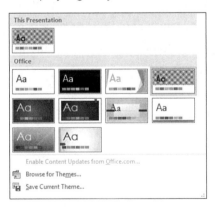

FIGURE 3.2

Choose a theme that best matches your presentation.

3. Pause your mouse over each theme to preview it in your active slide.

4. Select the theme you want to use.

5. Optionally, select a color variant in the Variants group on the Design tab. PowerPoint applies this new theme and its selected variant to your presentation.

Applying Multiple Themes to a Single Presentation

PowerPoint enables you to use more than one theme in a presentation. Multiple themes might be appropriate if you want to use one theme for your title slide and another for the rest of your presentation. Or if your presentation is divided into several distinct sections, you might want to use a separate theme for each. Figure 3.3 shows an example of a presentation with multiple themes.

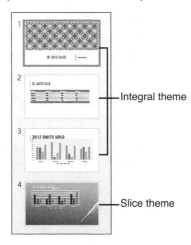

FIGURE 3.3

Use different themes to distinguish parts of a presentation.

 CAUTION   Although it's easy to apply multiple themes, you should carefully consider whether it's a good idea. Too many contrasting styles and designs can make your presentation confusing and difficult to follow. Even if you decide to apply multiple themes, your best bet is to keep them reasonably similar or use a consistent color scheme.

To apply a different theme to a group of slides, select the slides whose theme you want to change (in Normal view or Slide Sorter view). On the Design tab, select the new theme in the Themes group. PowerPoint applies the new theme only to the selected slides. The unselected slides retain the original theme.

 CAUTION If you select only a single slide, PowerPoint applies the theme to the entire presentation. To apply a theme to a single slide, right-click the theme in the Themes group and then select Apply to Selected Slides from the menu.

 TIP You can also apply a new variant to selected slides by right-clicking a variant in the Variants group and selecting Apply to Selected Slides from the menu.

Applying a New Theme Variant

When you created your presentation, PowerPoint prompted you to select a new variant without changing your presentation's theme. To do so, select a new variant in the Variants group on the Design tab (refer to Figure 3.1).

Formatting Presentation Backgrounds

You can further customize your presentation by formatting its background. In addition to applying specific background colors, you can also apply gradient or texture fills, hide background graphics, apply artistic effects, and modify pictures.

Formatting Your Presentation's Background

Formatting a background is an easy way to change the appearance of your presentation and its theme.

To format a background, follow these steps:

1. On the Design tab, click the Format Background button. The Format Background pane opens (see Figure 3.4).

2. Click one of the following buttons to display related content on the pane:

   - **Fill**—Format fills or hide background graphics.

   - **Effects**—Apply artistic effects such as Paintbrush and Watercolor Sponge. Note that this option isn't available with all themes.

   - **Picture**—Apply picture corrections and color.

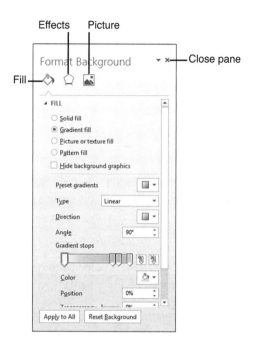

FIGURE 3.4

The Format Background pane enables you to make many changes in one place.

3. After specifying your background preferences in this pane, click the Apply to All button. The new background displays on your presentation slides, overriding the theme's background.

The tools available on the Format Background pane are very similar to those found on the Format Shape pane. See Chapter 10, "Working with Shapes," for more information about this pane.

 TIP Another option is to apply a background style. On the Design tab, click the down arrow in the lower-right corner of the Variants group and select Background Styles. A gallery opens with several background style options to choose from.

Omitting Background Graphics

If you want to omit the background graphics included with the template you applied to your presentation, click the Fill button on the Format Background pane and then select the Hide Background Graphics check box. For example, selecting this check box on a presentation whose theme includes pictures or shapes removes these objects but retains the original colors.

Resetting a Background

If you customize your background and decide you prefer the original, you can easily reset it. To reset the background to the theme default, click the Format Background button on the Design tab and click the Reset Background button on the Format Background pane.

Customizing Themes

If PowerPoint's built-in themes don't suit your needs, you can customize the fonts, colors, and effects in a theme and create your own theme.

Customizing Theme Color Schemes

Every PowerPoint theme includes a color scheme, a set of 12 coordinated colors used in the following parts of your presentation:

- Text and background (two light and two dark)
- Accents (six colors for graphs, charts, and other objects)
- Hyperlinks
- Followed hyperlinks

Applying a New Slide Color Scheme

If you don't like the colors in a particular theme, you can apply another color scheme.

To apply a new scheme, follow these steps:

1. On the Design tab, click the down arrow in the lower-right corner of the Variants group and select Colors. A gallery of color schemes displays, as shown in Figure 3.5.

2. Pause your mouse over each scheme to preview it on your presentation.

3. Click the scheme you prefer to apply it to your presentation.

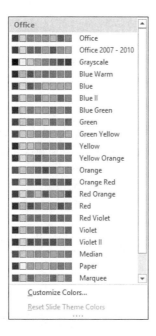

FIGURE 3.5

You can modify your presentation's color scheme.

Applying Multiple Color Schemes to a Single Presentation

PowerPoint also enables you to apply multiple color schemes within a single presentation. As with applying multiple themes, be sure that you have a good reason to do this before applying many different colors to your presentation. To apply multiple color schemes to your presentation, follow these steps:

1. Select the slides to which you want to apply a separate color scheme. You can do this on the Slides panes on the left side of your screen or in Slide Sorter view.

2. On the Design tab, click the down arrow in the lower-right corner of the Variants group and select Colors. The theme colors gallery displays.

3. In the gallery, right-click the new color scheme, and choose Apply to Selected Slides. PowerPoint applies the color scheme to only the selected slides. The unselected slides retain the original color scheme.

To return to a single color scheme, select that scheme from the gallery.

CAUTION Although the capability to apply multiple color schemes to your presentation adds flexibility and creativity, be sure not to overdo it. Consider carefully before applying more than one color scheme to verify that your presentation is still consistent and readable.

Creating a Custom Color Scheme

Occasionally, you might want to customize the individual colors in a color scheme. For example, you might like a particular scheme but want to modify one of the text/background colors. Or you might want to use colors that match your company's logo or other design elements.

To create a custom color scheme, follow these steps:

1. On the Design tab, click the down arrow in the lower-right corner of the Variants group and select Colors to open the colors gallery.

2. In the gallery, select Customize Colors to open the Create New Theme Colors dialog box (see Figure 3.6).

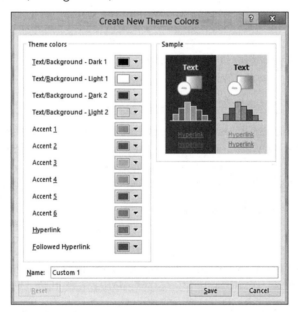

FIGURE 3.6

Change the color of certain areas of your presentation to customize it.

3. In the dialog box, select theme colors for text, backgrounds, accents, and hyperlinks from the drop-down lists. The Sample box previews your selections.

4. Enter a name for your new color scheme.

5. When you're happy with your choices, click the Save button. Your new color scheme now displays as a custom color scheme, available for selection from the gallery.

To edit custom color schemes, right-click the appropriate color scheme in the gallery, and select Edit from the shortcut menu. Make your changes in the Edit Theme Colors dialog box, and click Save.

To delete a custom color scheme, right-click the appropriate color scheme in the gallery, and select Delete from the shortcut menu. Click Yes to confirm the deletion. The custom scheme no longer displays in the gallery.

Customizing Theme Fonts

Although each theme comes with coordinating fonts, you can apply new fonts to your presentation—or create your own.

Applying New Theme Fonts

To apply new theme fonts, follow these steps:

1. On the Design tab, click the down arrow in the lower-right corner of the Variants group and select Fonts. The font gallery displays, as shown in Figure 3.7.

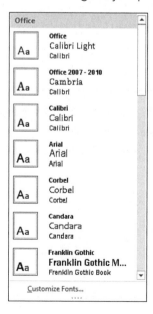

FIGURE 3.7

Select the fonts you want to use in your presentation.

2. Pause your mouse over each font pair to preview on your presentation. The font gallery shows two fonts in each pair. The first is for headings (both titles and subtitles) and the second is for body text, which includes all text other than title text such as text in tables, charts, and so on.

3. Choose the font pair you prefer from the font gallery.

Creating New Theme Fonts

To create new theme fonts, follow these steps:

1. On the Design tab, click the down arrow in the lower-right corner of the Variants group and select Fonts.

2. In the font gallery, click Customize Fonts to open the Create New Theme Fonts dialog box (see Figure 3.8). If you enable multiple language support, this dialog box might contain additional options.

FIGURE 3.8

Select your own heading and body text fonts.

3. Select a new Heading Font and a new Body Font from the drop-down lists. The Sample box previews your selections.

4. Enter a name for your custom font pair.

5. Click the Save button. Your new custom font pair now displays in the font gallery.

 TIP Be sure that any new fonts you apply are readable on your slides. Theme fonts are designed to be easy to read with all theme color schemes.

Editing Custom Fonts

To edit custom fonts, follow these steps:

1. Right-click the custom font pair you want to edit in the font gallery, and choose Edit from the shortcut menu. The Edit Theme Fonts dialog box displays, which is nearly identical to the Create New Theme Fonts dialog box.

2. Make your changes in the Edit Theme Fonts dialog box.

3. Click the Save button.

 TIP To delete custom fonts, right-click the custom font pair in the font gallery, and choose Delete from the shortcut menu. Click Yes when prompted to confirm. Your custom fonts no longer display in the font gallery.

Customizing Theme Effects

In addition to colors and fonts, you can also apply new effects that coordinate with your theme. These effects affect the look of tables, text, charts, diagrams, shapes, and pictures. Theme effects play a particularly important role with objects to which you've applied shape styles.

On the Design tab, click the down arrow in the lower-right corner of the Variants group and select Effects. A gallery of theme effects displays, as shown in Figure 3.9.

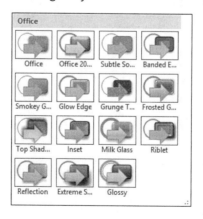

FIGURE 3.9

Select a theme effect to apply to your presentation.

Pause your mouse over each effect to preview it on your presentation. Note that changes display only if your slide content is affected by theme effects. Click the effect you prefer to apply it to your presentation.

Working with Custom Themes

If you modify the fonts, colors, and effects of a theme, you might want to save it to apply to future presentations. For example, you might want to create a custom theme to use throughout your company.

Creating and Saving a Custom Theme

To create a custom theme, follow these steps:

1. Make any theme changes such as changes to your theme's colors, fonts, and effects.

2. On the Design tab, click the down arrow in the lower-right corner of the Themes group.

3. Select Save Current Theme from the gallery. The Save Current Theme dialog box opens, as shown in Figure 3.10.

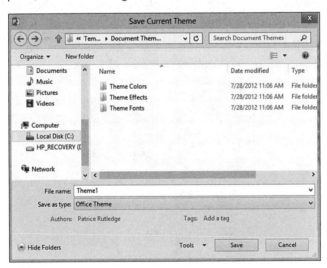

FIGURE 3.10

Save your custom theme for later reuse.

4. Enter a filename for your new theme.

5. Click the Save button to save your theme as an Office Theme file type stored in the Document Themes folder.

Your theme is now available to select from the gallery.

 TIP   In addition to creating custom themes, you can also create custom layouts. See Chapter 19, "Customizing PowerPoint," for more information.

THE ABSOLUTE MINIMUM

Here are the key points to remember from this chapter:

- If you don't like the theme you applied to your presentation, you can switch to another in a matter of seconds.

- PowerPoint enables you to use more than one theme in a presentation, but you need to think about clarity and consistency before using this feature.

- Applying a new color variant is another way to change your presentation's appearance quickly.

- You can further customize your presentation by formatting its background, including fills, artistic effects, and pictures.

- For more creative control, you can customize theme colors, fonts, and effects.

4

WORKING WITH TEXT

Adding and formatting text is a straightforward process in PowerPoint. If the standard formatting isn't enough, however, PowerPoint also offers sophisticated text formatting and customization. In addition, it automates many formatting tasks if you're in a hurry or have limited design skills. In this chapter, you find out how to add and format text, text boxes, bullets, numbered lists, and WordArt, and you also discover how to spell check the text in your presentation.

Adding Text to a Placeholder

In PowerPoint, the most common place to add text is in a placeholder that's part of a PowerPoint slide layout. Placeholders enable you to add both title text and body text to your slides. See Chapter 2, "Creating a Basic Presentation," for more information about adding slide layouts that contain placeholders.

Figure 4.1 shows a sample slide with two placeholders.

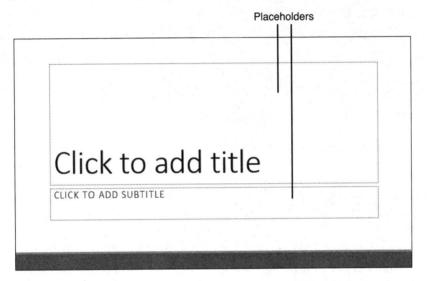

FIGURE 4.1

In PowerPoint, a placeholder is a tool for entering text.

You can also add text in a text box, table, WordArt object, chart, shape, or SmartArt graphic.

To move or resize a placeholder, see the section, "Moving and Resizing a Text Box," later in this chapter.

Using AutoFit

Sometimes you might have slightly too much text to fit into a placeholder. AutoFit resolves this problem by shrinking the text size until it fits. It works as you type; as soon as your text spills outside the placeholder, AutoFit starts shrinking the text size. When it does, the AutoFit Options button displays next to the placeholder. Figure 4.2 shows an example.

⊚	AutoFit Text to Placeholder
○	Stop Fitting Text to This Placeholder
⇆	Control AutoCorrect Options...

FIGURE 4.2

Make your text more readable with AutoFit.

When you click the AutoFit Options button, a menu of formatting options displays:

- **AutoFit Text to Placeholder**—Shrink the text in the placeholder until it fits.

- **Stop Fitting Text to This Placeholder**—Restore the text to its original size.

- **Control AutoCorrect Options**—Open the AutoCorrect dialog box to the AutoFormat as You Type tab, which you use to turn AutoFit on or off. Use the AutoFit Title Text to Placeholder check box to enable or disable AutoFit in title placeholders. Use the AutoFit Body Text to Placeholder check box to enable or disable AutoFit in text placeholders. Click OK to keep your changes.

See Chapter 19, "Customizing PowerPoint," for more information about AutoCorrect.

 CAUTION AutoFit shrinks text until it's so tiny your audience can't read it. When any text on your slide is smaller than 20 points, consider reformatting rather than reducing font size.

Using Text Boxes

Use a text box when you need to add text to a slide outside its original placeholders or when you need to frame special text. Text boxes are also useful for wrapping text around an object.

Inserting a Text Box

To insert a text box, follow these steps:

1. On the Insert tab, click the Text Box button.

2. Click where you want to place the text box on the slide.

3. Enter your text.

Figure 4.3 shows a text box.

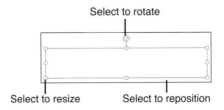

FIGURE 4.3

A text box calls attention to something you want to say and lets you place the text exactly where you want it.

Moving and Resizing a Text Box

If your text box isn't exactly right when you first create it, you can take the following actions:

- Position the mouse over one of the text box handles to resize it. The mouse pointer displays as an arrow when you resize.

- Position the mouse over the text box outline and drag it to a new location. The mouse pointer displays as a crosshair when you reposition.

- Position the mouse over the rotation handle (the small circle at the top of the text box) to rotate the box. The mouse pointer displays as an open circle when you rotate.

 TIP You can also move and resize placeholders, shapes, and WordArt objects using these techniques.

Formatting a Text Box

You can format text in a text box as you would any other text, including formatting the font, size, color, and style. See the section, "Formatting Text," later in this chapter.

You can also format a text box using the Format Shape pane. To view the options available in this pane, follow these steps:

1. Right-click the text box you want to format.

2. Select Format Shape from the menu that displays to open the Format Shape pane.

3. In the Format Shape pane, click the Text Options link and then the Textbox button.

4. Modify your text box using the options available on the pane (see Figure 4.4). For example, you can specify alignment, text direction, margins, and more. For more information about these options, see the section, "Using the Format Shape Pane" in Chapter 10, "Working with Shapes."

FIGURE 4.4

The Format Shape pane offers a variety of text box formatting options.

5. When you're finished, click the Close (x) button in the upper-right corner of the pane to close it.

You can also apply formatting to the text inside a text box. See the next section for more information.

Formatting Text

PowerPoint's themes include colors, fonts, and other design elements designed to work well and look good together. In this way, PowerPoint frees you to focus on your message. For maximum flexibility, however, PowerPoint offers numerous options for text formatting and customization.

You can format text in several ways:

• Use the options available in the Font and Paragraph groups on the Home tab.

- Use the Font and Paragraph dialog boxes to make a number of changes in one place and to set defaults. Open these dialog boxes by clicking the dialog box launcher (down arrow) in the lower-right corner of the Font and Paragraph groups.

- Apply text formatting individually by right-clicking the target text and using options on the mini toolbar.

- Use the text formatting options on the Format Shape pane (right-click text and select Format Shape from the menu). See Chapter 10 for more information about this pane.

Enhancing Presentation Text

The following are some changes you might consider to enhance the presentation of your slides:

- **Enlarge or reduce font size**—If you have too little text on a slide, you can increase the font size to fill the page. You can also shrink the text in a placeholder so that it can hold more text. Be sure, however, that the font size is still appropriate for the presentation. Verify that all text is still readable on the slide, and if you're going to do an onscreen presentation, that it isn't too small to be seen by viewers at the back of a room.

- **Replace one font with another**—You might have a particular font you prefer to use in presentations. Be careful, however, not to be too creative with unusual fonts. You want to be sure that everyone can read your presentation clearly. In addition, don't choose an unusual font if you're going to run your presentation from a computer other than the one you used to create it just in case the second computer doesn't have the font.

- **Add boldface, italic, or color**—Use these to emphasize a point with a certain word or words.

- **Add text effects**—Apply text effects such as shadow, reflection, glow, bevel, and 3-D rotation.

Using the Formatting Tools on the Home Tab

The Home tab (see Figure 4.5) includes an extensive collection of text formatting tools.

FIGURE 4.5

The Home tab includes buttons for commonly used text effects.

Table 4.1 lists the formatting options in the Font group on the Home tab.

TABLE 4.1 Font Group Buttons

Name	Description
Font	Apply a font to the selected text.
Font Size	Set the selected text's size. Choose any common size from 8 to 96 points, or type any size in the edit box.
Increase Font Size	Increase the selected text's size by a few points.
Decrease Font Size	Decrease the selected text's size by a few points.
Clear All Formatting	Clear all formatting from selected text.
Bold	Bold the selected text.
Italic	Italicize the selected text.
Underline	Underline the selected text.
Text Shadow	Apply a shadow to the selected text.
Strikethrough	Draw a line through selected text.
Character Spacing	Adjust spacing between characters.
Change Case	Change the case of the selected text. Options include Sentence case, lowercase, UPPERCASE, Capitalize Each Word, and tOGGLE cASE.
Font Color	Apply the color you choose from the drop-down list to the selected text.

To apply one of these formatting elements, select the text you want to format and click the appropriate button. Clicking the Bold, Italic, Underline, Text Shadow, or Strikethrough button a second time acts as a toggle and removes the formatting.

With the Font drop-down list, you can preview what each font actually looks like.

 CAUTION Remember that an unusual use of case might be difficult to read, particularly uppercase and toggle case. With text, go for readability and clarity.

Table 4.2 lists the formatting options in the Paragraph group on the Home tab.

TABLE 4.2 Paragraph Group Buttons

Name	Description
Bullets	Apply or remove bullets to the selected text.
Numbering	Apply or remove automatic numbering to the selected text.
Decrease List Level	Decrease the indent level of the selected text.
Increase List Level	Increase the indent level of the selected text.
Line Spacing	Determine the number of spaces between lines, such as single or double spacing.
Align Left	Align text to the object's left margin.
Center	Center text within the object.
Align Right	Align text to the object's right margin.
Justify	Space words and letters within words so that the text touches both margins in the object.
Add or Remove Columns	Set the number of columns to apply to the selected text.
Text Direction	Specify directional formatting, including horizontal, rotated, and stacked text options.
Align Text	Align text to the top, middle, or bottom of the text box, with an option to center as well.
Convert to SmartArt Graphic	Convert text to a SmartArt diagram.

Formatting Text with Options in the Font Dialog Box

The Font dialog box offers some advanced formatting options not available on the Home tab.

To format selected text with the options in the Font dialog box, follow these steps:

1. On the Home tab, click the dialog box launcher (down arrow) in the lower-right corner of the Font group. The Font dialog box displays, as shown in Figure 4.6.

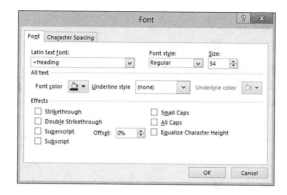

FIGURE 4.6

Make font changes quickly with the Font dialog box.

2. In the Latin Text Font list, select the font you want to use. Scroll down the list to see the available fonts.

3. In the Font Style list, choose whether the font should be regular (neither bold nor italic), bold, italic, or bold and italic.

4. In the Size field, enter a specific font point size in the box or scroll through the available options.

5. Choose a font color from the palette that displays when you click the button next to the Font Color field. For additional color choices, click More Colors from the palette to open the Colors dialog box. See Chapter 10 for more information about the Colors dialog box.

6. If you want to underline text, select an Underline Style and Underline Color from the drop-down lists.

7. Apply other effects by selecting the check box next to any of the following:

   • **Strikethrough**—Place a horizontal line through the selected text.

   • **Double Strikethrough**—Place two horizontal lines through the selected text.

   • **Superscript**—Raise the text above the baseline and reduces the font size. Set the Offset to 30%, which you can adjust.

   • **Subscript**—Lower the text below the baseline and reduce the font size. Set the Offset to –25%, which you can adjust.

NOTE *Offset* refers to the percentage the text displays above or below the baseline, which is the invisible line on which the characters sit. For example, because subscript text is below the baseline, its offset will be a negative number.

- **Small Caps**—Format the text in small caps.

- **All Caps**—Capitalize the selected text.

- **Equalize Character Height**—Make all letters the same height. For additional character spacing options, select the Character Spacing tab in the Font dialog box.

8. Click the OK button to close the dialog box and apply the font formatting.

Formatting Text with Options in the Paragraph Dialog Box

The Paragraph dialog box offers some advanced formatting options not available directly on the Home tab. To open this dialog box, select the text you want to format and click the down arrow in the lower-right corner of the Paragraph group on the Home tab. The Paragraph dialog box appears, as shown in Figure 4.7.

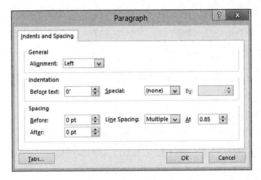

FIGURE 4.7

Set alignment, indentation, and spacing in the Paragraph dialog box.

In this dialog box, you can do the following:

- Set alignment, including right-aligned, left-aligned, centered, justified, and distributed text.

- Specify indentation requirements such as hanging and first-line indentation.

- Set line spacing. When a slide looks crowded or too sparse, the *line spacing*, or the amount of space between lines of text, might be at fault. Adjust line spacing until the text looks right.

- Establish tab stop parameters by clicking the Tabs button and setting the tab stop position.

Formatting Text with the Mini Toolbar

To access the mini toolbar, right-click the text you want to format. The mini toolbar appears (see Figure 4.8) either above or below a menu that includes options for Font, Paragraph, Bullets, and Numbering.

FIGURE 4.8

The mini toolbar enables you to quickly access common text formatting options.

The mini toolbar contains selected text formatting buttons, most of which you should be familiar with from the Font and Paragraph groups on the Home tab. These include the following:

- Font
- Font Size
- Increase Font Size
- Decrease Font Size
- Decrease List Level
- Increase List Level
- Bold

- Italic
- Underline
- Align Left
- Center
- Align Right
- Font Color
- Format Painter

See Chapter 5,"Formatting and Organizing Objects, Slides, and Presentations," for more information about the Format Painter.

Using Bullets

Creating a bulleted list is a common PowerPoint task, but one you should choose judiciously. A PowerPoint presentation that's just a series of slides with bullets isn't nearly as effective as one that uses a combination of graphic and visual elements for emphasis. You can add a bulleted list to any slide that contains text. You can also add bulleted lists within a table.

To format text as a bulleted list, select the text and click the Bullets button in the Paragraph group on the Home tab. PowerPoint uses the theme's default bullet style, but you can change to another bullet style if you want.

TIP   Consider using a list-style SmartArt graphic instead of a bullet list for greater visual impact. See Chapter 11, "Working with SmartArt," for more information about SmartArt options.

Changing the Bullet Style of Selected Text

To change the bullet style of selected text, follow these steps:

1. On the Home tab, click the down arrow to the right of the Bullets button.

2. Select Bullets and Numbering in the gallery that displays. The Bullets and Numbering dialog box opens, as shown in Figure 4.9.

FIGURE 4.9

You can choose from many different bullet types.

3. On the Bulleted tab, select one of the seven bullet styles that appear. Choosing None removes the bulleted list.

4. Set Size as a percentage of the text. The default is 100%. Lower the number to reduce the size; increase the number to enlarge the size.

5. Choose a color from the Color drop-down list. For additional color choices, click More Colors to open the Colors dialog box. See Chapter 10 for more information about the Colors dialog box.

6. Click the OK button to apply the bullet style.

To change the bullets in your entire presentation, make the change on the master slide. See Chapter 19 for more information.

Applying Picture Bullets

If none of the seven default bullet styles suits your needs, you can also use picture bullets, which display a small graphic as the bullet point.

To apply a picture bullet to a selected list, follow these steps:

1. On the Home tab, click the down arrow to the right of the Bullets button.

2. Select Bullets and Numbering in the gallery to open the Bullets and Numbering dialog box.

3. Click the Picture button to open the Insert Pictures dialog box (see Figure 4.10). If you're not connected to the Internet, PowerPoint prompts you to connect.

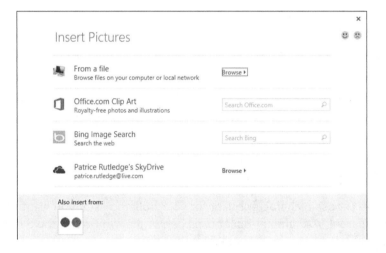

FIGURE 4.10

A picture bullet can enhance a creative presentation.

4. In the Office.com Clip Art field, enter **web bullets** and press the Enter key.

5. Select a bullet from the available options (see Figure 4.11) and click the Insert button to apply the bullet to your list.

NOTE To use one of your own images as a picture bullet (such as a logo), click the Browse button on the Insert Pictures dialog box (see Figure 4.10) and select the image you want to use. Other options include using an image from your SkyDrive or Flickr account, searching for images on Bing, and searching for other images in the Office.com clip art collection.

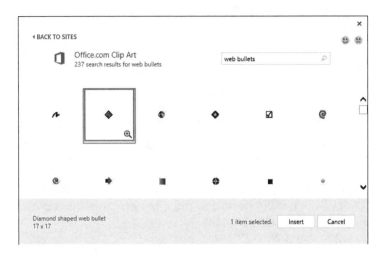

FIGURE 4.11

The Office.com clip art collection offers a variety of picture bullet choices.

 TIP It's best if your bullet is small—between 10 and 20 pixels square. PowerPoint shrinks larger images to fit, but the larger the image, the less desirable the result.

Applying Character Bullets

You can choose a character bullet for your bulleted list if you want something a little different. A character bullet uses one of the symbols in the Symbols dialog box as a bullet point in your presentation.

To apply character bullets to a selected list, follow these steps:

1. On the Home tab, click the down arrow to the right of the Bullets button.

2. Select Bullets and Numbering in the gallery to open the Bullets and Numbering dialog box.

3. Click the Customize button to open the Symbol dialog box, as shown in Figure 4.12.

4. Select a font from the Font drop-down list (Wingdings or Webdings are good options) and then choose the bullet you want from the display area.

5. Click the OK button to apply the character bullet.

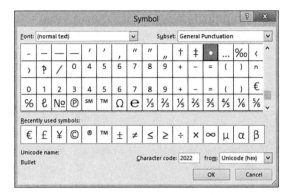

FIGURE 4.12

Use a font such as Wingdings for character bullets.

 TIP To speed up the process, you can view and choose from character bullets you've recently applied to a bulleted list from the Recently Used Symbols section of the Symbols dialog box.

Using Numbered Lists

For a sequence of items, creating a numbered list is a good alternative to a bulleted list. For example, a series of procedural steps works well in a numbered list. You can create numbered lists with actual numbers, Roman numerals, or letters of the alphabet.

To format text as a numbered list, select the text and click the Numbering button on the Home tab. PowerPoint applies the default numbering to your text.

If the default numbered list formatting doesn't suit your needs, you can choose an alternative. To change the numbering style of selected text, follow these steps:

1. On the Home tab, click the down arrow to the right of the Numbering button.

2. Select Bullets and Numbering in the gallery that displays. The Bullets and Numbering dialog box opens.

3. On the Numbered tab, as shown in Figure 4.13, select one of the seven number styles that display. Choosing None removes the numbered list.

4. Set Size as a percentage of the text. The default varies but is typically 100%. Lower the number to reduce the size; increase the number to enlarge the size.

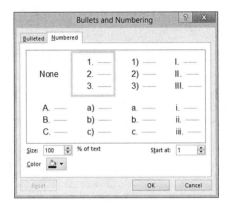

FIGURE 4.13

A numbered list can put a series of items in order.

5. Choose a color from the Color drop-down list. For additional color choices, click More Colors to open the Colors dialog box. See Chapter 10 for more information about the Colors dialog box.

6. If you want to start numbering at something other than 1 (or lettering at something other than a), select a starting value in the Start At field.

7. Click the OK button to apply the numbering.

Using WordArt

WordArt enables you to create special text effects such as shadowed, rotated, stretched, and multicolored text. PowerPoint treats WordArt as both an object and text, so you can apply object formatting such as fills and 3-D as well as apply text formatting. You can also check the spelling in your WordArt text.

 CAUTION   Be careful not to overuse WordArt in your presentation, or it can become cluttered and confusing. Use WordArt only for emphasis.

Inserting WordArt

Inserting WordArt is a simple, three-step process:

1. On the Insert tab, click the WordArt button. The WordArt gallery displays, as shown in Figure 4.14.

2. Click the WordArt style you prefer. A text box displays on your slide.

3. Replace the placeholder text with text you want to format using WordArt.

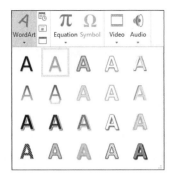

FIGURE 4.14

Preview WordArt styles before you choose one.

 TIP   To move or resize a WordArt object, see the section, "Moving and Resizing a Text Box," earlier in this chapter.

Formatting WordArt

If you want to change your initial WordArt selection, you can select a different style or customize it. Many WordArt formatting options are similar to those for shapes. See Chapter 10 for more information about these options.

To format WordArt, select a WordArt object and click the Drawing Tools – Format tab. Figure 4.15 shows the WordArt Styles group, where you can do the following:

- Click the down arrow to the right of the sample styles that display in the WordArt Styles group. The WordArt gallery opens, where you can apply a new WordArt style to selected text or all text in the shape. You can also click the Clear WordArt option to remove WordArt formatting.

- Click the down arrow to the right of the Text Fill button to choose another theme color, remove the fill color, or apply gradients and textures.

- Click the down arrow to the right of the Text Outline button to choose an outline color, remove the outline, or specify a weight or dash type.

- Click the down arrow to the right of the Text Effects button to apply special effects such as shadows, reflections, glows, bevels, 3-D rotation, and transforms (unusual text formations).

- Click the dialog box launcher (down arrow) in the lower-right corner of the WordArt Styles group to open the Format Shape pane. See Chapter 10 for more information about the text formatting options available on this pane.

FIGURE 4.15

Format your WordArt for additional emphasis.

If you click the Text Fill, Text Outline, or Text Effects button directly, you apply the default formatting. You must select the down arrow to the right of these buttons to view all available options.

 TIP You can also apply the formatting options in the WordArt Styles group to other text, not just WordArt.

Proofing Your Text

Creating a quality, error-free, and easy-to-read presentation is a natural objective when you use PowerPoint. Fortunately, PowerPoint offers a spelling checker and a built-in thesaurus for finding just the right word. Keep in mind that, although an automated tool can help you catch errors, it isn't foolproof and doesn't take the place of thorough proofreading by a real person.

PowerPoint's proofing tools are on the Review tab. See Chapter 8, "Reviewing Presentations," for more information about the other tools on the Review tab.

Setting Spelling Check Options

To set options for spelling, click the File tab, select Options, and go to the Proofing tab on the PowerPoint Options dialog box, as shown in Figure 4.16.

You can choose any of the following spelling options:

- **Ignore Words in UPPERCASE**—Don't check spelling of any word that is all uppercase.

- **Ignore Words That Contain Numbers**—Don't check spelling of any word that includes a number.

- **Ignore Internet and File Addresses**—Don't flag Internet addresses, such as www.microsoft.com, as spelling errors.

- **Flag Repeated Words**—Highlight incidents of duplicate words, such as "the the."

- **Suggest from Main Dictionary Only**—Suggest only alternative spellings from your designated main dictionary. Click the Custom Dictionaries link to select from the dictionary list.

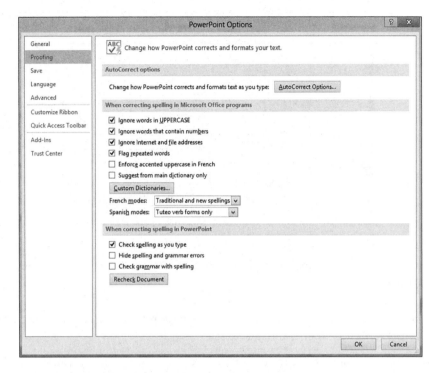

- **Check Spelling as You Type**—Place a red squiggly line under each suspected spelling error as you type it.

- **Hide Spelling and Grammar Errors**—Don't display red underlining for suspected spelling and grammar errors.

- **Check Grammar with Spelling**—Check for grammar errors while you check spelling.

NOTE Options for AutoCorrect formatting and languages such as French and Spanish might also be available. See Chapter 19 for more information.

Checking Your Spelling

After you set the spelling options you want, you can spell check your presentation.

If you set the option to have PowerPoint check spelling as you type, you know immediately when you've possibly misspelled a word. PowerPoint places a red squiggly line under all suspected misspellings, as Figure 4.17 shows. You can either fix the error yourself or right-click to see some suggested alternatives from which to choose.

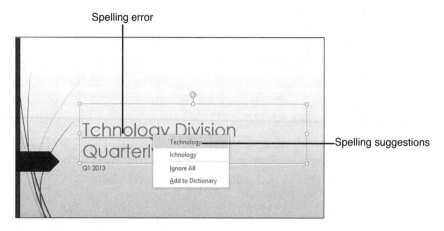

FIGURE 4.17

When you right-click a spelling error, PowerPoint suggests some possible alternative spellings.

You can also spell check your entire presentation at once. To check the spelling in your presentation, follow these steps:

1. On the Review tab, click the Spelling button. Alternatively, press F7. When PowerPoint encounters an error, it displays the Spelling pane, shown in Figure 4.18.

FIGURE 4.18

The Spelling pane offers several options for handling potential misspellings.

2. Review the word that the spelling checker suspects is misspelled.

3. If the word is correct, click the Ignore button (to ignore this instance of the word) or the Ignore All button (to ignore all instances of the word).

4. If the word is misspelled and the highlighted suggestion is correct, click the Change button (to change the individual misspelled word) or the Change All button (to change all instances of this misspelled word).

5. If you want to add the suspect word to the custom dictionary as a correctly spelled word, click the Add button.

6. If the word is misspelled and none of the suggestions is correct, enter the correct spelling directly on the slide and click the Resume button.

7. Continue steps 2 through 6 until you finish checking your presentation's spelling. PowerPoint displays a dialog box that informs you the process is complete and closes the Spelling pane.

Looking Up a Synonym in the Thesaurus

If you ever have trouble coming up with just the right word, PowerPoint can help you with its thesaurus.

To find a synonym in the thesaurus, follow these steps:

1. Select the word you want to look up. If you can't think of the exact word, type a word that's close to it.

2. On the Review tab, click the Thesaurus button (or press Shift+F7). The Thesaurus pane opens, as Figure 4.19 shows.

FIGURE 4.19

The Thesaurus pane helps you find the perfect word.

3. Pause the mouse over the word you want to use. A down arrow displays to the right of this word.

4. Click the down arrow and select Insert from the shortcut menu that displays. PowerPoint places the new word in your presentation.

TIP A quick way to find a synonym is to right-click the word in question and choose Synonyms from the menu. A list of possible synonyms displays.

 NOTE The Research pane also offers access to a thesaurus as well as a dictionary, translation tools, and several other research sources. Click the Research button on the Review tab to access this pane.

THE ABSOLUTE MINIMUM

Here are the key points to remember from this chapter:

- In PowerPoint, the most common place to add text is in a placeholder that's part of a PowerPoint slide layout.

- If you have too much text to fit into a placeholder, AutoFit shrinks the text size until it fits.

- Use a text box when you need to add text to a slide outside its original placeholders or when you need to frame special text.

- PowerPoint offers numerous ways to format text: the formatting tools on the Home tab, the mini toolbar, and the Format Shape pane.

- Creating a bulleted list is a common way to format text in PowerPoint, but be sure to consider other—often more effective—ways to communicate your message.

- For a sequence of items, creating a numbered list is an alternative to a bulleted list.

- WordArt lets you create special text effects such as shadowed, rotated, stretched, and multicolored text.

- Create an error-free presentation with PowerPoint's proofing tools such as the spelling checker.

- If you have trouble coming up with just the right word, PowerPoint's built-in thesaurus can help.

5

FORMATTING AND ORGANIZING OBJECTS, SLIDES, AND PRESENTATIONS

After you create a presentation, you most likely will want to modify its appearance. Fortunately, it's easy to modify slides, objects, and entire presentations in PowerPoint.

PowerPoint offers numerous ways to manage and format slide objects, including several automatic formatting options and the optional use of gridlines and guides. You can also organize entire presentations using tools such as Slide Sorter view.

Manipulating Objects

In PowerPoint, an *object* refers to any of the components you include on your slides, such as shapes, pictures, text boxes, placeholders, SmartArt, charts, WordArt, and so forth.

You can easily cut, copy, paste, move, and resize PowerPoint objects.

Cutting an Object

To cut a selected object, click the Cut button in the Clipboard group on the Home tab or press Ctrl+X. To cut more than one object, hold down the Shift key while selecting objects, or drag a selection box around all the objects with the mouse.

 TIP If you cut something by mistake, click the Undo button to retrieve it.

Copying an Object

To copy a selected object, click the Copy button on the Home tab or press Ctrl+C.

 TIP To copy the attributes of one object and apply them to another object, use the Format Painter button on the Home tab. For example, if you select an object with 3-D effects, click the Format Painter button and then select another object so that new object gets the same 3-D effects.

 NOTE When you copy an object, it displays on PowerPoint's Clipboard. To view the Clipboard, click the down arrow to the right of the Clipboard group on the Home tab to open the Clipboard pane. You can also select which item to paste on this pane.

Pasting an Object

To paste a cut or copied object, follow these steps:

1. Click the down arrow below the Paste button to open the Paste Options box, as shown in Figure 5.1, where you can preview the appearance of the pasted object on your slide. If you don't want to preview, click the Paste button directly (or press Ctrl+V) and skip to step 4.

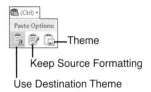

FIGURE 5.1

Preview an object before pasting it.

2. Pause your mouse over each option button to preview what the pasted object would look like on your slide before actually pasting it into your presentation. Depending on what you paste and the context in which you paste it, any of the following option buttons could display in the Paste Options box:

- **Keep Source Formatting**—Format the object as it was formatted in the location from which you copied it. This displays only when your destination slide has a different theme than the source.

- **Use Destination Theme**—Apply the current theme formatting to the object. This is the default when you paste the object directly.

- **Picture**—Convert the pasted item to a picture. To select a specific picture format, click the Paste Special link in the Paste Options box and choose a format from the Paste Special dialog box.

- **Keep Text Only**—Remove all formatting from pasted text. This displays only when you paste text without having a text placeholder open first. PowerPoint creates a placeholder for the text as it pastes it.

3. Click a button in the Paste Options box to paste using the selected paste option.

4. After you paste an object, the Paste Options button displays to its lower-right. If you aren't satisfied with the initial paste option you selected, you can click this button and select another option.

 TIP If the Paste Options button doesn't display below a pasted object, verify that this feature is active. To do so, click the File tab, select Options, and go to the Advanced tab on the PowerPoint Options dialog box. Select the Show Paste Options Button When Content Is Pasted check box and click OK.

Moving and Resizing an Object

To move an object, select it and drag to a new location.

You can resize an object using resizing handles, which display around an object's edges when you select it. Figure 5.2 illustrates these handles.

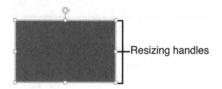

FIGURE 5.2

Resizing handles make it easier to adjust the size and shape of your object.

Drag the handles with the mouse to make the object smaller, larger, or a different shape. Notice that depending on which sizing handle you select—a corner or interior handle—you can either enlarge the entire object or change its shape. To resize the object proportionately so that it keeps its shape, press the Shift key and drag a corner handle.

Arranging Objects

If your presentation includes multiple objects, you might need to order, group, align, or rotate them to achieve your desired effect. Using the tools available when you click the Arrange button on the Home tab, you can maintain complete control over the appearance of your presentation objects.

These tools are also available on the contextual Drawing Tools – Format tab that displays when you select an object.

Layering Objects

When you place two or more objects on a slide, you might want part of one to display on top of part of another. This is called *layering* the objects. You can do this for pure visual effect or to indicate that the overlapping objects have a relationship to each other. PowerPoint lets you control each object's layering, so if two objects are layered and you want the one below to display on top, you can change it.

To specify an object's layer order in relation to the other objects on a slide, follow these steps:

1. Select the object whose order you want to arrange. If the object you want to select is hidden from view, press the Tab key to cycle through all objects to find the one you want.

2. On the Home tab, click the Arrange button to view a menu with the following options:

   • **Bring to Front**—Bring the selected object to the front layer of the stack, placing all other objects behind it.

   • **Send to Back**—Send the selected object to the back layer of the stack so that all other objects display above it.

   • **Bring Forward**—Bring the selected object one layer closer to the front. This is most useful when more than two objects are layered.

   • **Send Backward**—Send the selected object one layer to the back. This is also most useful when more than two objects are layered.

3. Click the order option you prefer from the menu. PowerPoint applies it to your selected object.

Figure 5.3 shows two sets of layered objects.

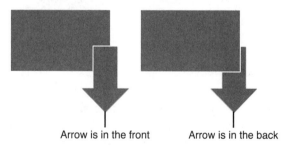

Arrow is in the front   Arrow is in the back

FIGURE 5.3

You can layer objects for a special effect.

 TIP   You can also access these layering options if you select an object, right-click, and choose from the submenu options that display.

Grouping Objects

It's difficult to move several objects on your slide and keep them positioned in proportion to each other. Fortunately, you can group two or more objects so that PowerPoint treats them as one object. For example, if you combine WordArt with a clip art image to create a logo, you can group these objects so that they stay together when you move them. A grouped set of objects moves in unison, always remaining in the same relative positions.

When you format grouped objects, the formatting applies to all the objects. For example, let's say you have two grouped objects that were originally different colors. If you now recolor them, the new color applies to both objects, not just one. To make individual changes, you have to ungroup the objects.

To group multiple objects on a slide, follow these steps:

1. Select the objects you want to group by pressing the Shift key and clicking individual objects.

2. On the Home tab, click the Arrange button.

3. Select the Group option on the menu that displays.

The object handles now treat the objects as one, as shown in Figure 5.4.

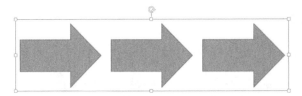

FIGURE 5.4

Group objects to treat them as one.

If you don't like the way you grouped objects and want to remove this grouping, click the Arrange button and select Ungroup from the menu. To revert back to the grouping, click the Arrange button and select Regroup.

Aligning Objects

To align and distribute objects relative to each other or to the slide, follow these steps:

1. Select the objects you want to align by pressing the Shift key and clicking individual objects.

2. On the Home tab, click the Arrange button, and choose Align. A submenu displays.

3. If you want to align or distribute relative to the slide itself, select Align to Slide. If you want to align or distribute relative to the objects, select Align Selected Objects. For example, let's say you select several objects and want to align

them to the left. If you choose Align to Slide, all the objects move to the leftmost edge of the slide. If you choose Align Selected Objects, they align to the left side of the leftmost object.

4. Choose from one of the following menu options:

   - **Align Left**—Move the objects horizontally to the left.
   - **Align Center**—Move the objects horizontally to the center.
   - **Align Right**—Move the objects horizontally to the right.
   - **Align Top**—Move the objects vertically to the top.
   - **Align Middle**—Move the objects vertically to their midpoint.
   - **Align Bottom**—Move the objects vertically to the bottom.
   - **Distribute Horizontally**—Move the objects horizontally, spaced evenly.
   - **Distribute Vertically**—Move the objects vertically, spaced evenly.

PowerPoint aligns your objects based on the direction you specify.

 TIP Alternatively, you can also select an object and use the arrow keys to nudge the object in the direction of the arrow.

Rotating and Flipping Objects

Many times when you add a shape or clip art image, it ends up facing the wrong direction. For example, you might add a callout to draw attention to specific text, but the callout is pointing the wrong way.

 TIP To rotate or flip a single object in a group, you need to ungroup the objects first and then regroup the objects when you finish.

To quickly rotate an object, follow these steps:

1. Select the object you want to rotate.
2. Place the mouse pointer over the green rotation handle that displays at the top of the object, as shown in Figure 5.5.

Drag to rotate

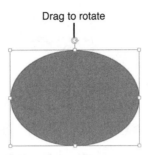

FIGURE 5.5

Use the rotation handle to quickly rotate an object.

3. Drag this handle to rotate the object. Pressing the Ctrl key while rotating changes the rotation angle 15° at a time.

You can also select rotation options by clicking the Arrange button on the Home tab and selecting Rotate from the menu. Then, select one of the following options from the submenu:

- **Rotate Right 90°**—Move the object clockwise 90°.

- **Rotate Left 90°**—Move the object counterclockwise 90°.

- **Flip Vertical**—Reverse the object vertically.

- **Flip Horizontal**—Reverse the object horizontally.

- **More Rotation Options**—Open the Format Shape dialog box, where you can specify size and position options.

Using the Selection Pane

Using the Selection pane, you can reorder slide objects and specify their visibility. Choosing to hide a specific object is temporary. This action doesn't delete it from the slide, and you can choose to make it visible again at any time.

To open this pane, click the Selection Pane button on the Drawing Tools – Format tab. Figure 5.6 shows the Selection pane.

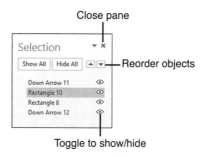

FIGURE 5.6

Temporarily hide objects in your presentation.

Working with Gridlines and Guides

Another way to align slide objects is to use gridlines and guides. These useful tools help you align objects on the slide or place objects in a precise location.

Gridlines display on your slides as small squares. Select the Gridlines check box on the View tab to display gridlines. Figure 5.7 displays a slide with gridlines.

FIGURE 5.7

Gridlines help you align objects.

Guides divide your slide into quarters, as shown in Figure 5.8. Select the Guides check box on the View tab to display guides.

FIGURE 5.8

Guides are another useful alignment tool.

You can drag a guide to reposition it up, down, left, or right.

If you want to add another guide, right-click your slide and select either Add Vertical Guide or Add Horizontal Guide from the menu.

 NOTE Gridlines and guides are invisible during a slide show and don't display on a printed presentation.

Using Smart Guides

By default, PowerPoint uses smart guides to help you align objects. When you start to reposition an object in relation to another object, PowerPoint recognizes this and displays temporary guides to help you align correctly. To deactivate—or activate—this feature, right-click your slide and select Grid and Guides, Smart Guides from the menu.

Using the Grid and Guides Dialog Box

Using the Grid and Guides dialog box offers several advanced alignment features. To open this dialog box, shown in Figure 5.9, right-click your slide and select Grid and Guides from the menu.

FIGURE 5.9

You can snap objects to a grid.

In the Grid and Guides dialog box, you can perform the following tasks:

- Choose to snap objects to a grid.

- Indicate the spacing of your grid in inches (from 1/24th of an inch to 2 inches).

- Select the Display Grid on Screen check box to activate the grid. You see horizontal and vertical dotted lines on your screen in the spacing width you specified, which helps you position your objects. Although the grid displays on the screen, it doesn't display in print or during a slideshow.

- Use adjustable drawing guides by selecting the Display Drawing Guides on Screen check box. This places one adjustable vertical line and one adjustable horizontal line on your screen, which you can drag to position where you want them. These, too, are invisible in print or during a slide show.

- Display smart guides when shapes are aligned. These dashed-line guides display only when you move an object on a slide that contains multiple objects.

- To set these options as your default, click the Set as Default button. Click OK to close the Grid and Guides dialog box.

Organizing Slides

In addition to organizing and formatting slide objects, you can also organize slides. Organizing slides is easy in PowerPoint: Select the slide you want to move and drag it to a new location.

You can organize and rearrange slides using three different PowerPoint views:

- **Normal view**—A good choice if you know exactly what you want to move and want to do it quickly.

- **Slide Sorter view**—Suited to major slide reorganizations, this view provides more flexibility and enables you to see thumbnails of multiple slides on a single page.

- **Outline view**—Useful if you just want to read the content of your slides as you reorganize.

See Chapter 1, "Introducing PowerPoint 2013," to learn more about PowerPoint views.

Using Slide Sorter View

To open Slide Sorter view, click the Slide Sorter icon on the lower-right corner of the PowerPoint window, or click the Slide Sorter button on the View tab. Figure 5.10 displays Slide Sorter view.

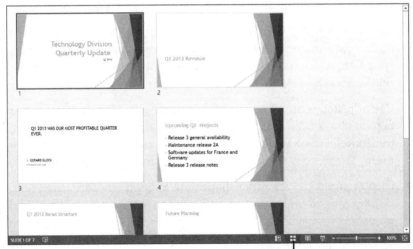

Open Slide Sorter view

FIGURE 5.10

Analyze and organize slides in Slide Sorter view.

In this view, you see smaller versions of your slides in several rows and columns. By viewing the basic content of each slide, you can more easily rearrange their order.

To move a slide in the Slide Sorter, select it and drag it to a new location. To view a particular slide in more detail, double-click it. To delete a slide in Slide Sorter view, select it and press the Delete key. To select multiple slides to delete, press Ctrl, select the slides, and then press the Delete key.

Copying and Moving Slides from One Presentation to Another

Using the Slide Sorter view, you can copy or move slides from one presentation to another. To do so, follow these steps: :

1. Open both the source and destination presentations in Slide Sorter view.

2. On the View tab, click the Arrange All button. PowerPoint displays both presentations in different window panes in Slide Sorter view, as shown in Figure 5.11.

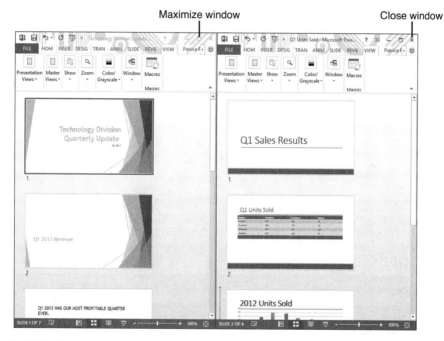

FIGURE 5.11

By splitting panes between two presentations, you can copy or move slides between them.

3. To copy a slide, select it and then drag it to the desired location in the other presentation. PowerPoint places the slide in the destination presentation, but it also remains in the source.

4. To move a slide, select it, press Ctrl+X, position the mouse in the new destination location, and press Ctrl+V. The slide is removed from the source presentation and inserted in the destination presentation.

5. To move or copy more than one slide at a time, press Ctrl as you drag slides from the source presentation.

6. If each presentation uses a different theme, the slide changes to the formatting of the new presentation, and the Paste Options button displays. If you want to retain the formatting of the source presentation, click the down arrow to the right of the Paste Options button and choose Keep Source Formatting. To go back to the formatting of the target presentation, choose Use Destination Theme.

 CAUTION   Although you can combine multiple themes in a single presentation, think carefully before doing so. Combining can make your presentation confusing.

7. To remove the dual-window view, click the Close button in the upper-right corner of the presentation you no longer want to view.

8. Click the Maximize button in the upper-right corner of the presentation you want to keep active. :

 TIP   If more than one presentation is open at a time and each is in a maximized window, you can press Ctrl+F6 to cycle through them. This helps when you want the full-screen view and want to copy/move from one presentation to the next without having to use the Window menu.

Deleting Slides

If you no longer need a slide or make a mistake and want to start again, you can delete it. You can delete slides in Normal view, Outline view, or Slide Sorter view.

To delete a slide, select the slide or slides you want to remove and press the Delete key. To delete multiple consecutive slides, press the Shift key and then select the slides. To delete multiple nonconsecutive slides, hold down the Ctrl key and then select the slides.

Changing Slide Size

In addtion to rearranging slides, you can also change slide size. In PowerPoint 2013, the default slide size is now widescreen (16:9) to match the dimensions of most computers and projectors. If you prefer, you can change your slide size to the former default (4:3) by clicking the Slide Size button on the Design tab.

THE ABSOLUTE MINIMUM

Here are the key points to remember from this chapter:

- You can cut, copy, and paste PowerPoint objects with the click of a button.

- PowerPoint offers a multitude of ways to manage and format slide objects, including aligning, layering, grouping, rotating, and flipping objects to meet your presentation needs.

- Gridlines, guides, and smart guides help you align slide objects and place objects in a precise location.

- You can organize your presentation and move slides from one presentation to another using Slide Sorter view.

WORKING WITH TABLES

Tables offer a great option for presenting and structuring related data on a PowerPoint slide in ways that are easy to read and aesthetically pleasing.

Understanding Tables

A *table* is an object that conveys related information in columns and rows. If you've created tables in other applications, such as Word, you know how valuable they are for communicating information. Tables are also efficient and flexible. For example, rather than creating three separate bullet list slides, each listing the five most important features of your three main products, you can summarize all this information in a table on a single slide. Alternatively, you can present information on individual slides and then summarize everything in a table at the end of the presentation.

You can include a table in a PowerPoint presentation in several ways:

- **Insert a table from the content palette**—PowerPoint's basic table-insertion feature places a table into a slide, based on the number of rows and columns you specify. You can then format, customize, and add data to the table.

- **Draw a table**—When you need to create a complex table, one that the basic table feature can't make, you can draw it right on your slide. It takes longer to draw your own table, though.

- **Insert an Excel table**—Insert a table that takes advantage of the table formatting and calculation options available only in Excel.

Inserting a Table

One of the easiest ways to insert a table in a PowerPoint presentation is to start with a slide layout that includes the content palette.

To add a new slide that contains a table, follow these steps:

1. On the Home tab, click the down arrow below the New Slide button. A gallery of slide layouts displays.

2. Select one of the layouts that includes a content palette, such as the Title and Content, Two Content, Comparison, or Content with Caption layout from the gallery. A new slide displays.

3. On the content palette, click the Insert Table button to open the Insert Table dialog box, illustrated in Figure 6.1.

 TIP You can also open the Insert Table dialog box by clicking the Table button on the Insert tab. This option works best if you want to insert a table on a blank slide.

Insert Table button

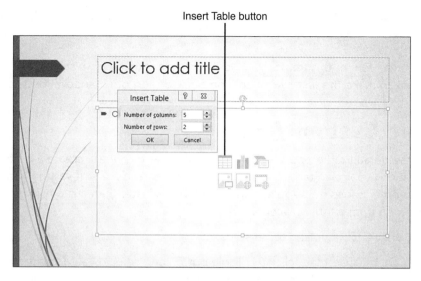

FIGURE 6.1

Choose the number of rows and columns you want to include.

4. Choose the number of columns and rows to display and click the OK button. A blank table displays in your slide, as shown in Figure 6.2.

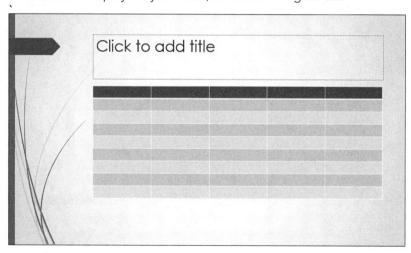

FIGURE 6.2

Enter table text to complete your table.

5. Click the title placeholder to remove the placeholder text and then enter a title for the slide.

6. Add the text you want in each cell of the table, clicking inside the table and then either tabbing to the cell or clicking in the cell.

You can format this text as you would any other text. For example, you might want to make the first row or column bold, or add other special formatting.

Drawing Custom Tables

If the default table options don't give you what you need, create a custom table. Drawing your own table lets you make columns and rows of varying widths, for example. For some people, drawing a table is faster than customizing a table created from a table placeholder.

To draw a table, follow these steps:

1. On the Insert tab, click the Table button and select Draw Table from the menu that displays. The mouse pointer becomes a pencil.

2. Drag the mouse diagonally across the slide to create a box about the size you think the table should be (see Figure 6.3).

FIGURE 6.3

Draw your own tables for total control.

3. On the Table Tools – Design tab, click the Draw Table button in the Draw Borders group. The mouse pointer becomes a pencil again.

4. Select the type of lines you want to draw from the Pen Style, Pen Weight, and Pen Color drop-down buttons.

5. Use the pen to draw lines inside the box to make columns and rows.

If you make a mistake or want to imitate the Merge Cell feature, select the line you want to delete and then click the Eraser button on the Table Tools – Design tab. Use this eraser to remove the lines between rows and cells as necessary.

 TIP To make it easier to create rows and columns, on the View tab, click Gridlines.

Inserting Excel Spreadsheets

If you want to take advantage of Excel's formatting and calculation features in your table, you can insert an Excel table in your PowerPoint presentation. You can insert an Excel table on any PowerPoint slide, but this works best on blank slides or slides with the Title Only layout.

To insert a table you can format as an Excel spreadsheet, follow these steps:

1. On the Insert tab, click the Table button and choose Excel Spreadsheet. An Excel table displays on your slide.

2. Using the table handles, resize your table to fit your slide.

3. Enter your table data as you would in an Excel spreadsheet. The Ribbon now presents many Excel options, including the Formulas and Data tabs. Figure 6.4 shows a sample Excel table.

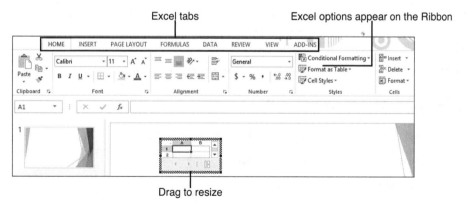

Drag to resize

FIGURE 6.4

An Excel table enables you to use Excel's formatting and calculation features in PowerPoint.

4. Click anywhere outside the Excel table to return to the normal PowerPoint interface.

Formatting Tables

When you click in a table cell, a contextual tab displays called the Table Tools tab. This tab includes two subtabs: Design and Layout. These tabs are contextual in that they display only in context with a table. If you're not working on a table, they don't display on the Ribbon.

 TIP The Table Tools tab doesn't display when you click a table formatted as an Excel spreadsheet. Instead, double-click the Excel table to display Excel Ribbon tabs you can use for formatting.

Figure 6.5 illustrates the Table Tools – Design tab. Figure 6.6 illustrates the Table Tools – Layout tab. Combined, they contain the majority of the tools you need to format tables.

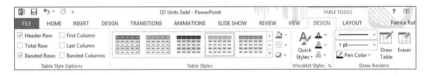

FIGURE 6.5

Choose formatting options for your table, including styles and borders.

FIGURE 6.6

Manipulate table rows and columns as well as set alignment.

PowerPoint lets you format tables in a number of ways, including the following:

- Applying different border styles, widths, and colors
- Inserting and deleting rows and columns
- Merging and splitting cells
- Applying table effects, including gradients, textures, background, and 3-D effects
- Aligning cell text to the top, bottom, or center

Setting Table Style Options

The Table Style Options group on the Table Tools – Design tab offers the following options for formatting the rows and columns in your table:

- **Header Row**—Apply a different color to the top row in a table and make its text bold.

- **Total Row**—Apply a different color to the bottom row in a table and make its text bold.

- **Banded Rows**—Highlight every other row in a table, using alternating colors, for easier viewing.

- **First Column**—Bold the text in the first column.

- **Last Column**—Bold the text in the last column.

- **Banded Columns**—Highlight every other column in a table, using alternating colors, for easier viewing.

Figure 6.7 shows a table with a header row and a total row.

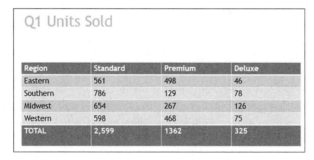

Q1 Units Sold			
Region	Standard	Premium	Deluxe
Eastern	561	498	46
Southern	786	129	78
Midwest	654	267	126
Western	598	468	75
TOTAL	2,599	1362	325

FIGURE 6.7

Applying row and column formatting makes your table easier to read and understand.

Applying a Table Style

The Table Styles group on the Table Tools – Design tab displays suggested table style options. To view other options, click the down arrow on the right side of this group, as illustrated in Figure 6.8. If you want to remove formatting, click Clear Table.

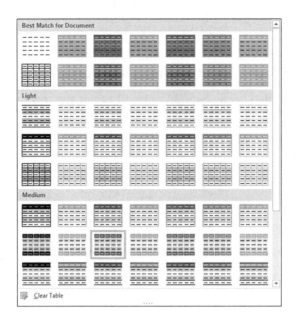

FIGURE 6.8

Apply any of a variety of formatting options to your table, or clear all formatting.

Creating a Border

Use borders to draw attention to your table or even to specific information in your table. New tables get a black, solid line border by default, but you can change this. To format the border, select the table and use the Table Tools tab to change the border style, width, and color and to set where borders display.

Setting the Border Style

To set the border style, click the Pen Style drop-down list on the Table Tools – Design tab, which is located in the Draw Borders group. Choose the border style you prefer from the list, which includes the option to apply no border, a solid line, or a variety of dashed line styles, as shown in Figure 6.9.

FIGURE 6.9

Choose the border style that suits your table.

Setting the Border Width

To set the border width, on the Table Tools – Design tab, click the Pen Weight drop-down list and choose the width you prefer. Options include point sizes from 1/4 point (a thin line) to 6 points (a thick line), as shown in Figure 6.10.

FIGURE 6.10

Use a thick border to create more emphasis, and a thin border to create less.

Setting the Border Colors

To set the border color, click the Pen Color button. The gallery that displays offers several possible colors, based on the presentation's theme colors. For more color choices, click More Border Colors to open the Colors dialog box. Learn more in Chapter 10, "Working with Shapes."

Creating Borders

You can specify which parts of your table contain borders: the whole table or only specific outside or inside areas. Applying creative borders such as diagonals is another option.

To set borders, on the Table Tools – Design tab, click the down arrow to the right of the Borders button. Select the border you prefer from the available options.

Setting Table Fill Color

You can change the color that fills one or more cells in your table.

 CAUTION Be sure that your table text is still readable if you change a cell's fill color. For example, if your text is black, don't fill cells with dark blue.

To change table fill color, follow these steps:

1. Select the cells whose fill color you want to change.

2. On the Table Tools – Design tab, click the down arrow next to the Shading button.

3. From the palette that displays, you can perform the following actions:

- Choose from the colors on the palette. You can choose colors that complement your theme or any of a variety of standard colors.

- Click More Fill Colors to open the Colors dialog box. You can either choose from a large number of colors in this dialog box or create a custom color.

- Apply pictures, gradients, textures, and table backgrounds. See Chapter 10 for more information about these options.

To remove a fill you no longer want, select No Fill from the palette.

Applying Table Effects

The Table Tools – Design tab also offers the option to apply formatting effects such as bevel, shadow, and reflection to your table. Click the down arrow next to the Effects button to view available formatting effects. You can also select table text and choose any of the formatting options in the WordArt Styles group. Learn more in Chapter 4, "Working with Text."

Working with Columns and Rows

It never fails: As soon as you create a table and format it just so, you find that you need to add or remove information.

To insert a row into your table, click in the row above or below where you want to insert the row. Then, from the Table Tools – Layout tab, choose Insert Above or Insert Below, as appropriate. PowerPoint inserts the row, as shown in Figure 6.11.

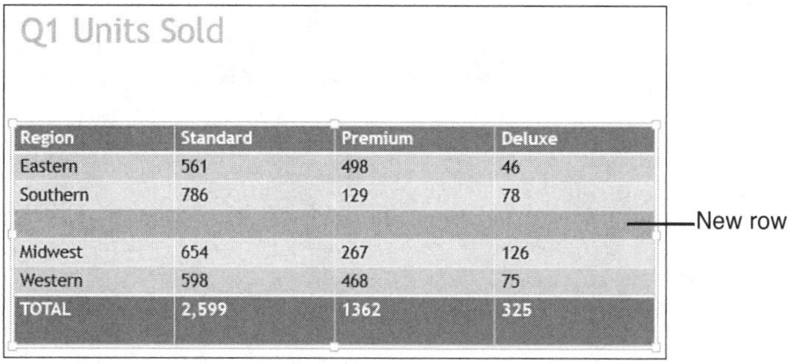

Q1 Units Sold			
Region	Standard	Premium	Deluxe
Eastern	561	498	46
Southern	786	129	78
Midwest	654	267	126
Western	598	468	75
TOTAL	2,599	1362	325

———New row

FIGURE 6.11

Add rows if you didn't create enough during the initial table creation.

When you add or delete rows and columns, your table might no longer fit well on the slide. You then need to resize the table by dragging a corner. Be careful, however, that you don't hide existing text by making the cells too small during resizing.If you want to insert multiple rows, select that number of rows before selecting the Insert command. For example, if you select two rows and then choose Insert Above in the Table Tools – Layout tab, PowerPoint inserts two rows above the selected rows.

To add a new column to your table, click in the column to the left or right of where you want to insert the column. Then choose Insert Left or Insert Right from the Table Tools – Layout tab.

Merging and Splitting Cells

One way PowerPoint makes tables flexible is by enabling you to *merge* and *split* table cells. For example, if you want a table to have a title centered at the top, you can merge all the cells across the top row. If you need to show two separate bits of information in one location, you can split one cell into two.

To merge cells, select the cells you want to merge. Then, on the Table Tools – Layout tab, click the Merge Cells button. Figure 6.12 illustrates five cells that were merged into one.

Q1 Units Sold

Eco Choice Division				— Row of merged cells
Region	Standard	Premium	Deluxe	
Eastern	561	498	46	
Southern	786	129	78	
Midwest	654	267	126	
Western	598	468	75	
TOTAL	2,599	1362	325	

FIGURE 6.12

Merged and split cells have a variety of applications within a table.

 NOTE If you already have text in each of the cells you merge, each cell text becomes a line of text in the new single cell.

To split a cell, select the cell you want to split, then, on the Table Tools – Layout tab, click the Split Cells button. The Split Cells dialog box displays, where you can specify the number of rows and columns you want to insert in this particular cell.

Specifying Other Layout Options

The Table Tools – Layout tab offers other formatting options to explore. In the Cell Size group, you can set cell size options, such as the following:

- **Table Row Height**—Apply the specified height to table rows you select.
- **Table Column Width**—Apply the specified width to the table columns you select.
- **Distribute Rows**—Resize the rows you select so that they're the same width.
- **Distribute Columns**—Resize the columns you select so that they're the same height.

In the Alignment group, you can specify alignment, text direction, margins, and table size:

- **Align Text Left**—Align selected text to the left.
- **Center**—Center selected text.
- **Align Text Right**—Align selected text to the right.

- **Align Top**—Align text to the top of the cell.

- **Center Vertically**—Align text to the vertical center of the cell.

- **Align Bottom**—Align text to the bottom of the cell.

- **Text Direction**—Set the text direction as horizontal, rotated 270°, rotated 90°, or stacked.

- **Cell Margins**—Set text margins in a normal, narrow, or wide format, changing how far your text is from the cell's edges. You can also remove all margins.

In the Table Size group, specify the exact height and width of the table. Optionally, you can also lock the aspect ratio as you make changes (to prevent the table from getting formatted out of perspective).

In the Arrange group, perform advanced multiple-object formatting, such as bringing objects to the front or sending them to the back.

Adding Bulleted and Numbered Lists Within Tables

To create a bulleted list within a table cell, select the cell. Then, on the Home tab, click the Bullets button.

To create a numbered list within a table cell, select the cell. Then, on the Home tab, click the Numbering button.

 TIP   For more bullet and numbering options, select the text you want to format; then click the down arrow next to the Bullets or Numbering button and choose Bullets and Numbering to open the Bullets and Numbering dialog box. This dialog box gives you more control over your lists by letting you choose a color for numbers and bullets, change numbering to alphabetical or outline, use picture bullets, and more.

Deleting Tables and Table Contents

If you no longer need your table or want to start over creating a table, you can delete an existing table in your PowerPoint presentation. You can also delete rows, columns, or selected table text.

To delete an entire table, on the Table Tools – Layout tab, click the Delete button, and then click Delete Table from the menu that displays.

TIP Another way to delete a table is to click the outside border of the table to select the entire table and then press the Delete key.

To delete rows or columns, select the rows or columns you want to delete. Then, on the Table Tools – Layout tab, click the Delete button. Select either Delete Rows or Delete Columns from the menu that displays. PowerPoint deletes the selected content.

To delete text in a cell, select the text (not just the cell) and press the Delete key.

THE ABSOLUTE MINIMUM

Here are the key points to remember from this chapter:

- Tables provide an easy and efficient way to summarize data on your PowerPoint slides.

- Drawing a custom table offers the most flexibility but the least automation.

- Insert an Excel spreadsheet to take advantage of that application's features and functionality.

- PowerPoint gives you a multitude of table formatting options, including borders, colors, shading, merging, and more.

- If you make a mistake, you can delete a table row or column, or even an entire table.

7

OUTLINING PRESENTATIONS

A solid, well-organized outline helps you achieve the goals of your presentation. Fortunately, PowerPoint offers features that simplify the outlining process. You can use Outline view to display and organize your outline in PowerPoint or create an outline in Microsoft Word or another application and insert it into a presentation.

Creating an Effective Presentation Outline

Before you actually create a presentation, you need to determine its purpose, organize your ideas, and establish the flow of what you're going to say. In other words, you need to create an outline, or storyboard.

A presentation can be outlined in a few ways: on paper, in another application such as Microsoft Word, and directly in PowerPoint. Which one is best depends on the type of presentation you're delivering, its length and complexity, and—most important—your personal preferences.

As you create your outline, keep several things in mind:

- Start your presentation with a title slide that introduces your topic and its presenter.

- Think of several main points to cover and design your presentation around those points.

- Try not to cover more than one main topic or concept in an individual slide.

- Remember that a PowerPoint outline is usually designed to accompany a verbal presentation. It's important to separate what you want your audience to see versus what you want them to hear during your presentation.

- Plan a balance of text and graphics in your outline. The best presentations contain both.

- When you use bulleted lists, be sure to maintain consistency. For example, a single bullet on a slide doesn't make sense; a list should contain at least two bullets. Too many bullets on one slide and too few on another might not work well.

- Consider using a summary slide to summarize the points you made during your presentation and conclude it.

Using Outline View

No matter which method you use to create your outline, you might want to use PowerPoint's Outline view to organize this information at some point.

 TIP You can change the size of any pane in PowerPoint by dragging its border to a new location. To do this, move the mouse over the border and, when the cursor changes to a double-headed arrow, click and drag.

To open Outline view, click the Outline View button on the View tab. Your presentation's outline displays in a pane on the left side of the window, replacing the Slides pane, and shares the interface with the slide itself and related notes. Figure 7.1 shows Outline view.

FIGURE 7.1

Outline view offers a flexible approach to creating an outline.

Each slide is numbered and followed by a slide icon and the title text. The body text is listed under each slide title. This body text includes bulleted and indented lists and other text information. The title text is also referred to as the *outline heading*, and each individual point in the body text is referred to as a *subheading*. Clip art, tables, charts, and other objects don't display in the outline.

Adding new outline information is simple. Enter the content and then press the Enter key to move to the next point. To delete a point you no longer need, select it and press the Delete key.

Modifying Your Outline

When you right-click the content of any slide in Outline view, a contextual menu displays, as shown in Figure 7.2.

Although some of the options on this menu are generic—such as Cut, Copy, and Paste—most focus on editing and formatting slide content in Outline view. Table 7.1 lists the options found on this menu.

FIGURE 7.2

Right-click to view this menu of outlining options.

TABLE 7.1 Outline Menu Options

Menu Option	Description
Collapse	Hide all body text for the selected slides. Select Collapse All to hide all body text in the entire outline.
Expand	Display all body text for the selected slides. Select Expand All to display all body text in the entire outline.
New Slide	Insert a new slide after the selected slide.
Delete Slide	Delete the selected slides.
Promote	Change the selected text's outline level to the previous level, applying that level's style and formatting. For example, promoting text at outline level two moves it to level one. Note that you can't promote slide title because they are already at the highest level. Pressing Shift+Tab also promotes selected text.
Demote	Change the selected text's outline level to the next level, applying that level's style and formatting. For example, demoting text at outline level three moves it to level four. Demoting a slide title moves the text of the selected slide to the previous slide. You can demote up to nine levels. Pressing the Tab key also demotes selected text.
Move Up	Move the selected text so that it displays before the previous item in the outline.
Move Down	Move the selected text so that it displays after the next item in the outline.
Hyperlink	Add a hyperlink to the selected text.
Show Text Formatting	Show the actual presentation font formatting in Outline view.

NOTE   Most of these menu options work best for slides that contain a lot of text, such as bulleted lists. If your slides emphasize other types of content, such as graphics and charts, you'll find it to be more convenient to rearrange content directly on your slides.

Promoting and Demoting Outline Points

You can demote outline headings, and promote and demote subheadings to reorganize and rearrange your presentation. Promoting a first-level subheading makes it a heading (slide title) in a new slide. Promoting a second-level subheading (such as indented text or lower-level bullet) moves it up to the next level. On the other hand, promoting indented text outdents it.

For example, if you right-click the text of a second-level bullet in the outline (see Figure 7.3) and select Promote from the menu, the bullet becomes a first-level bullet (see Figure 7.4).

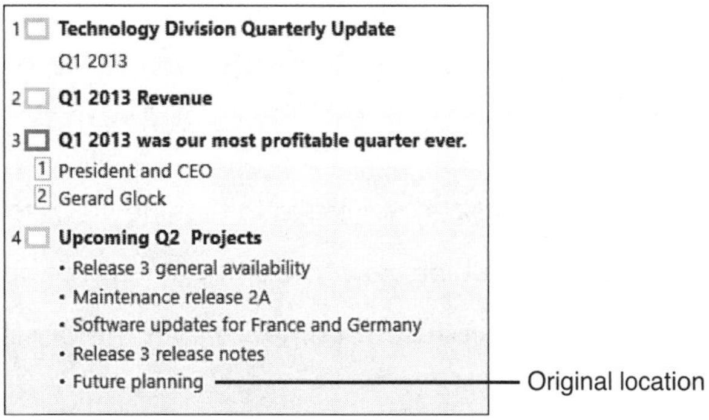

1 ☐ **Technology Division Quarterly Update**
     Q1 2013

2 ☐ **Q1 2013 Revenue**

3 ☐ **Q1 2013 was our most profitable quarter ever.**
  1 President and CEO
  2 Gerard Glock

4 ☐ **Upcoming Q2 Projects**
    • Release 3 general availability
    • Maintenance release 2A
    • Software updates for France and Germany
    • Release 3 release notes
    • Future planning ———————————— Original location

FIGURE 7.3

If a list item is at the wrong level, you can promote it.

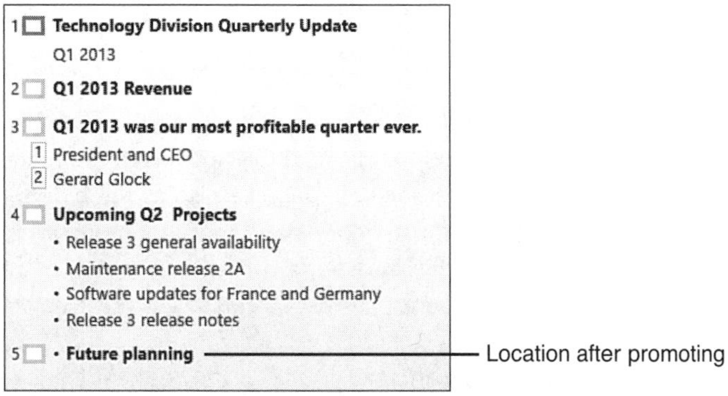

1 ☐ **Technology Division Quarterly Update**
     Q1 2013

2 ☐ **Q1 2013 Revenue**

3 ☐ **Q1 2013 was our most profitable quarter ever.**
  1 President and CEO
  2 Gerard Glock

4 ☐ **Upcoming Q2 Projects**
    • Release 3 general availability
    • Maintenance release 2A
    • Software updates for France and Germany
    • Release 3 release notes

5 ☐ • **Future planning** ———————————— Location after promoting

FIGURE 7.4

Promoting the list item moves it up one level but doesn't change its location.

If you promote a first-level bullet, it becomes a slide title, and PowerPoint inserts a new slide into the presentation. Demoting works in much the same way as promoting. Demoting a slide title makes it a first-level item and adds the slide's contents to the end of the previous slide. Demoting other text indents the text to the next outline level.

When you demote a slide, the text content remains and carries over to the previous slide, but any graphics or notes are deleted. To keep the notes and graphics, copy them to their destination using the Clipboard and then demote the slide.

Moving Outline Points Up and Down

You can also move each outline item up or down in the outline. To move an item up, right-click it and select Move Up from the menu. If you want to move an item down the outline, as you might expect, select Move Down from the menu.

Collapsing and Expanding Outline Points

To make it easier to read a long outline, collapse and expand slides and their body text.

To collapse the body text of slides in Outline view, follow these steps:

1. Right-click in Outline view to display a menu of options.

2. From the menu, pause your mouse over the Collapse option to display a submenu.

3. Select Collapse All from the submenu. On the outline, the slide numbers and titles remain, but the related body text is hidden from view.

To display your outline's detail again, right-click and select Expand and then Expand All from the menus.

 TIP To collapse the body text of an individual slide, right-click it and select Collapse from the menu. Right-click again and then select Expand to display the hidden text. If you want to collapse and expand more than one slide, but not all slides, press Shift, choose the consecutive slides, and then select Collapse or Expand. The slides you select must be consecutive.

Collapsing and expanding your outline makes it easier to print. You can print an entire outline in detail, only certain sections in detail, or only a collapsed summary outline. Learn more in Chapter 16, "Creating and Printing Presentation Materials."

Showing Slide Formatting

By default, Outline view displays each heading and subheading in the same font, bolding the headings for emphasis. If you want the outline to display using the actual fonts and formatting of the presentation, right-click the slide content and select Show Formatting from the menu.

Each item's specific font and attributes—such as size, bold, italic, underlining, and shadow—now display on the outline. The text's color is always black, though, regardless of the color formatting you've applied.

Inserting an Outline from Another Application

If you create an outline in another application, you can insert this file directly into PowerPoint, which can work with outlines in many different formats, such as the following:

- Word documents (.doc and .docx)
- Rich Text Format (.rtf)
- Text files (.txt)
- HTML (.htm or .html)

You can insert an outline into a blank presentation or into a presentation that already includes slide content. In the latter case, PowerPoint inserts the outline after the current slide.

To insert an outline from another application, follow these steps:

 CAUTION Be sure the file you want to insert is closed. If it's open in another application, PowerPoint gives you an error message.

1. On the Home tab, click the down arrow below the New Slide button.

2. At the bottom of the gallery, click Slides from Outline. Figure 7.5 shows the Insert Outline dialog box that displays.

 TIP The Insert Outline dialog box offers many of the same advanced options found in the Open dialog box. Learn more in Chapter 2, "Creating a Basic Presentation."

3. Navigate to the file you want to import and then click the Insert button. PowerPoint creates new slides and inserts the outline content onto these slides.

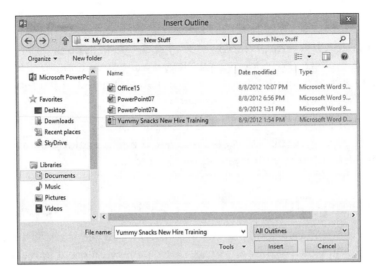

FIGURE 7.5

Insert an outline you created in another application.

For example, if you create an outline in Word, you can use Heading 1, Heading 2, and Heading 3 styles to format your document. When PowerPoint imports your outline, each Heading 1 becomes a slide title, each Heading 2 becomes first-level text, and each Heading 3 becomes second-level text. Other text isn't included in your outline. Figure 7.6 shows a PowerPoint slide with three heading levels inserted from a Word outline.

FIGURE 7.6

Outline in Word and then export your outline to PowerPoint.

If your outline doesn't insert as you anticipated, review your source document for any possible formatting problems. You can also use Outline view to revise your inserted content. Another option is to simply cut and paste your content onto your PowerPoint slides.

THE ABSOLUTE MINIMUM

Here are the key points to remember from this chapter:

- A solid, well-organized outline can make a big difference in the success of your presentation.

- Use Outline view to organize your slides, including promoting and demoting slide content.

- If you already have an existing outline in another application (such as Microsoft Word), you can import it into PowerPoint without retyping.

8

REVIEWING PRESENTATIONS

Providing feedback on PowerPoint presentations is an important part of the presentation design process in many organizations. Fortunately, PowerPoint simplifies this process with several powerful but flexible reviewing tools. Using the Review tab and Comments pane, you can add and manage presentation comments easily. If reviewers work on their own copies of a presentation, you can use the Compare feature to compare review copies to your master and incorporate any changes.

Understanding PowerPoint Reviewing Tools

If you're a longtime PowerPoint user, you're probably familiar with PowerPoint's commenting tools. In version 2010, PowerPoint introduced the capability to compare two presentations and collaboration through co-authoring—features that are new to many PowerPoint 2013 users as well.

This chapter focuses specifically on the reviewing tools you find on the Review tab. See Chapter 17, "Sharing Presentations," for more information about the many ways you can collaborate on the presentation review process.

 NOTE In addition to enabling you to manage comments and compare presentations, the Review tab also offers numerous proofing and language tools. See Chapter 4, "Working with Text," for more information about these tools.

Working with Comments

Using comments—the electronic version of Post-it Notes—is key to a successful presentation review. The Comments group on the Review tab offers five buttons that provide all the features you need to review and comment on a PowerPoint presentation (see Figure 8.1).

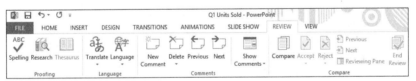

FIGURE 8.1

Use the buttons on the Review tab to add and manage presentation comments.

These buttons include the following:

- **New Comment**—Insert a comment about a slide or slide object.
- **Delete**—Delete a selected comment. Alternatively, click the down arrow to delete all comments on the current slide or all comments in the current presentation.
- **Previous**—Move to the previous comment in a presentation.
- **Next**—Move to the next comment in a presentation.
- **Show Comments**—Display the Comments pane or show markups.

Adding Comments to Slides

The best way to communicate your suggested changes to a presentation's author is to add a comment. You must use Normal view to add comments; Slide Sorter view doesn't support this feature.

To add a comment to a slide, follow these steps:

1. Select the slide object to which you want to add a comment, such as a text box, chart, or picture. If you want to comment on the slide as a whole, don't select anything.

2. On the Review tab, click the New Comment button. The Comments pane (see Figure 8.2) opens, displaying a comment box with your name and image.

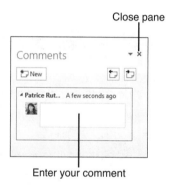

Close pane

Enter your comment

FIGURE 8.2

Comments are a great way to provide feedback on a presentation.

3. Enter your comment in the box.

4. Optionally, click the New button on the Comments pane to add another comment. If you want to comment on a specific slide object, select it before clicking the New button.

5. When you finish entering comments, click the Close button (x) to close the Comments pane.

PowerPoint displays comment markers for each comment you enter. PowerPoint places all general comment markers in the upper-left corner of the slide. If you add more than one general comment, the markers are stacked. If your comment relates to a specific slide object, the marker displays next to that object. Figure 8.3 shows a sample slide with two general comments, a comment about the slide title, and a comment about a chart.

Comments about the slide   Comment about the slide title

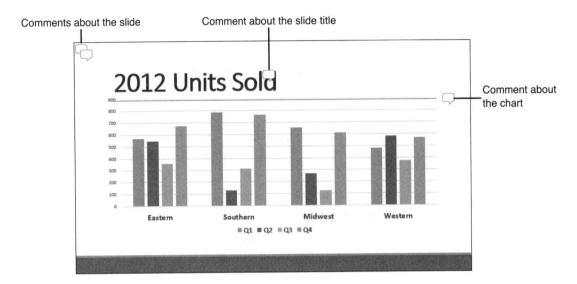

Comment about the chart

FIGURE 8.3

Add comments about overall slide content or about a specific slide object.

NOTE Optionally, you can move a comment marker from its default location by selecting it and dragging it with the mouse. This will make it more difficult to determine the focus of the comment, however.

Reviewing Comments

Use the Next and Previous buttons in the Comments group on the Review tab to move from comment to comment, evaluating each one on the Comments pane and making any needed presentation changes. When you reach the end of a presentation, clicking the Next button brings you back to the presentation's first comment.

TIP You can also use the Next and Previous buttons on the Comments pane (located just below the Close button) to move through comments.

Editing and Replying to Comments

To edit a comment, follow these steps:

1. Click the comment marker for the comment you want to edit; the Comments pane opens.

2. In the Comments pane, click the comment box to edit its contents (see Figure 8.4).

FIGURE 8.4

Edit comments on the Comments pane.

3. Make the appropriate changes and then click outside the comment box to close it.

 TIP   If comment markers don't display in your presentation, click the down arrow below the Show Comments button and select Show Markup from the menu.

To reply to a comment, select it on the Comments pane and enter your comment in the Reply box (refer to Figure 8.4).

Deleting Comments

After you read a comment and make any required presentation changes, you'll probably want to delete that comment. PowerPoint offers two ways to do this:

• Select a comment on the Comments pane and click the Delete button in its upper-right corner (refer to Figure 8.4).

• Select a comment marker on a slide and click the Delete button on the Review tab (the Comments pane also opens by default).

To delete all comments on the current slide, click the down arrow below the Delete button and then choose Delete All Comments and Ink on This Slide from the menu.

To delete all the comments in your entire presentation, click the down arrow below the Delete button and choose Delete All Comments and Ink in This Presentation.

Hiding Comments

If you don't want to delete comments, an alternative is to hide them so that they don't display on your presentation slides. To do so, click the down arrow below the Show Comments button and select Show Markup from the menu to remove its check mark.

Be aware that comments don't display in a slide show, so it isn't necessary to hide or delete them before presenting a show.

Comparing Presentations

Although it's best if all reviewers comment on and edit the same version of a presentation, such as one stored in a central location, there are times when they will enter comments in a separate version of your presentation. It can be a time-consuming process to determine what changes a reviewer made in this new version, particularly if your presentation contains lots of slides.

Fortunately, the Compare group on the Review tab (see Figure 8.5) offers several options for comparing presentations and accepting or rejecting potential changes.

FIGURE 8.5

The buttons on the Compare group simplify the consolidation of multiple presentation versions.

 NOTE   Until you click the Compare button and select another presentation to compare, none of the other buttons in this group are available.

To compare an open PowerPoint presentation with another presentation, follow these steps:

1. On the Review tab, click the Compare button. The Choose File to Merge with Current Presentation dialog box opens, as shown in Figure 8.6.

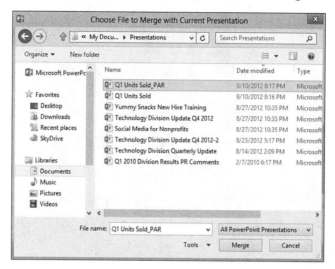

FIGURE 8.6

Select a presentation to compare.

2. Navigate to the presentation you want to compare and then click the Merge button. PowerPoint merges the two presentations and enables you to review, accept, and reject changes.

3. Manage your changes in one of the following ways:

    -   Use the Revisions pane.

    -   Use the Next and Previous buttons in the Compare group to scroll through changes.

    -   Click the Accept button to accept all changes.

Which option is best for you depends on your personal preferences and the number of suggested changes. The rest of this section covers the many ways you can view, edit, accept, and reject changes in a compared presentation.

Working with the Revisions Pane

When you click the Compare button, the Revisions pane opens with the Details tab selected by default (see Figure 8.7).

FIGURE 8.7

Quickly see presentation differences on the Revisions pane.

On the Details tab, you can view the following:

- Slide changes, such as comments or text replacements
- Presentation changes, such as the application of a new theme

On the Slides tab, shown in Figure 8.8, you can view slide changes by reviewer.

FIGURE 8.8

Click the down arrow in the Revisions pane for more slide review options.

To accept all the changes for a specific reviewer, select the check box to the left of that person's name. You can also click the down arrow to the right of each slide to do the following:

- Accept changes by this reviewer (for this slide).

- Reject changes by this reviewer (for this slide).

- Preview any animations added to the comparison presentation.

To close the Revisions pane, click the Close button (x) in the upper-right corner. Alternatively, on the Review tab, click the Reviewing Pane button, which serves as a toggle for this pane.

Viewing Revisions

You can also view and manage changes with buttons on the Review tab. Click the Next button in the Compare group to view each suggested change sequentially. PowerPoint highlights the change on the Revisions pane, letting you know what the suggested change is and who suggested it.

To accept the change, select the check box that precedes the change information. Continue to click the Next button until you finish cycling through all the changes. To go back, click the Previous button to return to the previous change.

Accepting Changes

If you want to accept an active change, click the Accept button. For more options, click the down arrow below the Accept button. From the menu that displays, you can do the following:

- Accept the current change (the same as clicking the Accept button).

- Accept all changes to the current slide.

- Accept all changes to the current presentation.

 TIP You can also accept changes on the Revisions pane or by clicking the check box to the left of any change that displays on a slide.

Rejecting Changes

After you accept a change, the Reject button on the Review tab becomes available. If you want to reject the active change, click the upper part of the Reject button. For more options, click the down arrow below the Reject button. From the menu that displays, you can do the following:

- Reject the current change (the same as clicking the Reject button).

- Reject all changes to the current slide.

- Reject all changes to the current presentation.

Ending the Review

When you finish comparing presentations, click the End Review button. PowerPoint opens a dialog box confirming that you want to proceed. All your accepted changes are applied to your original presentation; changes you didn't accept are discarded. Note that you can't undo this action.

THE ABSOLUTE MINIMUM

Here are the key points to remember from this chapter:

- PowerPoint offers a collection of reviewing tools that help you manage presentation feedback, an important part of the presentation design process in many organizations.

- The Comments group on the Review tab and the Comments pane offer everything you need to enter, edit, manage, reply to, and delete presentation comments.

- PowerPoint's Compare feature simplifies the process of comparing and consolidating feedback from multiple versions of your presentation.

9

WORKING WITH PICTURES

PowerPoint offers several ways to enliven your presentations with pictures, including inserting pictures from your computer or the Web, inserting screenshots, and creating photo albums.

After you add pictures to your presentation, PowerPoint provides a wide variety of customization and formatting options, including color correction, artistic effects, picture styles, borders, custom layouts, and much more.

Understanding PowerPoint Pictures

You can insert a variety of pictures into your PowerPoint presentations, including both illustrations and photographs. You do this by inserting a picture from your own computer or network or by inserting online pictures from the Office.com clip art collection, your SkyDrive account, or an external site such as Flickr.

PowerPoint works with two basic types of pictures. *Bitmap* pictures are composed of pixels: tiny dots of color. A single picture might contain hundreds of thousands of pixels. Bitmap pictures are the most common type of pictures on the Web. Photos from digital cameras are also bitmaps. Common bitmap file formats include .bmp, .gif, .jpg, .png, and .tif.

Vector pictures, on the other hand, are composed of points, lines, and curves. Because you can easily resize and change the color of vector pictures, they are popular for producing logos and other pictures that need to be repurposed. Common vector file formats include .eps and .wmf.

Table 9.1 lists the most common picture formats you can use in PowerPoint.

TABLE 9.1   Picture Formats

File Extension	Format
.emf	Windows Enhanced Metafile
.wmf	Windows Metafile
.jpg, .jpeg, .jfif, .jpe	JPEG File Interchange Format
.png	Portable Network Graphics
.bmp, .dib, .rle, .bmz	Windows Bitmap
.gif, .gfa	Graphics Interchange Format
.emz	Compressed Windows Enhanced Metafile
.wmz	Compressed Windows Metafile
.pcz	Compressed Macintosh PICT
.tif, .tiff	Tag Image File Format
.eps	Encapsulated PostScript
.pct, .pict	Macintosh PICT
.wpg	WordPerfect Graphics

Inserting Pictures

PowerPoint makes it easy to insert a picture from your computer or a network location. To do so, follow these steps:

1. On the Insert tab, click the Pictures button. The Insert Picture dialog box opens (see Figure 9.1), which is similar to the Open dialog box.

FIGURE 9.1

Find and insert a picture from the Insert Picture dialog box.

 NOTE   See Chapter 2, "Creating a Basic Presentation," for more information about the advanced features of the Open dialog box that are shared with the Insert Picture dialog box.

 TIP   Another way to insert a picture is to create a new slide using a slide layout that includes the content palette. Click the Pictures button on the palette to insert your picture.

2. Select the picture you want to insert.

 TIP   To select multiple pictures, hold down the Shift key as you select. If the pictures aren't contiguous, hold down the Ctrl key.

3. Click the Insert button to insert the selected picture on your slide. If you plan to make updates to this picture and would rather link to it instead, click the down arrow to the right of the Insert button and choose to link directly to the file. Alternatively, you can insert it and then link to it.

You can resize and reposition your picture and modify it in other ways. See "Modifying Pictures," later in this chapter, for more information.

Inserting Online Pictures

PowerPoint offers several options for inserting online pictures, including pictures from the Office.com clip art collection, your SkyDrive account, and other locations on the Web such as Bing Image Search and Flickr. After you insert an online picture, you can reformat, recolor, and redesign it to suit your needs.

Inserting Pictures from the Office.com Clip Art Collection

To insert a royalty-free photo or illustration from the Office.com clip art collection, follow these steps:

1. On the Insert tab, click the Online Pictures button. The Insert Pictures dialog box opens, as shown in Figure 9.2.

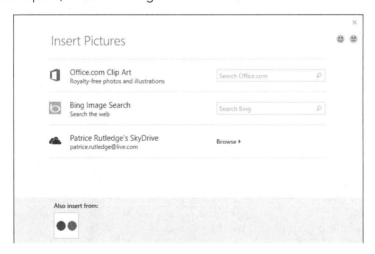

FIGURE 9.2

Insert pictures from Office.com.

TIP Another way to insert an online picture is to create a new slide using a slide layout that includes the content palette. Click the Online Pictures button on the palette to insert your picture.

2. Enter a keyword or keywords in the Search Office.com field and then click the Search button (the small magnifying glass to the right of the field). For example, you can search for pictures with computers, people, and so forth.

3. Scroll down the right side of the dialog box to view all results that match your keywords (see Figure 9.3).

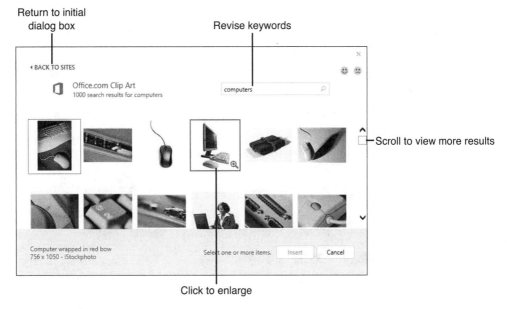

FIGURE 9.3

Viewing matching results.

4. Pause your mouse over a picture to display a description.

5. Click the View Larger button in the lower-right corner of a picture to enlarge it.

6. Select one or more pictures from the matching results. To select multiple pictures, hold down the Shift key as you select.

7. Click the Insert button to insert the picture into your presentation.

 TIP If your initial search doesn't yield the desired results, enter new keywords to search again.

Inserting Pictures from the Bing Image Search

To search Microsoft's search engine Bing for pictures licensed under Creative Commons, follow these steps:

 NOTE Creative Commons (creativecommons.org) enables content creators such as artists and photographers to let the public use their content under conditions they specify.

1. On the Insert tab, click the Online Pictures button to open the Insert Pictures dialog box (refer to Figure 9.2).

2. Enter a keyword or keywords in the Search Bing field and click the Search button (small magnifying glass to the right of the field).

3. Scroll down the right side of the dialog box to view all results that match your keywords (see Figure 9.4).

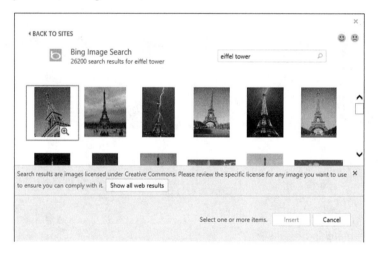

FIGURE 9.4

Bing displays matching pictures that are licensed under Creative Commons.

 CAUTION You can click the Show All Web Results button to view more options, but be aware that this could display pictures protected by copyright.

4. Pause your mouse over a picture to display a description.

5. Click the View Larger button in the lower-right corner of a picture to enlarge it.

6. Select one or more pictures from the matching results. To select multiple pictures, hold down the Shift key as you select.

7. Click the Insert button to insert the picture into your presentation.

Inserting Pictures from Your SkyDrive Account

To insert pictures stored on your SkyDrive account, follow these steps:

1. On the Insert tab, click the Online Pictures button to open the Insert Pictures dialog box (refer to Figure 9.2).

2. Click the Browse button.

3. Navigate to the folder that contains the picture you want to insert (see Figure 9.5).

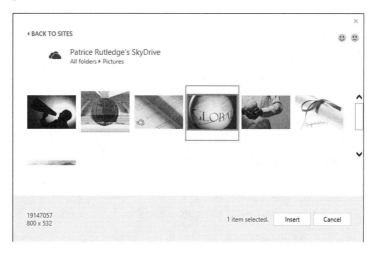

FIGURE 9.5

Insert pictures stored on SkyDrive.

4. Select one or more pictures from the matching results.

5. Click the Insert button to insert the picture into your presentation.

 TIP You can also insert pictures from your Flickr account. Click the Flickr button in the lower-left corner of the Insert Pictures dialog box to connect your Flickr account to your Microsoft account, enabling you to view your Flickr photos and videos in Office.

Inserting Screenshots

Rather than using an external application to take screenshots, PowerPoint offers its own screen capture tool.

To take a screenshot and insert it into your presentation, follow these steps:

1. Open the application from which you want to take a screenshot. For example, you might want to capture something from another Office application or from an external website.

2. Return to your PowerPoint presentation.

3. On the Insert tab, click the Screenshot button. A list of available windows appears, as shown in Figure 9.6.

FIGURE 9.6

Insert a screenshot of an open window or clip a section of a screen.

4. If you want to take a screenshot of the entire window and insert it into your PowerPoint presentation, select that window from the list.

5. If you want to select a specific area for your screenshot, select the Screen Clipping option on the menu. This minimizes PowerPoint and displays open applications and the desktop with a white semi-transparent layer.

6. If you're taking a clip of a screenshot, select the area you want to include in your presentation using your mouse pointer (which now appears as a crosshair).

Release the mouse and PowerPoint inserts the screenshot into your presentation.

Creating a Presentation from a Photo Album

With its Photo Album feature, PowerPoint enables you to automatically create a presentation composed of a series of pictures. For example, you could create a travel presentation consisting of a series of photos taken on a trip.

NOTE Be aware that PowerPoint creates a new presentation from your photo album, even if you start the process from an existing presentation.

To create a presentation based on a photo album, follow these steps:

1. On the Insert tab, click the Photo Album button. The Photo Album dialog box opens, as shown in Figure 9.7.

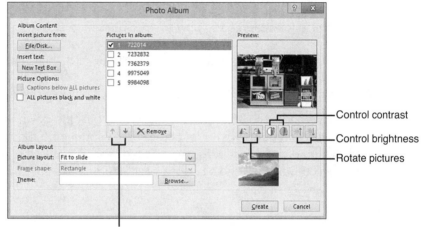

Move pictures up and down

FIGURE 9.7

Select and organize photos to insert in your presentation.

2. Click the File/Disk button to open the Insert New Pictures dialog box.

3. Navigate to the folder that contains the pictures you want to include in your album. To select all pictures, press Ctrl+A. Alternatively, press the Ctrl button on your keyboard and select individual pictures.

4. Click the Insert button to return to the Photo Album dialog box. PowerPoint lists the selected pictures in the Pictures in Album section.

5. Modify your photo album to suit your needs. For example, you can perform the following tasks:

    *   Insert a text box slide by clicking the New Text Box button. When you return to your presentation, you can enter text on this slide.

    *   Choose to display captions below all pictures or convert all pictures to black and white.

    *   Change the order of your pictures by clicking the Up and Down buttons (designated by arrows).

- Select a picture and click the Remove button to delete it from the album.

- Adjust the appearance of a picture using the Rotate, Brightness, and Contrast buttons (the small buttons below the picture).

- Select a layout from the Picture Layout drop-down list, such as one, two, or four pictures per page, with or without a title.

- Apply a frame shape such as a rectangle (the default), rounded rectangle, simple frame, or soft edge rectangle.

- Browse for a theme to apply to your presentation.

6. When you finish setting up your photo album, click the Create button.

PowerPoint creates a new presentation from your photo album.

To edit your photo album, go to the Insert tab, click the down arrow to the right of Photo Album button, and select Edit Photo Album from the menu. The Edit Photo Album dialog box opens, which is nearly identical to the original Photo Album dialog box you used to create your album. Make any changes and then click the Update button.

Modifying Pictures

After you insert a picture into a PowerPoint presentation, you can modify it to suit your needs. PowerPoint includes many image-editing features that can eliminate the need to edit your pictures in an external application.

The Picture Tools – Format tab, shown in Figure 9.8, appears whenever you select a picture. Using this contextual tab, you can make both minor and major adjustments to a picture, such as changing its color or adjusting its contrast. Although the buttons on this tab use the term *Picture*, these features also apply to photos and screenshots in your presentation.

FIGURE 9.8

The Picture Tools – Format tab offers a multitude of formatting options.

 NOTE   The Picture Tools – Format tab also displays when you select a shape that includes a picture fill.

NOTE Many of the options on the Picture Tools – Format tab include a link to the Format Picture pane, where you can customize a picture even further. You can also access this pane by right-clicking a picture and selecting Format Picture from the menu that appears. See the "Using the Format Picture Pane" section, later in this chapter, for more information.

Adjusting Pictures

The Adjust group on the Picture Tools – Format tab enables you to remove background areas from pictures, correct pictures, adjust color settings, and apply artistic effects. Be aware that not all these options are available, depending on the format of the picture you want to modify.

Removing a Picture Background

To remove the background of a selected picture, click the Remove Background button on the Picture Tools – Format tab. The Background Removal tab appears, as shown in Figure 9.9.

FIGURE 9.9

The Background Removal tab enables you to specify how and what to remove.

This tab offers the following options:

- **Mark Areas to Keep**—Designate the areas to keep with a Pencil tool.
- **Mark Areas to Remove**—Designate the areas to remove with a Pencil tool.
- **Delete Mark**—Remove the background areas you marked to remove.
- **Discard All Changes**—Restore the picture to its original state.
- **Keep Changes**—Save changes and close the Background Removal tab.

 CAUTION It takes some time to learn to use this powerful tool effectively. If you don't like the end result, click the Undo button in the upper-left corner of the PowerPoint screen to restore your picture's background.

Applying Picture Corrections

To brighten and sharpen a selected picture, follow these steps:

1. On the Picture Tools – Format tab, click the Corrections button.

2. From the gallery that appears, select an option in either the Sharpen/Soften section or the Brightness/Contrast section.

3. Pause your mouse over each style to preview what it looks like when applied to your picture.

4. When you find a style you like, click the style to apply it.

For additional picture correction options, click the Picture Corrections Options link at the bottom of the gallery to open the Format Picture pane.

Adjusting Picture Colors

To change or adjust a selected picture's colors, click the Color button on the Picture Tools – Format tab. In the gallery that appears, as shown in Figure 9.10, you can perform the following tasks:

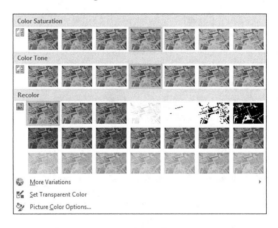

FIGURE 9.10

Specify exact colors for your picture.

- Modify your picture's color by specifying its purity based on a percentage (Color Saturation), specifying how light or dark the color is (Color Tone), or changing to a new color (Recolor).

- Click the More Variations link to open the Colors palette. You can choose a color from the palette or click the More Colors link to open the Colors dialog box. See Chapter 10, "Working with Shapes," for more information about this palette.

- Click the Set Transparent Color link to click a pixel in the selected picture, thereby making all pixels of the same color transparent.

- Click the Picture Color Options link to open the Format Picture pane.

Applying Artistic Effects

To apply artistic effects to a selected picture, such as a paintbrush effect or a pencil sketch effect, click the Artistic Effects button on the Picture Tools – Format tab. In the gallery that appears, select your desired effect. To apply additional effects in the Format Picture pane, click the Artistic Effects Options link.

Compressing Pictures

Compressing pictures enables you to reduce the file size of your presentation, which makes it easier to manage and deliver on the Web.

To compress a selected picture, follow these steps:

1. Click the Compress Pictures button on the Picture Tools – Format tab (a small button in the Adjust group). The Compress Pictures dialog box opens, as shown in Figure 9.11.

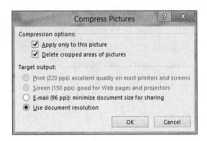

FIGURE 9.11

Specify compression options and select your target output.

2. The Apply Only to This Picture check box is selected by default. If you want to compress all the pictures in your presentation, remove this check mark.

3. The Delete Cropped Areas of Pictures check box is selected by default, which permanently removes any areas you cropped and reduces file size. If you don't want to do this, remove this check mark.

4. By default, the Use Document Resolution button is selected as your target output. Optionally, you can switch to a resolution suited to print, screen, or email. Depending on your picture format, all these options might not be available.

5. Click the OK button to compress your picture.

 NOTE If you remove the check mark next to the Apply Only to This Picture, PowerPoint compresses all pictures in your presentation. This process could take a while, especially if you are working on a large presentation with many pictures.

Changing to a Different Picture

If you decide to insert a different picture, but want to retain all the formatting you've applied to an existing presentation picture, on the Picture Tools – Format tab, click the Change Picture button (a small button in the Adjust group).

The Insert Pictures dialog box opens, where you can select a new picture from your computer or the Web. PowerPoint inserts the new picture and keeps all existing formatting.

Resetting a Picture

If you've made a lot of changes to a picture and then decide you want to go back to the original, on the Picture Tools – Format tab, click the Reset Picture button (a small button in the Adjust group). PowerPoint restores your picture to its original appearance. If you want to reset picture formatting *and* size (from compression, for example), click the down arrow to the right of the Reset Picture button and select Reset Picture & Size from the menu.

 NOTE If you compress a picture and select the Delete Cropped Areas of Pictures check box, you can't reset your picture.

Working with Picture Styles

The Picture Styles group on the Picture Tools – Format tab enables you to apply one of many preselected styles to your pictures. You can also add a border, apply special effects, and modify your layout.

Applying a Picture Style

To apply a picture style, select one of the styles in the Picture Styles group, or click the down arrow to the right of the group to open a gallery of additional options, as shown in Figure 9.12.

FIGURE 9.12

Choose to apply a picture style, such as a rotated white border or a soft-edge oval shape, to your picture.

This gallery displays additional picture styles such as Reflected Bevel Black, Rotated White, and Soft Edge Oval. Pause your mouse over each style to preview what it looks like when applied to your picture. When you find a style you like, click it to apply.

 TIP You can also apply a picture style by right-clicking a picture and then selecting the Style button that displays either above or below the shortcut menu depending on where you right-click the picture.

Applying Picture Borders

To add a border to a selected picture, on the Picture Tools – Format tab, click the Picture Border button. The Picture Border palette appears, as shown in Figure 9.13.

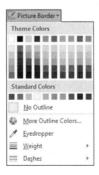

FIGURE 9.13

Specify the type of picture border to apply.

Choose from the following options:

- Apply one of the theme or standard colors. The theme colors are compatible with your slide's color scheme.

- Select No Outline to hide the existing border.

- Select More Outline Colors to open the Colors dialog box, in which you can select from many other colors or create a custom color. See Chapter 10 for more information about this dialog box.

- Select Eyedropper to select a fill color by clicking an existing color on the screen.

- Select Weight to specify the border weight—from 1/4 point to 6 points.

- Select Dashes to specify a dash style, such as square dot, dash dot, or long dash. Unless you create a thick outline, dashes probably won't be visible.

 TIP For more options, select More Lines from the Weight or Dashes menu to open the Format Picture pane.

Applying Picture Effects

You can add shadow, glow, bevel, and 3-D effects to pictures by using the tools on the Picture Effects palette. To apply picture effects to a selected picture, on the Picture Tools – Format tab, click the Picture Effects button. The Picture Effects menu appears. Each menu choice leads to a gallery of additional options.

Depending on the shape you select, not all options are available. To preview a potential effect on your presentation, pause the mouse over it in the gallery.

Choose from the following options on the Picture Effects menu:

- **Preset**—Apply one of 12 ready-made effects designed to work well with your picture.

- **Shadow**—Apply an outer, inner, or perspective shadow to the shape. Select No Shadow to remove the shadow.

- **Reflection**—Apply one of several reflection variations, such as a half or full reflection. Selecting No Reflection removes the shape effect.

- **Glow**—Apply one of several glow variations in different colors and sizes. Select No Glow to remove the glow effect. Select More Glow Colors to open the Colors palette, where you can select another color.

- **Soft Edges**—Apply a soft edge, ranging in width from 1 to 50 points. Select No Soft Edges to remove the effect.

- **Bevel**—Apply one of several bevel options, such as a circle or divot. Select No Bevel to remove the effect.

- **3-D Rotation**—Apply a parallel, perspective, or oblique rotation to the selected shape. Remove the effect by selecting No Rotation.

 TIP For more options, select the Options link at the bottom of each gallery to open the Format Picture pane. The exact wording of the Options link varies based on the name of the gallery, such as Shadow Options or 3-D Rotation Options.

Converting Pictures to SmartArt Graphics

If you want to convert a picture, or a series of pictures, to a SmartArt graphic, select the pictures, and then on the Picture Tools – Format tab click the Picture Layout button. From the gallery that appears, select the SmartArt style you want to apply to your pictures.

See Chapter 11, "Working with SmartArt," for more information about SmartArt graphics in PowerPoint.

Arranging Pictures

Like with other PowerPoint objects, you can arrange the pictures you insert into your presentation. The Arrange group on the Picture Tools – Format tab offers numerous options for arranging pictures. For example, you can align, group, and rotate pictures and send overlapping pictures backward or forward to achieve a desired effect.

See Chapter 5, "Formatting and Organizing Objects, Slides, and Presentations," for more information about using the options in the Arrange group.

Cropping Pictures

If you don't want to include an entire picture in your presentation, you can crop it to your exact specifications. For example, you might want to zero in on an object in the center of a picture, or remove extra content at the top of a picture.

To crop a selected picture, on the Picture Tools – Format tab, click the Crop button.

 TIP You can also crop a picture by right-clicking it and then selecting the Crop button that displays either above or below the shortcut menu depending on where you right-click the picture.

From the menu that appears, select one of the following options:

- **Crop**—Drag the mouse to determine your cropping area. Handles surround the picture, enabling you to specify the exact content you want to retain.

- **Crop to Shape**—Select a shape from the gallery that appears. PowerPoint modifies the picture to fit the selected shape.

- **Aspect Ratio**—Crop to a specific aspect ratio, such as a 1:1 square, 2:3 portrait, or 3:2 landscape.

- **Fill**—Resize the picture to fill the entire picture area, maintaining the original aspect ratio.

- **Fit**—Resize the picture to fit the specified picture area, maintaining the original aspect ratio.

Modifying a Picture's Height and Width

To modify a selected picture's height or width, on the Picture Tools – Format tab, enter a new measurement in the Shape Height and Shape Width boxes, located in the Size group. Alternatively, use the scrolling arrows to make incremental adjustments either smaller or larger.

For more picture-sizing options, click the arrow in the lower-right corner of the Size group to open the Format Picture pane, where you can specify size, rotation, scale, and more.

Using the Format Picture Pane

You can use the Format Picture pane to apply numerous formatting changes all in one place. This pane duplicates many of the functions available on the Picture Tools – Format tab, but also has some special features of its own.

To open the Format Picture pane, shown in Figure 9.14, right-click a picture and choose Format Picture from the menu that displays.

 TIP You can also access this pane from the Options menu in many of the palettes and galleries on the Picture Tools – Format tab. For example, click the Artistic Effects button and select Artistic Effects Options from the gallery to open the Artistic Effects section on the Format Picture pane.

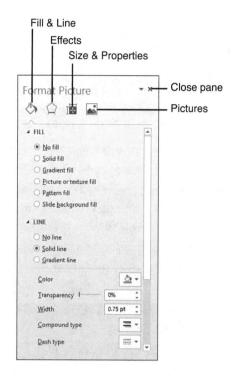

FIGURE 9.14

The Format Picture pane enables you to make many changes in one place.

Click one of the following buttons to display related content on the pane:

- **Fill & Line**—Format fills and lines.

- **Effects**—Apply shadows, reflections, glows, soft edges, 3-D formats, 3-D rotations, and artistic effects.

- **Size & Properties**—Format size, position, text boxes, and alt text.

- **Pictures**—Apply picture corrections, color, and cropping.

The tools available on the Format Picture pane are nearly identical to those found on the Format Shape pane. See Chapter 10 for more information about this pane.

THE ABSOLUTE MINIMUM

Here are the key points to remember from this chapter:

- You can insert a variety of pictures, photos, and illustrations into your PowerPoint presentation, including both bitmap and vector images.

- Inserting a picture from your computer or a network location is one of the most common ways to add pictures to a presentation.

- PowerPoint offers several options for inserting online pictures, including pictures from the Office.com clip art collection, your SkyDrive account, and other locations on the Web such as Bing and Flickr.

- You don't needs to use an external application to take screenshots. PowerPoint provides its own screen capture tool that lets you insert full or cropped screenshots.

- With a photo album, you can automatically create a presentation composed of a series of pictures.

- You can use the Picture Tools – Format tab or the Format Picture pane to modify a picture's color, appearance, or size as well as apply artistic effects, styles, borders, and layouts.

10

WORKING WITH SHAPES

A *shape* is an object you place on a slide, such as a line, arrow, rectangle, circle, square, or callout. You can quickly insert a basic shape in your presentation, but after you use PowerPoint for a little while, you'll probably want to modify the default shape formats. Fortunately, PowerPoint offers a variety of shape-formatting options that enable you to quickly customize a shape to meet the exact needs of your presentation.

Inserting Shapes

PowerPoint offers dozens of ready-made shapes that you can add to your presentation.

To insert a shape on your slide, follow these steps:

1. On either the Home tab or the Insert tab, click the Shapes button. The Shapes gallery opens, as shown in Figure 10.1.

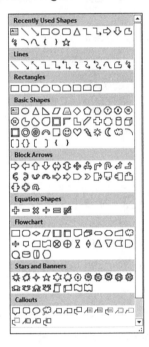

FIGURE 10.1

The Shapes gallery offers a variety of options.

 TIP If you've already inserted another shape and the Drawing Tools – Format tab appears, you can access the Shapes gallery from this tab as well.

2. From the gallery, select the shape you want to insert. Gallery options include the following:

    *   **Recently Used Shapes**—Insert one of the shapes you've most recently used in your PowerPoint presentations. If you have a new installation of PowerPoint 2013, this option won't appear.

- **Lines**—Insert a straight line or arrow, or insert a special line form such as a curve, scribble, or freeform. This option also includes six different connectors that draw lines between objects. When you move an object, the connector stays attached and moves with it.

 TIP   To force a connection between two objects to be the shortest distance, reroute the connector. To do this, go to the Drawing Tools – Format tab, click the Edit Shape button in the Insert Shapes group, and choose Reroute Connectors.

- **Rectangles**—Insert one of nine different rectangular shapes, including the Rounded Rectangle and Snip Single Corner Rectangle.

- **Basic Shapes**—Insert a common shape. Here are some options:

  - Polygons, such as a hexagon, a triangle, a parallelogram, and so on

  - 3-D shapes, such as a box and a cylinder

  - Fun shapes, such as a crescent moon, a smiley face, and a lightning bolt

  - Grouping and connecting shapes, such as brackets and braces

- **Block Arrows**—Insert a large block arrow, curved or bent arrow, or callout with arrows.

- **Equation Shapes**—Insert a plus, minus, multiplication, division, equal, or not equal sign.

- **Flowchart**—Insert a flowchart image such as a process, a decision, a document, an input, or a terminator.

- **Stars and Banners**—Insert a wave, a scroll, a ribbon, an explosion, or a pointed star.

- **Callouts**—Insert one of several kinds of callouts. A *callout* is a line with a text box connected to one end. You position the line's free end on something you want to highlight, place the text box to the side, and type descriptive text in it.

- **Action Buttons**—Insert an action button. Action buttons make your presentation interactive, performing actions such as navigating among slides, running programs, and playing sounds. See Chapter 18, "Working with Hyperlinks and Action Buttons," for more information about action buttons.

3. On your slide, click where you want the shape to appear and then drag until the shape is the size you want. You can then format the shape as you would any other object.

TIP Keep in mind that although PowerPoint shapes make it easy to create an attractive image, they aren't designed for complex graphic needs. If you need something more detailed, consider using SmartArt. See Chapter 11, "Working with SmartArt," for more information.

Inserting Lines and Arrows

You can add lines and arrows to your presentation to draw attention to something, show how things are connected, or show how one thing leads to another. For example, you might want to add a line to connect two shapes. Or you might use an arrow to point to text or an object of special importance. You can also create simple images with the line, rectangle, and oval shapes.

To draw a line or arrow on your slide, follow these steps:

1. On the Home tab or Insert tab, click the Shapes button to open the Shapes gallery (refer to Figure 10.1).

2. Click one of the buttons in the Lines section of the Shapes gallery. The mouse pointer becomes a plus sign.

3. Click and hold down where you want the line to begin and then drag to where you want the line to end.

If the line looks crooked or is the wrong length, you can adjust it. First, select the line. Then, pause your mouse over one of the handles that appear at the ends of the line. The mouse pointer becomes a line with an arrowhead at both ends. Click and drag the circle to lengthen the line or adjust its angle.

If the line isn't in the right place, you can move it. First, select the line. Then pause your mouse over the line. The mouse pointer becomes a cross with arrowheads at all four ends. Click and drag the line to move it.

 TIP Press the Shift key as you drag the mouse to create straight horizontal or vertical lines. This enables you to draw lines at angles evenly divisible by 15 (0, 15, 30, 45, and so forth), which makes it much easier to create a straight line. Press the Ctrl key as you drag the mouse to draw a line from a center point, lengthening the line in both directions as you drag.

 NOTE By using the options in the Shape Outline palette, you can easily change the appearance of a line or arrow by adjusting its width or converting it to a dashed line. See section, "Specifying Shape Outlines," later in this chapter, for more information.

Inserting Rectangles and Ovals

You can draw rectangular and oval shapes directly on your slide. Using rectangular shapes enables you to emphasize important information, group information, or illustrate other ideas or concepts.

To draw a rectangle, click one of the buttons in the Rectangles section of the Shapes gallery. The mouse pointer becomes a plus sign. Click where you want the rectangle to appear on your slide and then drag to draw the rectangle.

 TIP To draw a square, press the Shift key while you draw the shape.

To draw an oval, click the Oval button in the Basic Shapes section of the Shapes gallery. The mouse pointer becomes a plus sign. Click where you want the oval to appear and then drag to draw the oval.

 TIP To draw a perfect circle, press the Shift key while you draw the shape.

You can then reshape and resize these images or apply other formatting to them.

Another option is to add text to a rectangular or oval shape. If you want to add only a word or two, select the shape and type in the text you want to enter. Alternatively, click the Text Box button on either the Insert tab or the Drawing Tools – Format tab and create a text box inside the original object. Be sure, however, that the text box fits into the object without overlapping its borders.

Formatting Shapes Using the Drawing Tools – Format Tab

When you create or select a shape, the contextual Drawing Tools – Format tab appears, shown in Figure 10.2.

FIGURE 10.2

The Drawing Tools – Format tab offers numerous options for shape creation and formatting.

The Insert Shapes and Shape Styles groups on the Drawing Tools – Format tab are the centerpieces of PowerPoint's suite of shape-creation and shape-formatting tools. They offer a multitude of options for modifying and enhancing presentation shapes, such as specifying a shape's fill, outline, and effects. This rest of this chapter focuses on the many shape-formatting options available on this tab.

 NOTE The Home tab also offers most, but not all, of the shape-formatting features available on the Drawing Tools – Format tab.

Working with Shape Quick Styles

One way to format a shape quickly is to apply a Quick Style. Quick Styles offer numerous fill, shading, and border options in colors that coordinate with your chosen theme.

To apply a Quick Style to a shape, follow these steps:

1. Select the shape to which you want to apply the style.

2. On the Drawing Tools – Format tab, click the down arrow to the right of the Shape Styles box to open the Shape Styles gallery, as shown in Figure 10.3.

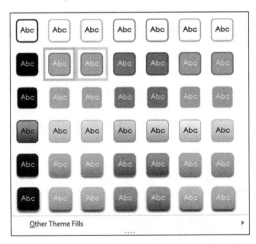

FIGURE 10.3

Choose a shape style that coordinates with your presentation theme.

3. Pause your mouse over an available style to preview the style's effect on your shape.

 TIP You can also open the Shape Styles gallery by clicking the Quick Styles button on the Home tab or by right-clicking a shape and clicking the Style button that displays either below or above the contextual menu.

4. Optionally, click Other Theme Fills at the bottom of the gallery to open a palette of additional options, including several grayscale options.

 TIP As a shortcut, you can click one of the styles that display in the Shape Styles box on the tab itself without opening the gallery. The default view shows several possible styles.

5. Click a style to apply it to the selected shape.

Specifying Shape Fill Color

To set a shape's fill color, select it, and on the Drawing Tools – Format tab, click the Shape Fill button. A palette displays, as shown in Figure 10.4.

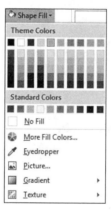

FIGURE 10.4

Add colors or patterns to fill an object.

You can do any of the following in this palette:

- Apply one of the theme, recent, or standard colors. The theme colors are compatible with your slide's color scheme.

- Select No Fill to make the object transparent. You see the slide background through the object.

- Select More Fill Colors to open the Colors dialog box, where you can choose from many other colors or create a custom color.

- Select Eyedropper to choose a fill color by clicking an existing color on the screen.

- Select Picture to fill your shape with a picture you select.

- Select Gradient to apply a light or dark gradient pattern.

- Select Texture to fill the shape with one of the available texture patterns in the gallery that appears.

 TIP You can also access fill options by right-clicking a shape and clicking the Fill button that displays below the contextual menu.

Using the Colors Dialog Box

Select More Fill Colors in the Shape Fill palette to open the Colors dialog box, as illustrated in Figure 10.5.

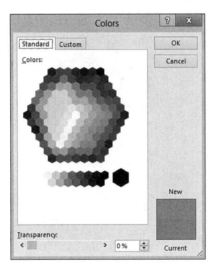

FIGURE 10.5

Choose from many common colors in the Colors dialog box.

To choose a new color, select it in the palette on the Standard tab. The color appears in the New section of the preview box to contrast with the Current color.

Click OK to keep the color or click Cancel to return to the original color.

 TIP You can set transparency (making the color appear transparent) by dragging the Transparency scrollbar or by entering a specific transparency percentage. The higher the percentage, the more transparent the color, which enables things behind the object to show through.

Using a Custom Color

To add a custom color, click the Custom tab on the Colors dialog box, as shown in Figure 10.6.

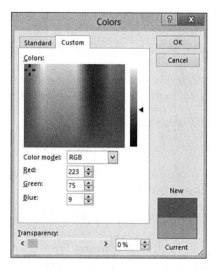

FIGURE 10.6

Create a custom color to suit your exact needs.

You can create a custom color in two ways. One way is to click and drag the crosshair in the Colors area until you find the color you want. The other way is to choose either RGB or HSL in the Color Model drop-down field and then adjust the color's level of red, green, and blue (for RGB) or hue, saturation, and luminance (for HSL). Click OK to keep the color or click Cancel to discard it.

 NOTE *Red, green,* and *blue* represent the amount of each of these primary colors in the color you create. The RGB color wheel used in PowerPoint is based on projected light—the kind you see with computer screen projection.

Hue represents the actual color, *saturation* represents the color's intensity, and *luminance* represents the color's brightness. In general, the lower the number, the lighter or less intense the color is.

Using the Eyedropper Fill

The Eyedropper fill enables you to choose a fill color by selecting an existing color on the screen. To use this tool, follow these steps:

1. Select the shape whose color you want to change.

2. On the Drawing Tools – Format tab, click the Shape Fill button and choose Eyedropper from the menu.

3. Click the shape whose color you want to copy. PowerPoint applies this color to the shape you selected in Step 1.

Applying a Picture Fill

You can even fill an object with a picture. For example, you could create a shape such as a circle and fill it with a logo, product image, or photo.

To apply a picture fill, follow these steps:

1. Select the shape to which you want to apply the picture fill.

2. On the Drawing Tools – Format tab, click the Shape Fill button and then choose Picture from the menu.

3. In the Insert Pictures dialog box, do one of the following:

- Click the Browse button next to the From a File field to open the Insert Picture dialog box, where you can select a picture on your computer to insert.

- Enter keywords in the Search Office.com field and press the Enter key to search the Office.com online clip art collection.

- Enter keywords in the Search Bing field to search Bing for relevant pictures.

- Click the Browse button next to the SkyDrive field to insert a picture you stored on your SkyDrive account.

- Click the Flickr button to insert a picture from your Flickr account.

See Chapter 9, "Working with Pictures," to learn more about the Insert Pictures dialog box.

 CAUTION Some pictures just don't work well as fills. Look at yours carefully. If it doesn't look good, press Ctrl+Z to undo it and then apply another fill.

Applying a Gradient Fill

A gradient creates a smooth transition from one color to another, using gentle blending. To apply a gradient to a selected shape, on the Drawing Tools – Format tab, click the Shape Fill button and select Gradient from the menu. From the gallery that appears, you can apply a light or dark gradient. Pause your mouse over each available gradient to preview its effect on your presentation. Click the gradient to apply to your presentation. To remove a gradient, select No Gradient in the gallery.

 TIP   For more gradient options, click More Gradients in the gallery to open the Format Shape pane. See section, "Using the Format Shape Pane," later in this chapter, for more information.

Applying a Textured Fill

To apply a texture to a selected shape, on the Drawing Tools – Format tab, click the Shape Fill button and then choose Texture from the menu. Select your preferred texture from the gallery (see Figure 10.7), pausing your mouse over each option to preview it on your presentation.

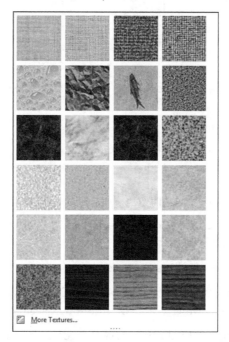

FIGURE 10.7

Textures can add visual depth to a shape.

 TIP   For more options, click More Textures in the gallery to open the Format Shape pane, described in section, "Using the Format Shape Pane," later in this chapter.

Specifying Shape Outlines

To specify the outline of a shape—either a line or any other shape such as a circle or rectangle—select the shape and click the Shape Outline button on the Drawing Tools – Format tab. The Shape Outline palette appears, as shown in Figure 10.8.

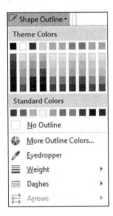

FIGURE 10.8

Specify the format of a shape's outline in the Shape Outline palette.

TIP You can also access outline options by right-clicking a shape and clicking the Outline button that displays below the contextual menu.

Choose from the following options:

- Apply one of the theme or standard colors. The theme colors are compatible with your slide's color scheme.

- Select No Outline to hide the existing line.

- Select More Outline Colors to open the Colors dialog box, where you can select from many other colors or create a custom color.

- Select Eyedropper to choose an outline color by clicking an existing color on the screen.

- Select Weight to specify the outline weight—from 3/4 point to 6 points.

- Select Dashes to specify a dash style, such as square dot, dash dot, or long dash. Unless you create a thick outline, dashes probably won't be visible.

- Select Arrows to specify an arrow style. Note that this option is available only for open shapes with a distinct beginning and end such as lines, arrows, curves, freeforms, and scribbles.

TIP   For more options, select More Lines or More Arrows from the Weight, Dashes, or Arrows menus to open the Format Shape pane, described in section, "Using the Format Shape Pane," later in this chapter.

Applying Shape Effects

You can add shadow, glow, bevel, and 3-D effects to shapes by clicking the Shape Effects button on the Drawing Tools – Format tab. The Shape Effects menu offers numerous effect choices, each leading to a gallery of additional options.

Depending on the shape you select, not all options are available. To preview a potential shape effect on your presentation, pause the mouse over it in the gallery.

Choose from the following shape effects:

- **Preset**—Apply one of 12 ready-made effects designed to work well with your shape.

- **Shadow**—Apply an outer, inner, or perspective shadow to the shape. Select No Shadow to remove the shadow.

- **Reflection**—Apply one of several reflection variations, such as half or full reflection. Selecting No Reflection removes the shape effect.

- **Glow**—Apply one of several glow variations in different colors and sizes (see Figure 10.9). Select No Glow to remove the glow effect. Select More Glow Colors to open the Colors palette, where you can select another color. Refer to section, "Using the Colors Dialog Box," earlier in this chapter, for more information about colors.

- **Soft Edges**—Apply a soft edge, ranging in width from 1 to 50 points. Select No Soft Edges to remove the effect.

- **Bevel**—Apply one of several bevel options, such as a circle or divot. Select No Bevel to remove the effect.

- **3-D Rotation**—Apply a parallel, perspective, or oblique rotation to the selected shape. Remove the effect by selecting No Rotation. Figure 10.10 illustrates the 3-D Rotation gallery.

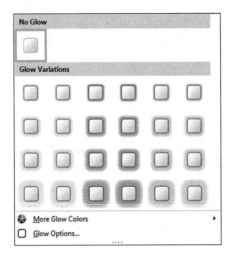

FIGURE 10.9

Get dramatic with glow effects.

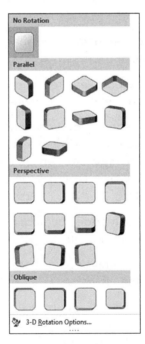

FIGURE 10.10

Get creative with 3-D effects, but be sure that your object doesn't become too distorted.

Editing Shapes

On the Drawing Tools – Format tab, click the Edit Shape button in the Insert Shapes group to open a submenu with the following choices:

- **Change Shape**—Change the applied shape to another shape available in the Shapes gallery.

- **Edit Points**—Edit the points of selected shapes. This enables you to select and drag a shape's existing points to create a new shape design.

- **Reroute Connectors**—Force a connector (line connecting two shapes) to be the shortest distance. Be aware that although doing this creates a more direct connection, the connector might overlap other shapes or text.

 CAUTION Be aware that depending on the type of shape you select, not all editing options are available.

Merging Shapes

PowerPoint 2013 introduces the capability to merge shapes using the Merge Shapes button. To merge two or more selected shapes, follow these steps:

1. Select the shapes you want to merge.

2. On the Drawing Tools – Format tab, click the Merge Shapes button (it's a small button in the Insert Shapes group).

3. From the menu that displays, specify the merge option you want to apply: Union, Combine, Fragment, Intersect, or Subtract. Figure 10.11 shows several examples of these merge options.

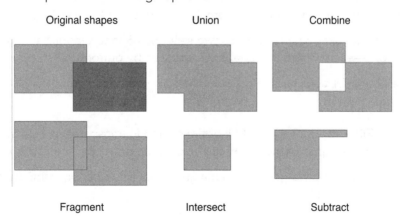

FIGURE 10.11

Try out some creative shape merge options.

TIP Several of these merge options work best with shapes that overlap.

Merging shapes using the Union option is similar to grouping shapes, but there are two distinct differences (for more information about grouping, see Chapter 5, "Formatting and Organizing Objects, Slides, and Presentations").

When you merge shapes, PowerPoint applies the attributes of the first selected shape to the other selected shapes. For example, if you select a green rectangle and then a blue rectangle and merge them using the Union option, both rectangles become green in the merged shape. When you group shapes of different colors, the coloring doesn't change.

In addition, grouping objects is reversible using the Ungroup option, which isn't available when you merge shapes (unless you use the Undo button above the Ribbon).

Using the Format Shape Pane

You can use the Format Shape pane to apply numerous formatting changes all in one place. The Format Shape pane duplicates some of the functions available on the Drawing Tools – Format tab, but also has some special features of its own.

NOTE If you select a picture to format, the name of the pane is Format Picture, but contains many of the same features as the Format Shape pane.

To open the Format Shape pane, right-click a shape and choose Format Shape from the menu that displays. Figure 10.12 shows the Format Shape pane.

The Format Shape pane includes two sections—Shape Options and Text Options—each with multiple tabs represented by buttons.

The Shape Options section includes the following tabs (refer to Figure 10.12):

- **Fill & Line**
    - **Fill**—Apply a variety of fill options, modify transparency, customize gradient presets, and change the scale and alignment of picture and texture fills.
    - **Line**—Apply a gradient line, adjust presets, and apply compound line styles and line joins.

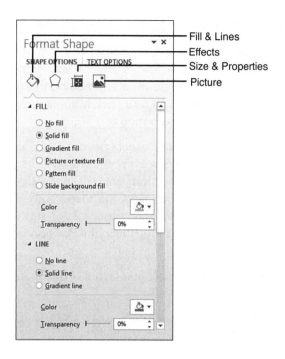

FIGURE 10.12

The Format Shape pane enables you to make many changes in one place.

- **Effects**
  - **Shadow**—Adjust the blur, distance, and angle of shadow presets.
  - **Reflection**—Apply a preset reflection and modify its transparency, size, distance, and blur.
  - **Glow**—Apply a preset glow and modify its colors, size, and transparency.
  - **Soft Edges**—Apply a preset soft edge and modify its size.
  - **3-D Format**—Apply 3-D formatting options, such as bevel, depth, contour, material, and lighting.
  - **3-D Rotation**—Apply preset rotation options; rotate the x, y, or z axis; and specify the distance from the ground.
  - **Artistic Effects**—Apply an artistic effect to a picture such as Watercolor Sponge, Chalk Sketch, or Crisscross Etching. This option is available only for shapes with picture or texture fills.

- **Size & Properties**
  - **Size**—Specify the exact height and width of an object, rather than resizing it with the mouse. This is useful if you want to create several objects of the same size and need greater precision than you can achieve by resizing with the mouse. You can also specify an exact rotation percentage rather than rotate using menu options.
  - **Position**—Enter the exact horizontal and vertical positions for the object. For example, to place an object so that its upper-left corner is exactly 1" left of the slide's center, enter **-1** in the Horizontal Position field and **0** in the Vertical Position field and then choose Center in both of the From fields. To move an object that's 2.75" from the slide's left edge 1" to the left, enter **1.75** in the Horizontal Position field and make sure that the From field specifies the Top Left Corner.
  - **Text Box**—Establish text layout, AutoFit, and internal margin settings for text boxes.
  - **Alt Text**—Apply alternative text to assist users with accessibility issues.
- **Picture**
  - **Picture Corrections**—Sharpen or soften a picture. Also modify brightness and contrast.
  - **Picture Color**—Modify color saturation and tone.
  - **Crop**—Specify exact cropping parameters including height and width. You can crop a picture if it contains things you don't need to show in your presentation. For example, you can crop a portrait to show just the person's face. You can also crop a picture with the mouse, which many people find easier. To do so, select the picture. Then, on the Drawing Tools – Format tab, click the Crop button.

 NOTE The Picture tab is available only for shapes with picture or texture fills.

The Text Options section includes the following tabs (see Figure 10.13):

- **Text Fill & Outline**
  - **Text Fill**—Apply a solid, gradient, picture, texture, or pattern fill and specify fill color and transparency.
  - **Text Outline**—Apply a solid or gradient line, adjust presets, and apply compound line styles and line joins.

- **Text Effects**—This tab includes options that are nearly identical to the Effects tab in the Shape Options section.

- **Textbox**—Apply text box formatting, including alignment, AutoFit, margins, and columns.

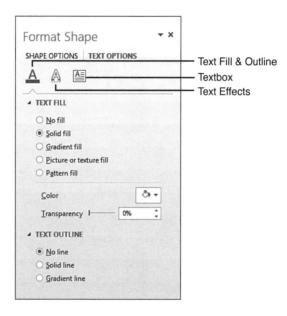

FIGURE 10.13

The Text Options section of the Format Shape pane offers additional ways to enhance text.

THE ABSOLUTE MINIMUM

Here are the key points to remember from this chapter:

- PowerPoint enables you to insert a wide variety of shapes on your slides, including lines, arrows, rectangles, circles, squares, callouts, and more.

- The Drawing Tools – Format tab provides an extensive array of shape-formatting tools.

- Using the Format Shape pane is another option for modifying and customizing shapes.

11

IN THIS CHAPTER

- Understanding SmartArt Graphics
- Inserting SmartArt Graphics
- Modifying and Formatting SmartArt Graphics

WORKING WITH SMARTART

SmartArt offers a unique opportunity to present slide content, such as an organization chart or a process, in a way that makes the most of PowerPoint's many sophisticated design features.

Understanding SmartArt Graphics

SmartArt takes the power and flexibility of PowerPoint shapes one step further. SmartArt enables you to combine shapes and text to create informative lists, matrices, pyramids, and more. Then, using PowerPoint's many shape and text formatting options, you can create a custom graphic that both conveys your message and gives your presentation the "wow" factor.

For example, you can create a detailed organization chart with SmartArt (see Figure 11.1). Or you can create a graphic that explains a step-by-step process (see Figure 11.2).

FIGURE 11.1

Use one of SmartArt's many organization chart layouts.

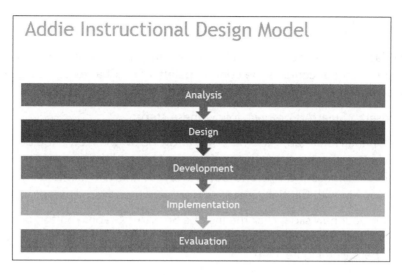

FIGURE 11.2

Highlight a process in your presentation.

Table 11.1 lists the PowerPoint SmartArt types, each offering a variety of layouts to choose from.

TABLE 11.1 PowerPoint SmartArt Types

Choose This SmartArt Type	To Display
List	Nonsequential data
Process	Steps in a process or a sequential timeline
Cycle	An ongoing process
Hierarchy	Hierarchical data such as an organizational chart
Relationship	Connected data
Matrix	Parts in relation to a whole
Pyramid	Proportions from small to large
Picture	A graphical representation of data

Inserting Smart Art Graphics

The fastest way to add a SmartArt graphic to your presentation is to apply a slide layout that contains the content palette. See Chapter 2, "Creating a Basic Presentation," for more information about PowerPoint slide layouts.

To insert a SmartArt graphic, follow these steps:

1. On the Home tab, click the down arrow below the New Slide button, and then choose an appropriate layout from the gallery that appears. For example, you could choose the Title and Content layout, the Two Content layout, or the Content with Caption layout.

2. On your new slide, click the Insert a SmartArt Graphic button on the content palette, as shown in Figure 11.3. The Choose a SmartArt Graphic dialog box opens (see Figure 11.4).

Insert SmartArt

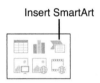

FIGURE 11.3

Use the content palette as an easy starting point for inserting SmartArt.

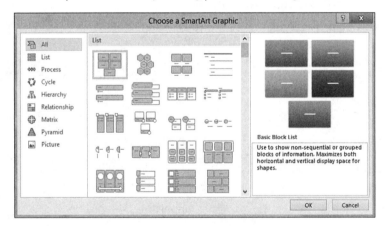

FIGURE 11.4

Choose from a variety of SmartArt graphic layouts.

3. In the Choose a SmartArt Graphic dialog box, select the button for the SmartArt layout types you want to view. Alternatively, select the All button to scroll through a list of all options. Refer to Table 11.1 for an explanation of each SmartArt type.

NOTE If you're new to SmartArt, it's often difficult to determine which graphic best suits your needs. When you click each graphic icon in the Choose a SmartArt Graphic dialog box, the right side of the screen displays a detailed example of the selected SmartArt graphic and describes its use in the box below. Reviewing all your options at least once gives you a clearer idea of what's available and can provide some inspiration as well.

4. Select the icon for the graphic type you want to insert, and click the OK button. The graphic appears on your slide (see Figure 11.5).

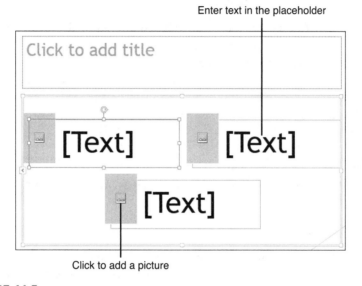

FIGURE 11.5

A blank SmartArt graphic appears on your slide.

Each SmartArt graphic includes text placeholders where you can enter the appropriate text. To enter text, click the [Text] placeholder and start typing. If you enter more text than the shape can hold, PowerPoint resizes the text. You can also enter text in the Text pane, described in the section, "Using the Text Pane," later in this chapter.

If you choose a graphic that includes pictures, click the picture placeholder to open the Insert Pictures dialog box.

Modifying and Formatting SmartArt Graphics

PowerPoint offers two contextual tabs that enable you to modify the design and format of your SmartArt graphics: the SmartArt Tools – Design tab and the SmartArt Tools – Format tab.

Note that these contextual tabs appear only when you have selected a graphic. If they disappear, select your graphic again to view them. Also, be aware that depending on your choice of SmartArt graphic, not all options are available on the SmartArt Tools tabs.

TIP You can also apply animation effects to your SmartArt graphic, such as having the graphic fly in to the slide. Learn more in Chapter 14, "Working with Animation and Transitions."

Using SmartArt Design Tools

The SmartArt Tools – Design tab, as shown in Figure 11.6, enables you to create additional graphic objects, specify layout and style options, and convert your SmartArt graphic to other formats.

FIGURE 11.6

The SmartArt Tools – Design tab is one of two SmartArt Tools contextual tabs.

Adding a Shape to a SmartArt Graphic

Although SmartArt graphics already contain shapes by default, you can add more shapes if you need. For example, you could create a basic cycle graphic, which comes with five shapes, and then decide you need to add a sixth.

To add a shape to a SmartArt graphic, follow these steps:

1. Select the SmartArt graphic to which you want to add a shape.

2. On the SmartArt Tools – Design tab, click the down arrow to the right of the Add Shape button to display a menu of options.

3. Select from the following menu choices:

   - **Add Shape After**—Add an identical shape after a selected shape.

   - **Add Shape Before**—Add an identical shape before a selected shape.

   - **Add Shape Above**—Add an identical shape above a selected shape.

   - **Add Shape Below**—Add an identical shape below a selected shape.

   - **Add Assistant**—Add an assistant shape to an organization chart.

NOTE The options available are based on your choice of SmartArt. For example, the Add Assistant menu option is available only if your graphic is an organization chart.

If you want to place an additional shape in the default location for your graphic type (such as at the end of a list), you can click the Add Shape button directly, without viewing the menu options.

Adding Bullets

If your SmartArt graphic supports bulleted lists, you can add a text bullet by clicking the Add Bullet button on the SmartArt Tools – Design tab. You must select a specific graphic object for this button to become active.

Using the Text Pane

Although you can enter text directly on your SmartArt graphic, using the Text pane is a good idea if you have a lot of text or your graphic is more complex.

To open the Text pane, click the Text Pane button on the SmartArt Tools – Design tab. Figure 11.7 shows a sample Text pane.

FIGURE 11.7

Edit and organize text on the Text pane.

In this pane, you can enter and revise text, use the buttons in the Create Graphic group to promote or demote objects, and edit any pictures if you selected a graphic type that includes pictures.

To close the Text pane, click the Close button (x) in the upper-right corner or click the Text Pane button on the SmartArt Tools – Design tab again, which acts as a toggle.

Organizing SmartArt Content

The Create Graphic group on the SmartArt Tools – Design tab (refer to Figure 11.6) also includes several buttons that help you organize the content in your graphic. For example, you can promote, demote, or reorder objects to customize your graphic exactly the way you want. Be aware that like other options on the SmartArt Tools – Design tab, the availability of these buttons depends on your graphic type and what object is selected.

The buttons include the following:

- **Promote**—Move selected object up a level. You can also use this with the Text pane.

- **Demote**—Move selected object down a level. You can also use this with the Text pane.

- **Right to Left**—Change layout from the right to the left.

- **Move Up**—Move selected object up in a sequence.

- **Move Down**—Move selected object down in a sequence.

- **Layout**—Modify the layout of an organization chart, such as displaying subordinates to the left or to the right.

Modifying Your SmartArt Layout

The Layouts group on the SmartArt Tools – Design tab offers several layout options that you can apply to your SmartArt graphic. Three options appear on the tab itself, but you can click the down arrow to the right of the group to open a gallery of additional options. Pause the mouse over each option to preview it on your slide. These layouts correspond to the layouts that appear on the Choose a SmartArt Graphic dialog box.

Changing SmartArt Colors

If you don't like your graphic's default color scheme, you can quickly change it by clicking the Change Colors button on the SmartArt Tools – Design tab. Figure 11.8 shows the gallery that displays, offering color choices suited to your specific SmartArt graphic type.

You can choose a primary theme color, select something more colorful, or opt for one of your theme's accent colors.

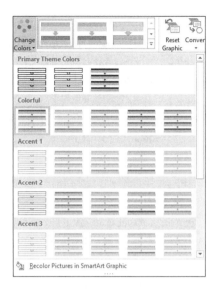

FIGURE 11.8

Get colorful by changing your SmartArt colors.

Applying a SmartArt Style

If you want to quickly dress up your SmartArt graphic, apply one of the many ready-made styles designed to complement your presentation's theme. To do so, select a style in the SmartArt Styles group on the SmartArt Tools – Design tab. For more options, click the down arrow to display a gallery where you can choose a style that's a good match for your document, or try out a 3-D style.

Resetting a SmartArt Graphic

If you've made a lot of changes to your SmartArt graphic and decide you don't like what you've done, click the Reset Graphic button on the SmartArt Tools – Design tab. PowerPoint deletes all the formatting changes you've made to your graphic and restores its original format. PowerPoint doesn't delete any text you've added, however.

Converting a SmartArt Graphic

If you decide that you don't want to use a SmartArt graphic you created but would like to retain your text as a bulleted list, click the Convert button on the SmartArt Tools – Design tab and then select Convert to Text from the menu.

Another option is to convert your SmartArt graphic to a shape so that you can take advantage of shape-formatting options. To do this, click the Convert button and then select Convert to Shapes from the menu. Learn more in Chapter 10, "Working with Shapes."

Formatting SmartArt Graphics

The SmartArt Tools – Format tab, as shown in Figure 11.9, offers numerous SmartArt formatting options, many of which are shared with other PowerPoint objects.

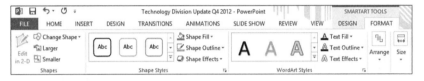

FIGURE 11.9

Create a custom look with the options on the SmartArt Tools – Format tab.

On this tab, you can perform the following tasks:

- Edit a 3-D graphic in 2-D.

- Format and change individual SmartArt shapes.

- Apply shape style, fills, outlines, and effects. Learn more in Chapter 10.

- Apply WordArt styles, fills, outlines, and effects to SmartArt text. Learn more in Chapter 4, "Working with Text."

- Arrange SmartArt objects, such as moving objects forward and backward and aligning, grouping, and rotating objects. Learn more in Chapter 5, "Formatting and Organizing Objects, Slides, and Presentations."

- Change the height and width of your SmartArt graphic by clicking the Size button.

Editing in 2-D

If you applied a 3-D style to your SmartArt graphic, you can temporarily return to 2-D to edit it by clicking the Edit in 2-D button on the SmartArt Tools – Format tab. When you finish editing, click this button again to return to your 3-D style.

Changing the Appearance of SmartArt Shapes

Although SmartArt graphics include default shapes, you might prefer a different shape. For example, if you select a Basic Block List, your graphic includes several basic rectangles. Your preference, however, might be rounded rectangles.

To change the appearance of the shapes in your SmartArt graphic, follow these steps:

1. Select the shape or shapes you want to change. To select multiple shapes, press the Ctrl key while clicking the shapes you want to change.

2. On the SmartArt Tools – Format tab, click the Change Shape button. A gallery of shape options appears, as shown in Figure 11.10.

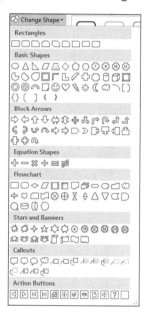

FIGURE 11.10

Select a new shape in this gallery.

3. Select the shape option you prefer to change your selected shapes.

Resizing Shapes

If you want to resize selected shapes on your graphic, click either the Larger or Smaller button on the SmartArt Tools – Format tab. You can continue clicking these buttons until you reach your desired size.

THE ABSOLUTE MINIMUM

Here are the key points to remember from this chapter:

- SmartArt graphics combine shapes and text to create informative, eye-catching slide content.

- You can insert a SmartArt graphic from any slide layout that includes the content palette.

- PowerPoint's extensive SmartArt formatting tools provide hundreds of options for colors, borders, styles, and other design elements.

12

WORKING WITH CHARTS

Charts enliven your presentation with visual impact and convey routine data in a way that your audience can easily understand and analyze. PowerPoint offers a variety of chart types, including the popular column, pie, and bar charts as well as more creative options such as line, stock, surface, radar, and combo charts.

You can create charts directly in PowerPoint or import charts from Excel. From there, use PowerPoint's plentiful chart formatting, design, and style tools to enhance and customize charts to meet your presentation needs.

Understanding Charts

Charts enable you to display, analyze, and compare numerical data in a graphical format. For example, you could use a column chart to compare sales revenue by region over a period of time (see Figure 12.1). Or you could create a pie chart that illustrates the percentage of revenue each of your product lines contributes to your total company revenue (see Figure 12.2).

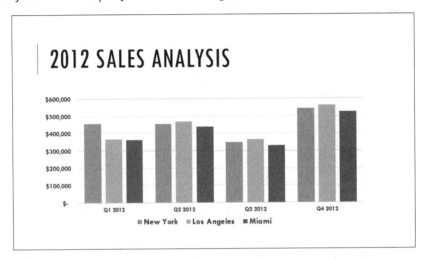

FIGURE 12.1

Compare data with a column chart.

FIGURE 12.2

Analyze percentages with a pie chart.

PowerPoint also offers a vast array of design and formatting options to make your charts as aesthetically pleasing as they are informational, enhancing the presentation's appearance.

You can use the default worksheet in PowerPoint to enter your chart data or take advantage of the formatting and charting tools available in Excel to create charts. You can also insert an existing Excel chart into your presentation.

Understanding Chart Terminology

Before creating a chart, it's a good idea to learn—or refresh your memory about—basic chart terminology. Table 12.1 lists the basic concepts you need to understand to make the most of PowerPoint chart functionality.

TABLE 12.1 Chart Terminology

Term	Definition
Axis	A line defining the chart area. PowerPoint charts have two axes: a vertical axis that displays data (the y-axis) and a horizontal axis that displays categories (the x-axis).
Chart area	The entire chart and all its components.
Data label	A label that provides information about a data marker.
Data points	Values that display on a chart in the form of columns, bars, or pie slices, for example. A *data marker* represents each individual data point.
Data series	A group of related data points on a chart, identified by a specific color or pattern.
Legend	A small box that describes the patterns or colors used to distinguish chart data series or categories.
Plot area	The area of the chart included inside the axes.

Understanding Chart Types

PowerPoint offers multiple chart types, each with several variations to choose from. For example, if you want to create a column chart, PowerPoint offers several variations of the basic column chart, including options for creating stacked, clustered, and 3-D column charts.

CAUTION The number of available chart options can become overwhelming. To choose the right chart type, think carefully about the information you want to present and the message you want to convey with this data, and then select a chart type suited to your data. From there, choose the variation that provides the optimal visual impact and works well with your PowerPoint theme. If you don't have a lot of experience creating charts, you might need to experiment to find just the right match.

Table 12.2 lists PowerPoint chart types.

TABLE 12.2   PowerPoint Chart Types

Chart Type	Description
Column	Compare data in two or more vertical columns. This chart type works well if you want to compare categories or data across a specific time span.
Line	Display data across a line with markers for each value.
Pie	Display a round pie-shaped chart with percentages of a total.
Bar	Compare data in two or more horizontal bars.
Area	Display value trends in a single area.
X Y (Scatter)	Compare data with points.
Stock	Display stock data (or other scientific data) in terms of volume and open, high, low, and close value.
Surface	Display numeric data in 3-D columns and rows.
Radar	Compare the value of several series of data.
Combo	Combine two different chart types, such as a column and line chart.

Inserting Charts

The fastest way to add a chart to your presentation is to apply a slide layout that contains the content palette. See Chapter 2, "Creating a Basic Presentation," for more information about PowerPoint slide layouts.

To insert a chart, follow these steps:

1. Click the down arrow below the New Slide button on the Home tab and then choose an appropriate layout from the gallery that displays. For example, you could choose the Title and Content, Two Content, Comparison, or Content with Caption layout.

2. On your new slide, click the Insert Chart button on the content palette, as shown in Figure 12.3. The Insert Chart dialog box opens (see Figure 12.4).

Insert Chart button

FIGURE 12.3

Click the Insert Chart button to get started.

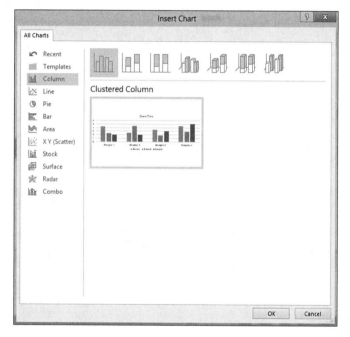

FIGURE 12.4

Choose from a variety of chart types.

  TIP Another way to insert a chart is to click the Chart button on the Insert tab.

3. In the Insert Chart dialog box, select the button for the chart type you want to insert. Refer to the section, "Understanding Chart Types," for an explanation of each chart type.

NOTE You can also view any chart templates you've saved by clicking the Templates button. See the section, "Saving Your Chart as a Template," later in this chapter, for more information about creating chart templates. On the Templates tab of the Insert Chart dialog box, you can also click the Manage Templates button to rename and delete your saved charts.

4. Select the icon for the specific chart type you want to insert and then click the OK button. PowerPoint displays the chart on your slide and opens a worksheet with sample data in the format needed for the selected chart type (see Figure 12.5).

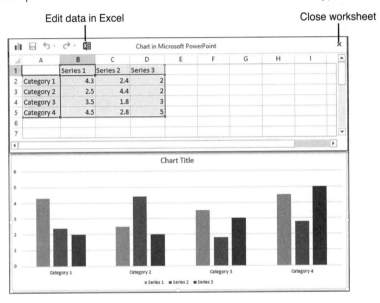

FIGURE 12.5

Enter your chart data in the worksheet.

5. Replace the sample data that displays in the worksheet with your actual data. The format of the sample data varies based on the chart type you selected in the Insert Chart dialog box.

 TIP Click the Edit Data in Microsoft Excel button to open Excel, which offers more formatting options.

6. When you're done entering data, click the Close (x) button in the upper-right corner of the worksheet.

7. PowerPoint displays the chart on your slide. From here, you can add a chart title and format your chart as needed.

Inserting a Chart from Excel

If you want to reuse an existing chart you created in Excel, you can quickly copy and paste it into PowerPoint.

To insert a chart from Excel, follow these steps:

1. Open the Excel worksheet that contains the chart you want to use in PowerPoint.

2. Select and copy (Ctrl+C) the chart you want to use.

3. Open your PowerPoint presentation and paste (Ctrl+V) the chart on the slide where you want to insert it.

4. Click the Paste Options button below the lower-right corner of the chart and select one of the following buttons, as shown in Figure 12.6:

   - **Use Destination Theme & Embed Workbook**—Embed the chart in your presentation and apply formatting from your presentation theme. You can modify the chart in PowerPoint, but any changes you make to the source in Excel aren't carried over.

   - **Keep Source Formatting & Embed Workbook**—Embed the chart in your presentation and retain the formatting applied in Excel. You can modify the chart in PowerPoint, but any changes you make to the source in Excel aren't carried over.

   - **Use Destination Theme & Link Data**—Insert the chart in your presentation (with a link to the source in Excel) and apply formatting from your presentation theme. Any changes you make to the source chart in Excel are carried over to PowerPoint.

   - **Keep Source Formatting & Link Data**—Insert the chart in your presentation (with a link to the source in Excel) and retain the formatting applied in Excel. Any changes you make to the source chart in Excel are carried over to PowerPoint.

   - **Picture**—Insert the chart as a picture. You can format your chart as you would any other picture in PowerPoint, but you can't change or update the chart data.

You can then format and modify your chart based on the constraints of your Paste Options selection.

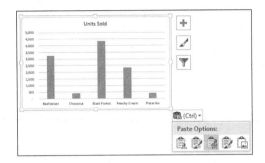

FIGURE 12.6

Specify how to paste Excel charts in PowerPoint.

Modifying and Formatting Charts

PowerPoint offers a variety of ways to modify and format your charts, which you explore in this section. New to PowerPoint 2013 are three buttons that display to the right of a selected chart: Chart Elements, Chart Styles, and Chart Filters.

PowerPoint also includes two contextual tabs that enable you to modify the design and format of your charts. These are, appropriately named, the Chart Tools – Design tab and the Chart Tools – Format tab. These tabs are nearly identical to the Chart Tools tabs in Excel.

NOTE Contextual tabs display only when a chart is selected. If they disappear, select your chart again to view them. Also be aware that depending on your choice of chart type, not all options are available on the Chart Tools tabs. For example, not all chart types have axes, trendlines, and so forth. In addition, some options pertain only to 3-D charts.

TIP You can also apply animation effects to your charts, such as having each series fly in separately. See Chapter 14, "Working with Animation and Transitions," for more information about chart animations.

Displaying, Hiding, and Modifying Chart Elements

PowerPoint charts include a variety of titles and labels that you can display, hide, and modify using the Chart Elements menu.

Select a chart and click the Chart Elements button to display this menu (see Figure 12.7). Here you can specify whether you want to show or hide each element by selecting or deselecting its check box and, optionally, choosing additional options from the menus that display. You can also specify your preferred formatting options.

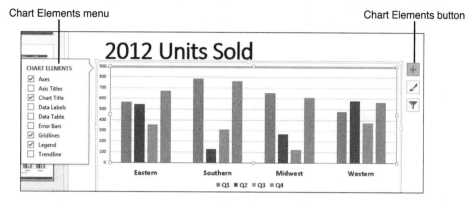

FIGURE 12.7

Specify the chart elements you want to display on your chart.

The available menu options vary by chart type and could include the following:

- **Axes**—Display the primary horizontal axis or the primary vertical axis.

- **Axis Titles**—Display the primary horizontal axis title or the primary vertical axis title.

- **Chart Title**—Display your chart title above the chart or as a centered overlay.

- **Data Labels**—Display data labels in one of five ways in relation to the data point (centered, inside the end, inside the base, outside the end, or as a data callout).

- **Data Table**—Display a data table with or without a legend key.

- **Error Bars**—Display error bars using standard error, by percentage, or with standard deviation.

- **Gridlines**—Display any or all of the following gridlines: primary major horizontal, primary major vertical, primary minor horizontal, or primary minor vertical.

- **Legend**—Display the legend at the right, top, left, or bottom.

- **Lines**—Displays drop lines or high-low lines.

- **Trendline**—Display a linear, exponential, linear forecast, or two-period moving average trendline based on a specific series in your chart.

- **Up/Down Bar**—Display up/down bars.

TIP It's sometimes hard to imagine how all these label options will actually look on your chart, so you might need to experiment a bit to find the format that works best.

Select the More Options link at the end of each menu to open the Format pane where you can select from additional options.

Modifying Chart Design

The Chart Tools – Design tab, as shown in Figure 12.8, enables you to change your chart type, edit chart data, and apply chart layouts and styles.

FIGURE 12.8

The Chart Tools – Design tab is one of two Chart Tools contextual tabs.

Adding a Chart Element

Click the Add Chart Element button on the Chart Tools – Design tab to add and format chart elements including axes, axis titles, chart titles, data labels, and more. You can also modify chart elements by clicking the Chart Elements button to the right of a selected chart. Refer to the section, "Displaying, Hiding, and Modifying Chart Elements," for more information.

Applying a Quick Layout

Click the Quick Layout button on the Chart Tools – Design tab to display a gallery of layout options you can apply to your chart. Pause over each option to preview its effect.

Applying a Chart Style

If you want to quickly dress up your chart, you can apply one of many chart styles designed to complement your presentation's theme. To do so, select one of the suggested styles in the Chart Styles group on the Chart Tools – Design tab. For more options, click the down arrow to the bottom-right of this group.

 NOTE You can also apply chart styles by clicking the Chart Styles button that displays to the right of a selected chart.

Modifying Chart Data

PowerPoint enables you to edit the data in your charts at any time or refresh data from a linked Excel chart.

The Data group on the Chart Tools – Design tab includes the following buttons:

- **Switch Row/Column**—Reverse the x- and y-axes.

- **Select Data**—Open the Select Data Source dialog box, where you can specify the chart data range and edit series and category labels.

- **Edit Data**—Open the worksheet where you can edit your chart data. Optionally, open in Excel for more formatting options.

- **Refresh Data**—Update a PowerPoint chart with data from a linked Excel worksheet.

Changing the Chart Type

If you don't like the way your chart looks and would like to try a different chart type, click the Change Chart Type button on the Chart Tools – Design tab to open the Change Chart Type dialog box. This dialog box is nearly identical to the Insert Chart dialog box, covered in the "Inserting a Chart" section earlier in this chapter. Select a new chart type and then click the OK button to return to your slide.

Formatting Charts

The Chart Tools – Format tab, as shown in Figure 12.9, enables you to apply formatting to specific chart areas, such as the axes, legend, gridlines, and series.

FIGURE 12.9

Apply subtle or sophisticated formatting on the Chart Tools – Format tab.

To format specific chart areas, follow these steps:

1. Select the area of the chart you want to format from the drop-down list in the upper-left corner of the Chart Tools – Format tab. The options that appear in the menu vary based on the chart type. For example, a pie chart doesn't have axes.

2. Click the Format Selection button to open the Format pane. Again, the exact name of the pane and its content vary based on your chart type and what you selected to format. For example, Figure 12.10 shows the Format Axis pane, which opens if you choose to format a chart axis.

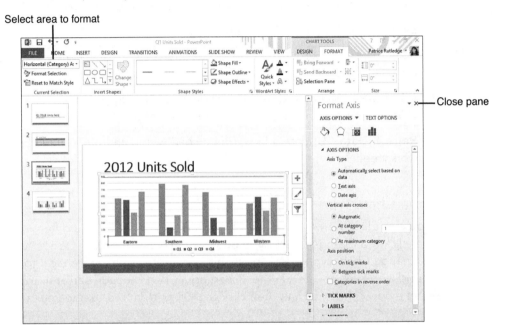

FIGURE 12.10

The Format pane takes many forms, such as the Format Axis pane.

3. Specify your formatting changes on the Format pane.

4. Click the Close (x) button to apply your changes and return to your chart.

The Chart Tools – Format tab also offers features shared with the Format tabs that appear in context when you're performing other tasks in PowerPoint, such as inserting shapes, applying shape styles and WordArt styles, and arranging chart elements. See Chapter 10, "Working with Shapes," for more information about this tab.

Applying Chart Filters

Chart filters enable you to hide chart data without actually deleting it.

To apply a filter, follow these steps:

1. Select a chart and click the Chart Filters button to its right (see Figure 12.11).

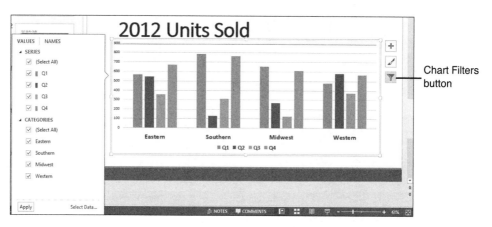

Chart Filters
button

FIGURE 12.11

Filter the data that displays on your chart.

2. On the Values tab, deselect the series and categories you don't want to display.

3. Click the Apply button.

NOTE Optionally, you can choose not to display series or category names on the Names tab (PowerPoint displays numbers instead). Or, you can click the Select Data link to open the Select Data Source dialog box, where you can add, edit, and remove data.

Saving Your Chart as a Template

If you make changes to your chart's design, layout, and format and would like to reuse it again, you can save it as a template.

To create a template based on your current chart, follow these steps:

1. Right-click the chart and select Save as Template from the menu that displays. Figure 12.12 shows the Save Chart Template dialog box that opens.

2. Verify that the default folder is the Charts folder. PowerPoint looks for chart templates in this folder when it populates the Templates section in the Insert Chart dialog box.

3. Enter a name for your template in the File Name field.

4. Click the Save button to save your template and return to your chart.

FIGURE 12.12

Reuse a common chart format as a template.

This template now displays as a choice in the Insert Chart dialog box for future use.

THE ABSOLUTE MINIMUM

Here are the key points to remember from this chapter:

- Charts enable you to display, analyze, and compare numerical data in a graphical format.

- PowerPoint offers a variety of chart types, including column, pie, bar, and line charts.

- You can create a chart directly in PowerPoint or import a chart from Excel.

- PowerPoint's chart formatting tools are plentiful; you can apply a variety of chart styles, change chart colors and appearance, specify the exact chart content you want to display, and much more.

13

WORKING WITH AUDIO AND VIDEO

The selective use of audio and video is a great way to add impact to any presentation. With PowerPoint, you can insert audio and video from a variety of sources, including the Office.com clip collection and YouTube, edit your media files without having to use an external application, and create videos from your presentation.

Understanding Audio and Video Formats

PowerPoint offers a multitude of options when it comes to incorporating audio and video into your presentation, including several ways to insert clips and a vast array of formatting and playback options. PowerPoint also supports a variety of common audio and video file formats.

Table 13.1 lists the audio and video file formats PowerPoint supports.

TABLE 13.1 Audio and Video File Formats

Audio File Formats	Video File Formats
Audio Interchange File Format (.aiff), the standard audio format for Apple computers	Advanced Systems Format (.asf), a Windows media file format for streaming media
Audio format used by Sun, Java, and Unix (.au)	Audio Video Interactive (.avi), a Windows video file format
Musical Instrument Digital Interface (.midi), an audio file format common with electronic musical instruments	Moving Picture Experts Group (.mpeg), a common movie file format
MPEG-1 Audio Layer 3 (.mp3), a common audio format for digital music	Windows Media Video (.wmv), a video file format developed by Microsoft for streaming video
Waveform Audio File Format (.wav), the standard audio format for Windows-based PCs	QuickTime video file (.mov), Apple's proprietary multimedia framework that handles both audio and video formats
Windows Media Audio (.wma), an audio format developed by Microsoft	Adobe Flash Media, multimedia format created with Adobe Flash (.swf)
QuickTime Video (audio component)	MP4 video (.mp4)

Inserting Audio Clips

PowerPoint offers three ways to insert audio clips into your presentation:

- Insert an online audio clip from Office.com
- Insert an audio clip stored on your computer or network
- Record an audio clip and insert it

When you select an audio clip on a slide, the player control bar displays below it. The Audio Tools – Format tab and Audio Tools – Playback tab also display.

See sections, "Formatting Audio and Video Clips" and "Specifying Audio and Video Playback Options," later in this chapter, for more information about these tabs.

Inserting Online Audio

To search for and insert an online audio clip from the Office.com royalty-free clip collection, follow these steps:

1. Navigate to the presentation slide where you want to insert your audio clip.

2. On the Insert tab, click the Audio button and select Online Audio.

3. Enter keywords related to the audio you want to insert in the text box and click the Search button (the small magnifying glass), as shown in Figure 13.1.

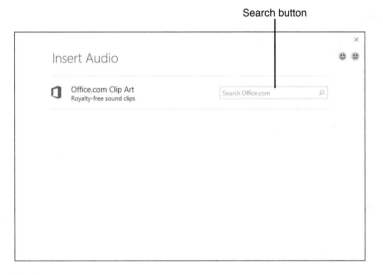

FIGURE 13.1

Add online audio to complement your presentation.

4. PowerPoint displays audio clips that match your search keywords. Select the audio clip you want and click the Insert button (see Figure 13.2).

 TIP   Preview an audio clip by clicking it. Be aware that the preview takes a few seconds to load.

5. PowerPoint downloads and inserts the audio into your slide in the form of an audio clip icon (see Figure 13.3). Modify and format the audio clip as desired.

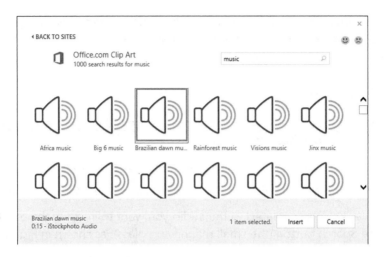

FIGURE 13.2

Select an audio clip from Office.com's extensive collection.

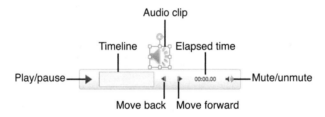

FIGURE 13.3

Play and control the playback of your audio clip.

Inserting Audio Clips from Your Computer

To insert an audio clip stored on your computer or on a network location, follow these steps:

1. Navigate to the presentation slide where you want to insert your audio clip.

2. On the Insert tab, click the Audio button and select Audio on My PC to open the Insert Audio dialog box, as shown in Figure 13.4.

 NOTE The Insert Audio dialog box shares many advanced options with the Open dialog box. See Chapter 2, "Creating a Basic Presentation," for more information about these options.

FIGURE 13.4

Insert an audio clip stored on your computer.

3. Navigate to the audio clip you want to insert and then click the Insert button. PowerPoint inserts the audio into your slide in the form of an audio clip icon (refer to Figure 13.3).

4. Modify and format the audio clip as desired.

You can reposition your audio clip elsewhere on your slide by clicking and dragging the clip to a new position.

 NOTE   If you are upgrading to PowerPoint 2013 from PowerPoint 2007 or earlier, be aware that PowerPoint now embeds audio clips in the PowerPoint file itself.

Recording Audio Clips

You can record your own audio clips to insert in your PowerPoint presentation. You need to have a microphone (built-in or external) on your computer to do this.

To record an audio clip, follow these steps:

1. Navigate to the presentation slide where you want to insert your audio clip.

2. On the Insert tab, click the Audio button and select Record Audio to open the Record Sound dialog box, as shown in Figure 13.5.

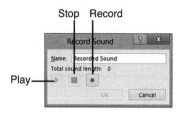

FIGURE 13.5

Record a sound to play with a particular slide.

4. Enter a description for this sound in the Name field.

5. Click the Record button to begin recording your sound.

6. Click the Stop button when you finish recording. To play back the sound, click the Play button.

7. Click the OK button to save the sound with the presentation; click Cancel to exit and start over.

An audio clip icon now displays in your presentation. You can reposition and resize it if desired. For example, you might want to place this icon in the lower-right corner of your slide to keep your audience focused on the slide content.

Deleting Audio Clips

To delete an audio clip from a slide, select it and press the Delete key.

 CAUTION   Be aware that you can't undo an audio clip deletion. If you change your mind after deletion, you have to insert or record the clip again.

Inserting Video Clips

PowerPoint offers two ways to insert video clips into your presentation:

- Insert an online video—from an external website or the Office.com clip collection.

- Insert a video clip from your computer.

Inserting Online Video

Inserting online video is an easy way to add a visual element to your presentation. PowerPoint enables you to insert video clips from an external website, such as YouTube. You can also search for videos on Bing, insert a video from one of your SkyDrive folders, or insert a video embed code.

To insert online video, follow these steps:

1. Navigate to the presentation slide where you want to insert your video clip.

2. On the Insert tab, click the Video button and select Online Video from the menu.

 TIP Another way to insert online video is to use a slide layout that includes the content palette and click the Insert Video button on the palette.

3. In the Insert Video dialog box, shown in Figure 13.6, you can do the following:

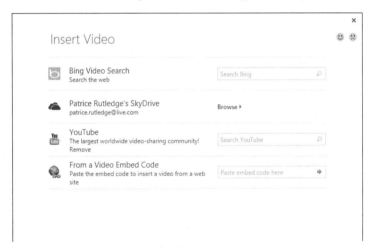

FIGURE 13.6

Insert videos from several online sources.

- Search for a video on Bing by entering keywords in the Search Bing field and clicking the Search button. PowerPoint displays matching videos from across the Web. Select the video you want and click the Insert button.

- Insert a video from your SkyDrive account by clicking Browse, selecting the video, and clicking the Insert button.

- Search for a video on YouTube by entering keywords in the Search YouTube field and clicking the Search button. PowerPoint displays matching videos (see Figure 13.7). Select the video you want and click the Insert button.

FIGURE 13.7

YouTube offers millions of videos you can insert in your presentations.

- Enter a video embed code in the Paste Embed Code Here field and press the Enter key.

 NOTE A video embed code enables you to share web videos in other locations, including PowerPoint presentations. Clicking a Share link or button usually leads to a video's embed code.

Figure 13.8 shows a sample video inserted from YouTube.

FIGURE 13.8

A sample online video inserted from YouTube.

You can resize and reposition a video by dragging the handles that surround it when it's selected.

Inserting a Video Clip from Your Computer

To insert a video clip from your computer or a network location, follow these steps:

1. Navigate to the presentation slide where you want to insert your video clip.

2. On the Insert tab, click the Video button and select Video on My PC to open the Insert Video dialog box, as shown in Figure 13.9.

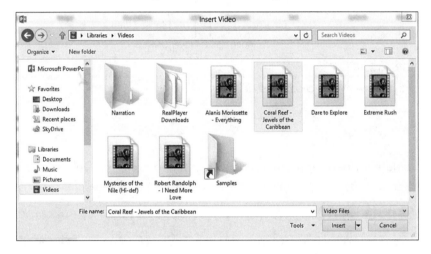

FIGURE 13.9

Select your own video to insert.

 NOTE The Insert Video dialog box shares many advanced options with the Open dialog box. See Chapter 2 for more information about these options.

3. Navigate to the video you want to insert and then click the Insert button. PowerPoint inserts the video into your slide, as shown in Figure 13.10.

4. Modify and format the video clip as desired.

Select the video to display the player controls below it, including the Play/Pause button, a timeline, the Move Back and Move Forward buttons, an elapsed time counter, and a volume control. The Video Tools – Format tab and Video Tools – Playback tab also display.

Play/pause ─→ | Timeline | Move back | Move forward | 00:13.55 | Elapsed time | Mute/unmute

FIGURE 13.10

Insert your own video clip on a slide.

Deleting a Video Clip

To delete a video clip from a slide, select it and press the Delete key.

Formatting Audio and Video Clips

The Audio Tools – Format tab and Video Tools – Format tab display when you select an audio or video clip on a PowerPoint slide. Figures 13.11 and 13.12 show these two tabs, which offer many options for formatting your media clips. With a few exceptions, these tabs are nearly identical and are also similar to the options on the Picture Tools – Format tab covered in detail in Chapter 9, "Working with Pictures." This chapter focuses on formatting issues unique to audio and video clips.

FIGURE 13.11

Format the appearance of an audio clip icon.

FIGURE 13.12

Dress up your video with a variety of video-formatting options.

Adjusting Audio and Video Clips

The Adjust group on the Audio Tools – Format tab and the Video Tools – Format tab enable you to remove background images from the audio clip icon, correct images, adjust color settings, and apply artistic effects. Be aware that not all these options are available, depending on the format of the image or video you want to modify.

See section, "Adjusting Pictures," in Chapter 9 for more information.

Specifying a Video Poster Frame

If you inserted a video clip, you can specify the appearance of the initial preview image, referred to as the *poster frame*. For example, you can display a static image from the video, a company logo, or even the photo of a speaker in the video.

To specify a poster frame for a selected video, go to the Video Tools – Format tab and click the Poster Frame button.

Select one of the following options from the menu:

- **Current Frame**—Use the current frame as the poster frame. To activate this option, you must play your video on your slide and pause it at the specific frame you want to use.

- **Image from File**—Open the Insert Pictures dialog box, where you can select an image from your computer, network location, or the Web.

- **Reset**—Restore the default poster frame.

Working with Audio and Video Styles

The Picture Styles group on the Audio Tools – Format tab and the Video Styles group on the Video Tools – Format tab enable you to do the following:

- Apply one of many preselected styles to your media clips, ranging from subtle to moderate to intense

- Add a border around your clip

- Apply special clip effects

- Modify your video shape

Note that for video, these effects apply to the video's preview image; for audio, the effects apply to the audio clip icon.

Figure 13.13 shows an example of the rotated, gradient style applied to a video clip.

FIGURE 13.13

Apply varied styles to your videos to give them a new look.

See section, "Working with Picture Styles," in Chapter 9 for more information.

Arranging Audio and Video Clips

The Arrange group on the Audio Tools – Format tab and the Video Tools – Format tab offers numerous options for arranging media clips. For example, you can align, group, and rotate images and send overlapping clips backward or forward to achieve a desired effect.

See Chapter 5, "Formatting and Organizing Objects, Slides, and Presentations," for more information about using the options in the Arrange group.

Resizing Audio and Video Clips

If you don't want to include an entire clip image in your presentation, you can crop it to your exact specifications. For example, you might want to zero in on an object in the center of a clip or remove extra content at the top of a clip. To do so, select the clip and click the Crop button on the Format tab. Handles surround the image, enabling you to specify the exact content you want to retain. Drag the mouse to determine your cropping area.

NOTE   *Cropping a clip* refers to reducing the size of its physical image. If you want to play only a certain section of the clip's audio or video content, you need to trim it, which you can do on the Playback tab.

Alternatively, enter precise size specifications in the Height and Width boxes.

Specifying Audio and Video Playback Options

The Audio Tools – Playback tab or Video Tools – Playback tab appears when you select an audio or video clip on a PowerPoint slide. The Playback tab offers many options for specifying how you want to play your clips in an actual slide show. Figures 13.14 and 13.15 show these two tabs.

FIGURE 13.14

Specify how you want to play an audio clip.

FIGURE 13.15

On the Video Tools – Playback tab, you can trim video content and determine how to start your video.

CAUTION   Be aware that not all playback options are available for online clips. If a specific button isn't active for your selected clip, that feature isn't supported.

Playing a Clip

To play a clip directly on your slide, click the Play button on the Playback tab. Alternatively, click the Play button on the player control bar that appears below your clip. This is a good way to preview clips before actually running a show.

Adding a Bookmark

If you want to return to a specific place in one of your clips, you can bookmark it. To create a bookmark, play the selected clip and then pause at the location where you want to place the bookmark. Next, click the Add Bookmark button on the Playback tab. PowerPoint inserts a bookmark on the clip's timeline (a yellow circle). Figure 13.16 shows a sample bookmark.

Bookmark

FIGURE 13.16

Use a bookmark to easily return to a specific location in your clip.

Bookmarks are useful if you want to start playing your clip at a certain location or want to replay a specific segment for emphasis. You can also bookmark start and stop times if you want to trim your clip.

Editing Audio and Video Clips

In the Editing group on the Playback tab, you can trim your clip by specifying exact start and stop times. You can also add fade-in and fade-out effects to your clip in increments of seconds.

To trim a selected audio clip, click the Trim Audio button on the Audio Tools – Playback tab. The Trim Audio dialog box displays, as shown in Figure 13.17.

To trim a selected video clip, click the Trim Video button on the Video Tools – Playback tab. The Trim Video dialog box displays, as shown in Figure 13.18.

FIGURE 13.17

Play only a certain section of an audio by trimming it.

FIGURE 13.18

PowerPoint makes it easy to trim your videos.

Although these dialog boxes differ in size, their fields are identical. To trim a clip, you can do the following:

- Enter times in the Start Time and End Time fields.

- Use the Play, Previous Frame, and Next Frame buttons to review your clip and determine start and end times.

- Use the sliders (green for start time and red for end time) to specify what to trim. This is particularly useful if you've already added bookmarks to your clip.

When you finish trimming, click the OK button to return to your slide.

NOTE Be aware that trimming clips doesn't actually remove any content; PowerPoint just plays the trimmed portions. To physically remove trimmed content, you must compress your files. See section, "Compressing Media Files for Improved Performance," later in this chapter for more information.

Specifying Audio and Video Options

The Audio Options group and Video Options group on the Playback tab share many of the same buttons and features, including the following:

- **Volume**—Specify the volume level: low, medium, high, or mute.

- **Start**—Specify whether to start a clip automatically, start it with a mouse click, or play it across slides (audio only).

- **Play Across Slides**—Play audio across all slides (audio only).

- **Loop Until Stopped**—Repeat playing a clip until you manually stop it.

- **Hide During Show**—Hide the Audio Clip icon during a slide show (audio only). You should play your clip automatically if you select this option.

- **Play Full Screen**—Select this check box to play a video full screen during a slide show (video only).

- **Hide While Not Playing**—Hide the video preview image when it's not playing (video only).

- **Rewind After Playing**—Return to the beginning of a clip after you play it.

Compressing Media Files for Improved Performance

To improve the playback performance of your media files and save disk space, you can compress these files. To compress the media files in an open presentation, follow these steps:

1. Click the File tab to open Backstage view.

2. Click the Compress Media button, shown in Figure 13.19, and select from the following menu of options:

   - **Presentation Quality**—Maintain high-quality audio and video.

   - **Internet Quality**—Maintain quality suitable for streaming media on the Internet.

- **Low Quality**—Maintain basic quality while reducing file size to that suitable for emailing a presentation.

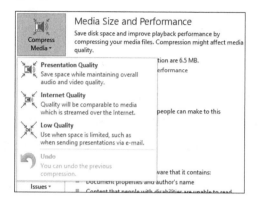

FIGURE 13.19

Compress your audio and video files to improve playback performance.

 CAUTION Be aware that the Compress Media button is available only if your presentation contains an audio or video file you can compress.

3. Review the Compress Media dialog box, which shows you the compression in progress. Depending on the number of media files in your presentation, this could take several minutes. When the compression process completes, the dialog box informs you how much space you saved, such as 1.4MB.

4. Click the Close button to close the dialog box.

Remember that compressing files affects presentation quality. Be sure to preview your presentation after compression to evaluate its impact.

 TIP To restore your presentation to its original status, select the Undo menu option.

Creating Videos from PowerPoint Presentations

PowerPoint lets you create full-fidelity video from your PowerPoint presentation in either a MPEG-4 Video (.mp4) or Windows Media Video (.wmv) format. You can distribute your video on the Web or mobile device, or through more traditional methods, such as on a DVD or through email.

TIP Before creating your video, decide what format you want to use and then verify that your slide content will work with this format. For example, if you want to run your video on portable devices, using small text isn't a viable option. In addition, you need to create any timings or narration before creating your video. See Chapter 15, "Presenting a Slide Show," for more information.

To create a video, follow these steps:

1. Open the presentation you want to save as a video.

2. Click the File tab and select Export to open the Export window in Backstage view.

3. Select Create a Video. The right side of the page shows the Create a Video section, as shown in Figure 13.20.

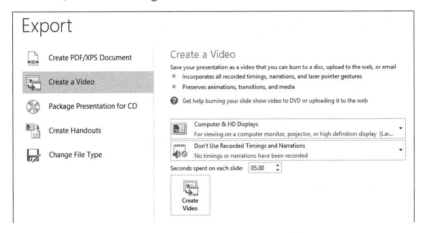

FIGURE 13.20

PowerPoint enables you to create videos from your presentations.

4. From the first drop-down list, select one of the following video formats:

- **Computer & HD Displays**—Create a video that plays on a computer monitor, project, or high-definition display at 960×720 resolution. This generates a video with very high quality but a large file size.

- **Internet & DVD**—Create a video that you can upload to the Web or burn to a DVD at 640×480 resolution. This generates a video with medium quality and a moderate file size.

- **Portable Devices**—Create a video that plays on a mobile device or a smartphone at 320×240 resolution. This generates a video with lower quality and the smallest file size.

5. From the second drop-down list, select one of the following options:

   - **Don't Use Recorded Timings or Narrations**—Use timing specified in the Seconds to Spend on Each Slide box. The default is 5 seconds, but you can increase or decrease this as desired.

   - **Use Recorded Timings and Narrations**—Use the timings, narrations, and recorded laser-pointing directives you specified on the Slide Show tab. See Chapter 15 for more information. This option isn't available if you haven't recorded any timings or narrations.

 TIP If you would like to add timings and narrations, click the Record Timings and Narrations link to open the Record Slide Show dialog box. Click the Preview Timings and Narrations option to preview your presentation as it would display in your video with timings and narrations.

6. Click the Create Video button to open the Save As dialog box.

7. Enter a filename for your video, select a file type (MPEG-4 Video or Windows Media Video), and click the OK button. PowerPoint starts the video creation process. The time it takes to create your video depends on the number of slides in your presentation, your slide content, and the video format you choose.

From here, you can do the following:

- Play this video on your computer, by going to its folder location and double-clicking it.

- Upload your video to your website, blog, or a video-sharing site such as YouTube.

- Burn your video to a DVD using DVD-burning software, such as Windows DVD Maker, included with many versions of Windows.

- Save to a shared site such as SharePoint, SkyDrive, or Microsoft Office Live.

- Send to others via email, as described in Chapter 17, "Sharing Presentations."

THE ABSOLUTE MINIMUM

Here are the key points to remember from this chapter:

- PowerPoint supports a variety of common audio and video file formats, including .mp3, .wav, .wma, .avi, .mov, and .mp4.

- You can insert an online audio clip from Office.com, audio stored on your computer or network, or audio files.

- Video options include inserting online video from Office.com or the Web and inserting a video clip from your computer.

- The Audio Tools – Format tab and Video Tools – Format tab display when you select an audio or video clip on a PowerPoint slide, offering a wide variety of media-formatting options.

- The Playback tab offers many options for specifying how you want to play your clips in an actual slide show.

- To improve the playback performance of your media files and save disk space, you can compress these files.

- PowerPoint enables you to create full-fidelity video from your PowerPoint presentation in either a Windows Media Video (.wmv) or MPEG-4 Video (.mp4) format.

14

WORKING WITH ANIMATION AND TRANSITIONS

PowerPoint offers numerous options for animating your slide content and enlivening your presentation. You csan animate the transition from one slide to another or animate how text, shapes, SmartArt, charts, and other objects display on a slide.

If the default settings don't meet your needs, you can also customize animations in a variety of ways using tools on the Animation pane, including special effects, timings, and more.

Understanding Animation and Transitions

Like most of PowerPoint's capabilities, animation can be either simple or complex. It all depends on how creative and sophisticated you want to make your presentation. Animation can definitely enhance any presentation, but as with any special effect, be careful not to overdo it. Too much animation can actually detract from your presentation. Animation also increases the presentation's file size.

PowerPoint offers two main ways to animate and add motion to your presentation:

- **Slide transitions**—Determine how to change from one slide to the next in your presentation. By default, when you move from one slide to another, the next slide immediately appears. With transitions, for example, you can make the old slide fade away to reveal the new slide or make the new slide move down from the top of the screen to cover the old slide.

- **Text and object animation**—Animate PowerPoint objects, such as text or shapes, using directional effects similar to slide transitions. For example, you can use an animation to wipe title text into your presentation. You can also specify more sophisticated animation options, such as the order and timing of multiple animation objects in one slide.

Setting Slide Transitions

Setting slide transitions is one of the most common animation effects. You can apply a slide transition to the entire presentation or just to the current slide. PowerPoint offers a variety of transition options, ranging from subtle to dynamic, including the capability to fade, wipe, reveal, or even introduce a slide with a honeycomb effect. If you aren't familiar with these effects, you can try them out on your slides before applying them. Most transitions enable you to choose a direction as well. For example, you can wipe up, down, left, or right.

CAUTION As with so many PowerPoint features, use restraint with slide transitions. For the most professional results, choose one transition to use for every slide in a presentation. Or if you want to highlight one or two particular slides, you can apply just the right transition to those, but don't apply transitions to the remaining slides. Too many different transitions can make your presentation confusing and inconsistent, detracting from your message.

To apply slide transitions, follow these steps:

1. On the Transitions tab, shown in Figure 14.1, choose one of the transitions that appears in the Transition to This Slide group.

FIGURE 14.1

Specify how you want to move from one slide to another slide during a presentation.

2. For more options, click the down arrow in the lower-right corner of the group and then choose one of the transitions from the gallery.

3. Click the Effect Options button to open a menu of effects that determine the direction your transition moves, such as from the top or from the bottom-right. Options vary based on the transition you select, and each includes an image that illustrates the direction.

4. To add a sound effect to your transition, select a sound from the Sound drop-down list. If you want to use a sound stored on your computer, choose Other Sound (at the bottom of the list) to open the Add Audio dialog box, select the sound to use, and click the Open button. If you want the sound to continue playing until the presentation encounters another sound file, select the Loop Until Next Sound option on the drop-down menu. See Chapter 13, "Working with Audio and Video," for more sound options.

 CAUTION Use sounds sparingly on slide transitions. They can unintentionally generate laughter or even annoyance in your audience.

5. In the Duration field, select the amount of time in seconds (or fractions of seconds) you want the transition to take introducing each slide.

6. If you want to advance to the next slide when you click the mouse or press a key (such as the spacebar, Enter, Page Up, or Page Down), verify that the On Mouse Click check box is selected and then skip to step 8. This is the default setting.

7. If you would rather have PowerPoint automatically change to the next slide after a specified amount of time, select the After check box and enter a specific time, in minutes and seconds, in the field beside it. Any timings you've already added to your slide show display in this box.

8. To preview your transitions, click the Preview button on the left side of the Transitions tab.

9. Click the Apply to All button to apply the transitions to all slides in your presentation.

TIP To remove slide transitions, click the None button in the Transition to This Slide group on the Transitions tab.

Applying Animation to Objects

You can apply basic animation to objects such as shapes, text placeholders, text boxes, SmartArt graphics, and charts using the options available in the Animation group on the Animations tab, as shown in Figure 14.2.

FIGURE 14.2

The Animations tab offers numerous options for adding motion to your slides.

To apply animations to objects, follow these steps:

1. Select the object or objects you want to animate. If you select more than one object, PowerPoint applies the animation to both objects at the same time. If you want the animations to occur in sequence, you must apply animation separately.

2. On the Animations tab, select the animation you want to apply from the Animation group. Several options appear on the Ribbon, but you can click the down arrow in the lower-right corner of the group and choose an option from the gallery (see Figure 14.3).

PowerPoint offers four categories of animations:

- **Entrance**—Determine how the text or object enters the slide.

- **Emphasis**—Add emphasis to the text or object.

- **Exit**—Determine how the text or object exits the slide.

- **Motion Paths**—Set a path that the selected text or object follows.

TIP Select More Entrance Effects, More Emphasis Effects, More Exit Effects, or More Motion Paths in the gallery to open a dialog box with additional options.

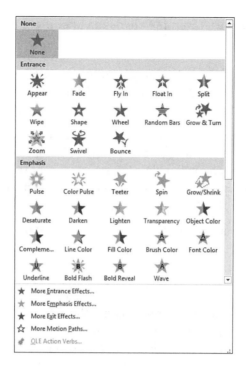

FIGURE 14.3

Choose from a variety of animation effects in the gallery.

3. Click the Effect Options button to choose the direction to apply the animation. The options that appear here vary based on the animation you chose. For example, if you choose the Fly In animation, this list includes eight options, including From Bottom and From Right. If the animation you selected doesn't offer effect options, you can't select this button.

 TIP If you're animating a chart, you can also specify a sequence. For example, you can animate a chart by series, by category, by element in a series, or as one object.

4. Click the Trigger button to specify what triggers this animation to start. Your choices include setting triggers based on the click of a specific object on the slide or on a bookmark.

5. Click the down arrow to the right of the Start button to specify when to start the animation:

   - **On Click**—Start the animation when you click the mouse.

   - **With Previous**—Start the animation when the previous animation in the list starts.

- **After Previous**—Start the animation after the previous animation in the list finishes.

6. Select a Delay setting, in seconds, between each animation. If you don't want a delay, select 00.00 in this field. Otherwise, you can specify delays in increments of 0.25 seconds or enter a custom increment.

7. Select a Duration setting, in seconds, to determine how long the animation should last. The smallest duration you can choose is 00.01, which introduces, and ends, your animation almost instantly. Otherwise, you can specify durations in increments of 0.25 seconds or enter a custom increment. If you choose a long duration, be aware that this creates a slow motion effect.

8. Click the Preview button to preview your animation choices.

Customizing Animations on the Animation Pane

The tools available on the Animations tab should suit most of your animation needs. However, if you want to customize your animations even more, you can do so on the Animation pane. For example, you use this pane to set animation effects for text, charts, SmartArt graphics, and media clips.

To open the pane (see Figure 14.4), click the Animation Pane button on the Animations tab.

 CAUTION Be aware that if you haven't applied any animations to the selected slide yet, the pane will be empty and its features and buttons will be inactive.

Each animation you applied from the Animations tab displays in the Animation pane in the order in which you applied it. The icon that precedes it tells you what kind of animation it is and corresponds to the icons that display in the Animation group on the Animations tab. The green bar that follows it indicates the duration of the animation. Pause the mouse over the animation in the list to display more information, such as the start option and effect type. If you have multiple animations in this list, the list is numbered, and the numbers also display on your slide to show where the animations are located. These numbers don't display in print or during a slide show, however.

Select an animated object in the list, and click the down arrow to its right to open a menu of additional options, described in more detail later in this section.

Click the Play All button to preview your animation effects. If you selected an animation on the pane, the Play From button displays instead.

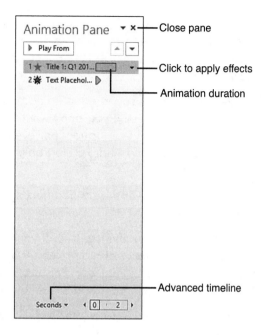

FIGURE 14.4

Further enhance your animation effects on the Animation pane.

Setting Additional Effects

To add additional effects to an animation listed in the pane—such as directional, sound, text, and color enhancements—click the down arrow to the right of an animation in the list and choose Effect Options from the menu that appears. A dialog box opens with the Effect tab selected (see Figure 14.5).

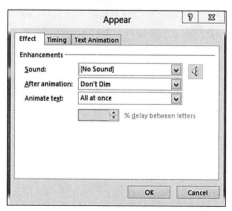

FIGURE 14.5

Continue to modify your custom animation with effect options.

The dialog box's name and content depend on the kind of animation event you're customizing. For example, if you choose the Appear entrance effect, the Appear dialog box opens. As an example, the Effect tab on the Appear dialog box offers the following options:

- **Sound**—If you want a sound effect to accompany the effect, select a sound from the drop-down list. If you don't want to include a sound, choose No Sound, which is the default option. For even more sounds, choose Other Sound to open the Add Audio dialog box. See Chapter 13 for information about using sounds.

- **Volume**—Raise or lower the sound effect's volume level. You can also choose to mute the effect.

- **After Animation**—Specify how to end your animation, such as by displaying the object in a new color or hiding it after animation. You can change the object's color after the animation finishes (select a color icon on the drop-down menu) or choose from one of the following options:

  - **Don't Dim**—Continue to display a static image of the object after animation.

  - **Hide After Animation**—Hide the object after animation.

  - **Hide on Next Mouse Click**—Hide the object when you click the mouse.

- **Animate Text**—From the drop-down list, choose a method for introducing text: All at Once (the default), By Word, or By Letter.

- **% Delay Between**—If you choose the By Word or By Letter option, you can set how long PowerPoint waits after starting to display one word or letter before starting to display the next word or letter. Fifty percent means that the previous word is 50% displayed when the next word begins to display.

Setting Timings

To set exact timing effects for your custom animations, click the down arrow next to an animation in the Animation pane and then choose Timing from the menu that appears. A dialog box opens with the Timing tab selected, as shown in Figure 14.6.

FIGURE 14.6

Make additional timing modifications on the Timing tab.

Remember that the name of this dialog box reflects the type of animation effect whose timing you want to customize. On the Timing tab, you can set the following options:

- **Start**—Specify when to start the animation:

  - **On Click**—Start the animation when you click the mouse.

  - **With Previous**—Start the animation when the previous animation in the list starts.

  - **After Previous**—Start the animation after the previous animation in the list finishes.

- **Delay**—Enter the delay in seconds.

- **Duration**—Choose a duration, from very slow to very fast.

- **Repeat**—Indicate how many times you want the animation to repeat. Options include none (which means that it plays once); two, three, four, five, or ten times; until the next mouse click; or until the next slide.

- **Rewind When Done Playing**—Click this check box if you want to return the animation to its original position when it finishes playing.

- **Triggers**—Click the Triggers button to display three more fields on this tab that let you determine what triggers this animation to start:

  - **Animate as Part of Click Sequence**—Animate as part of the click sequence in the Custom Animation list.

- **Start Effect on Click Of**—Choose a specific animation from the drop-down list on which to trigger this animation.

- **Start Effect on Play Of**—Animate at the start of a media file.

Animating Charts

You can add more effects to a chart to which you've applied an animation. To do so, click the down arrow next to the chart in the Animation pane and then choose Effect Options from the menu. Figure 14.7 shows the dialog box that displays. Remember that the dialog box name reflects the type of effect you've applied, such as Fly In or Fade.

FIGURE 14.7

Animating a chart is another possibility.

Click the Chart Animation tab and, from the Group Chart drop-down list, indicate how you want to introduce the chart elements. Options include As One Object, By Series, By Category, By Element in Series, and By Element in Category.

 NOTE If you choose any option other than As One Object, the Start Animation by Drawing the Chart Background check box activates, letting you begin the animation with a chart background and then filling it in.

See Chapter 12, "Working with Charts," for more information about inserting charts in your presentation.

Animating Text

If the object you animate includes text, such as a text placeholder or text box, you can apply special text effects to your animation. To do so, click the down arrow next to the object in the Animation pane, choose Effect Options from the menu, and click the Text Animation tab. Figure 14.8 shows this tab.

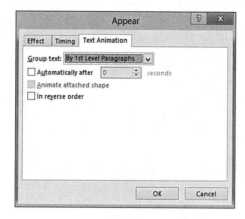

FIGURE 14.8

Emphasize specific words through text animation.

In the Group Text field, choose whether to animate as one object, all paragraphs at once, or by the level of paragraph (from 1st to 5th). You can also choose to animate text automatically after a certain number of seconds, animate an attached shape, or animate text in reverse order.

Depending on the type of text you animate, all these options might not be available. For example, let's say you want to animate a text box that includes several lines of text or perhaps a bulleted list. By choosing to animate by first-level paragraph, you can display each line individually rather than allow your audience to see your entire list at once.

Animating SmartArt Graphics

Animating SmartArt graphics is another animation customization you can apply. To do so, click the down arrow next to the graphic in the Animation pane, choose Effect Options from the menu, and click the SmartArt Animation tab (see Figure 14.9).

From the Group Graphic drop-down list, choose the way you want to introduce the graphic onto the slide. The choices depend on the kind of SmartArt graphic you animate.

FIGURE 14.9

You can animate SmartArt graphics for added emphasis.

Animating Audio and Video Files

You can also add customized animations to a media clip such as an audio or video file. For example, to customize an audio clip animation, click the down arrow next to the clip in the Animation pane and choose Effect Options from the menu. The Play Audio dialog box opens, where you can customize audio effects, timing, and volume.

Viewing the Advanced Timeline

The Animation pane also displays the Advanced Timeline (refer to Figure 14.4), which lets you further customize timings by dragging the timeline's scrollbar.

To close the timeline, click the down arrow to the right of any object and then select Hide Advanced Timeline from the menu that displays. To display the timeline again, select Show Advanced Timeline from this same menu. (The wording of the menu option changes based on whether the timeline is visible.)

Managing Animations

After you create animations, it's easy to reorder, modify, or even remove them.

Reordering Animations

Your animations are numbered in the order in which you create them, but you can change this order if you prefer. To do so, select an animated object and click the Move Earlier button or Move Later button on the Animation tab.

You can also reorder animations on the Animation pane by using the Reorder arrow buttons at the top of the pane. Another option is to drag an animation to another location in the pane.

Modifying Animations

After you apply custom animations to a slide, you might decide that you want to modify them. For example, you might want to change the type of effect you applied from Fade to Float In or from Pulse to Grow/Shrink. To do so, select the object and choose a new animation effect from the Animation group.

Removing Animations

To remove an animation from a selected object or objects, click the None button in the Animation group. Alternatively, select the animated object in the Animation pane, click the down arrow, and select Remove from the menu. To remove all animations, select the first animation in the list, press the Shift key, select the last animation in the list, click the down arrow, and select Remove. If you make a mistake and want to restore your deletions, click the Undo button on the Quick Access Toolbar.

Reusing Animations with the Animation Painter

To copy an animation you added to one object and apply it to another object, you can use the Animation Painter button on the Animations tab. This button works in much the same way as the Format Painter button.

To apply the animation from a selected object to another object, click the Animation Painter button and then select the new object. To apply animations to more than one object, double-click the Animation Painter button and then select the new objects.

THE ABSOLUTE MINIMUM

Here are the key points to remember from this chapter:

- Slide transitions let you automate how PowerPoint moves from one slide to another.

- You can animate PowerPoint objects—such as text, shapes, SmartArt, and charts—using directional effects similar to slide transitions.

- The Animation pane helps you customize animations with special effects, timings, and more.

- Use the Animation Painter to save time and reuse animation effects you applied to other objects.

PRESENTING A SLIDE SHOW

After you create all the slides in your presentation, you'll want to plan how to present them in a slide show. Fortunately, PowerPoint makes it easy to set up, rehearse, and present a show. In this chapter, you find out how to manage the slide show process, from setup to delivery, including how to present online and make the most of Presenter view.

Exploring the Slide Show Tab

In PowerPoint, all the tools you need to manage slide shows are on the Slide Show tab, shown in Figure 15.1.

FIGURE 15.1

Set up, manage, and run your slide shows from the Slide Show tab.

This tab is where you can set up and edit the slide show features you want to use, specify monitors, present online, and more.

 TIP Before you deliver a PowerPoint presentation, think through its entire visual flow. This is the time to rehearse in your mind what you want to present and how you want to present it, as well as plan for the technical aspects of your presentation.

Setting Up a Show

Although you can deliver your presentation instantly by pressing F5, it usually makes sense to set it up ahead of time to specify the exact options you want to use. To set up a PowerPoint slide show, follow these steps:

1. On the Slide Show tab, click the Set Up Slide Show button. The Set Up Show dialog box opens, as shown in Figure 15.2.

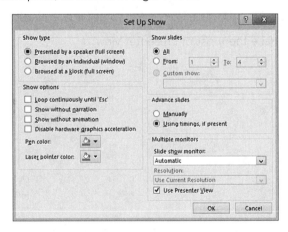

FIGURE 15.2

Use this dialog box to specify the type of presentation you want to make.

2. Select a show type. Options include the following:

- **Presented by a Speaker (Full Screen)**—This is the default option and most common method of delivering a PowerPoint presentation—full screen in front of an audience.

- **Browsed by an Individual (Window)**—This option lets someone view your presentation at any convenient time in a browser window with navigation elements such as a scrollbar.

- **Browsed at a Kiosk (Full Screen)**—This method lets you create a self-running presentation. It displays full screen and loops continuously; after the final slide, the presentation starts over. Timings you set determine how long each slide is visible. You might set up a kiosk show as part of a tradeshow demonstration. You can add voice narration if you want, but be sure that your show plays where the narration will be audible.

 NOTE If you don't set slide timings when you choose the Browsed at a Kiosk option then slides won't move from one to the next unless you set up action buttons or hyperlinks to move from slide to slide.

3. Specify the show options you want to set:

- **Loop Continuously Until 'Esc'**—Play your presentation over and over until you press the Esc key. This check box is available only if you select the Presented by a Speaker or Browsed by an Individual option. A presentation loops continuously by default if browsed at a kiosk.

- **Show Without Narration**—Temporarily deactivate any accompanying narrations you recorded in PowerPoint. For example, if you are presenting at a tradeshow, narrations might be either inaudible or distracting. See section "Recording Voice Narrations," later in this chapter, for more details about creating narrations.

- **Show Without Animation**—Temporarily deactivate any accompanying slide animations. For example, you might want to use animations in some situations, but not all. Refer to Chapter 14, "Working with Animation and Transitions," for more information about animation.

- **Disable Hardware Graphics Acceleration**—Turn off graphics acceleration, which increases performance but reduces presentation resolution.

- **Pen Color**—Specify the pen color to display when using the pen function during a show. This option is available only when you choose Presented by a Speaker as your show type. Click the arrow to the right of this field and either choose a default color or click More Colors to open the Colors dialog box and choose from a wider variety of colors. For more information, see section, "Using the Onscreen Pen to Mark Your Presentation" later in this chapter.

- **Laser Pointer Color**—Specify whether to use a red, green, or blue laser pointer during a show. The laser pointer enables you to activate a pointer by pressing the Ctrl key and clicking the left mouse button.

4. Choose the slides you want to include in your presentation. Options include all slides, a certain range of slides indicated in the From and To boxes, and a custom show (which you can select from the drop-down list). The Custom Show option is active only if you've created a custom show. See section, "Working with Custom Shows," later in this chapter, for more information about custom shows.

5. To advance slides, choose either Manually or Using Timings, If Present. To advance the slide manually, you need to press a key or click the mouse. Choosing Manually in this field overrides any timings you previously set. See section, "Rehearsing Timings," later in this chapter, for more information about timings.

 TIP Be sure that you chose the Using Timings, If Present option if you want to browse at a kiosk. Otherwise, you can't browse manually at a kiosk unless you have a touchscreen device and have created hyperlinks.

6. Select the Use Presenter View check box if you want to use the enhanced Presenter view feature. With this option, you can use one monitor to display just your slides and another to display speaker's notes, preview text, and the elapsed time of your presentation, among other useful tools. By default, when PowerPoint 2013 detects two displays, it automatically turns on Presenter view for the primary monitor. See section, "Using Presenter View," later in this chapter, for more information.

 TIP You can also set monitor options in the Monitors group on the Slide Show dialog box. By default, PowerPoint selects your monitor automatically, but you can specify a monitor if you prefer.

7. Click the OK button to close the Set Up Show dialog box.

Rehearsing Timings

PowerPoint can automate slide transitions, using transition timings that you set. PowerPoint shows a slide for the amount of time you choose and then transitions to the next slide. You can also set timings by rehearsing your presentation— PowerPoint keeps track of how long you spend on each slide. After you rehearse a presentation, you can save those timings. You might not always want PowerPoint to move you from slide to slide, however. For example, it can sometimes take you more or less time to discuss a slide in person, or an audience member might interrupt your presentation with a question. Even if you don't want to automate your slide transitions, rehearsing timings can be useful because it helps you adjust your presentation to fit into an allotted amount of time.

To rehearse and set timings, go to the Slide Show tab and click the Rehearse Timings button. The presentation displays in Slide Show view, opening the Recording toolbar in the upper-left corner, as shown in Figure 15.3. This toolbar contains the buttons Next, Pause Recording, Slide Time, Repeat, and Elapsed Time, which enable you to control and navigate your recording as well as manage the time you spend on each slide.

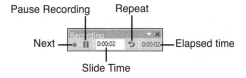

FIGURE 15.3

The Recording toolbar helps you rehearse and record slide timings.

Begin talking through your presentation, clicking the Next button in the toolbar (or clicking your mouse, or pressing any key) to advance to the next slide. If you need to stop temporarily, click the Pause Recording button. If you make a mistake and want to start over on your current slide, click the Repeat button.

The elapsed time of the current slide displays in the Slide Time box in the center of the toolbar. You can also enter a time manually in this box. The time field on the right side of the toolbar shows you the elapsed time of the entire presentation.

After you rehearse the last slide, PowerPoint asks whether you want to save the timings. If you click Yes, the presentation opens in Slide Sorter view with the timings displayed under each slide (see Figure 15.4). Alternatively, you can press the Esc key to stop rehearsal and optionally go to Slide Sorter view.

Elapsed time

FIGURE 15.4

View the elapsed time for each slide narration in Slide Sorter view.

Using Timings

If you want to use slide timings during a slide show, verify that the Use Timings check box is selected on the Slide Show tab, which is the default setting. You can also choose whether or not to use timings on the Set Up Show dialog box.

Deleting Timings

To delete slide timings, click the down arrow below the Record Slide Show button on the Slide Show tab and select Clear from the menu that displays. From the submenu, choose to clear timings on the current slide or clear timings on all slides. If you haven't set automatic timings for your presentation, the Clear menu option isn't available.

Recording Voice Narrations

You can record your own voiceover to accompany the following presentation types:

- A web-based presentation.

- An automated presentation, such as one you run continuously at a tradeshow booth.

- A presentation delivered by a speaker that includes special recorded commentary by a particular individual. An example of this would be a human resources representative delivering an employee orientation that includes voice narration from the CEO.

Before recording your narration, create a script and rehearse it several times until it flows smoothly and matches your presentation.

NOTE You need to have a microphone and a sound-enabled computer to record a narration. And remember, the better the quality of the equipment you use, the more professional your narration will sound.

To record a voice narration, follow these steps:

1. On the Slide Show tab, click the Record Slide Show button.

TIP If you want to start recording from the current slide, click the down arrow below the Record Slide Show button and choose Start Recording from Current Slide.

2. In the Record Slide Show dialog box (see Figure 15.5), specify whether you want to record slide and animation timings, narrations and laser pointer, or both, and then click the Start Recording button.

FIGURE 15.5

Specify what you want to record in the Record Slide Show dialog box.

3. The presentation displays in Slide Show view, opening the Recording toolbar in the upper-left corner (refer to Figure 15.3).

4. Record your presentation as you move through the slide show, by clicking the Next button on the Recording toolbar or by pressing the Page Down button on your keyboard. The toolbar displays your elapsed time on the current slide (time indicator in the middle of the toolbar) as well as your overall elapsed time (on the right).

TIP To pause your recording, click the Pause button on the Recording toolbar. When you're ready to resume recording, click the Pause button again.

5. When you reach the end of the presentation, it opens in Slide Sorter view with the slide timings listed below each slide (refer to Figure 15.4).

Rerecording Narrations

If you make a mistake in recording, you can rerecord your entire narration or rerecord a specific slide. To rerecord a specific slide, click the down arrow below the Record Slide Show button and choose Start Recording from Current Slide.

 TIP To avoid overwriting the recording of the next slide, insert a blank slide after the one you want to rerecord.

Playing Narrations

To play voice narrations during a slide show, verify that the Play Narrations check box is selected on the Slide Show tab, which is the default setting. If you insert media clips, such as sounds, and then add a voice narration, the narration takes precedence over the media clips. As a result, you'll hear only the narration. To resolve this, delete the narration if the media clips are of more importance, or include the clips in the narration you record.

Deleting Narrations

To delete slide narrations, click the down arrow below the Record Slide Show button and select Clear from the menu that displays. From the submenu that displays, you can choose to clear narration on the current slide or clear narrations on all slides.

Creating Custom Shows

At times, you might need to deliver a presentation to several audiences, but modify it to suit each individual audience's needs. With custom shows, you can create a presentation once and then specify customized versions that include only the individual slides you need. This saves you from creating several nearly identical presentations or updating the same slide in multiple presentations.

For example, you might want to create a sales presentation that you can use with three different types of prospective clients. Let's say that the first seven slides of your presentation cover information about your company and its history, which remains the same for all three types of prospects. But you've also created individual slides for each of your three prospect groups that detail your successes in those industries. You can then design three custom shows—each of which includes the seven main slides, plus the specific slides that pertain only to a certain prospect type. This helps save you time and effort when you need to update information in the seven main slides; you need to do it only once.

To create a custom show, follow these steps:

1. On the Slide Show tab, click the Custom Slide Show button.

2. Select Custom Shows from the menu to open the Custom Shows dialog box, shown in Figure 15.6.

FIGURE 15.6

Customizing your slide shows saves time and reduces duplication.

3. Click the New button to open the Define Custom Show dialog box, shown in Figure 15.7.

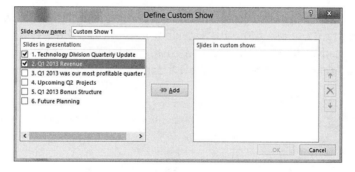

FIGURE 15.7

Add a new custom show in this dialog box.

4. Replace the default name in the Slide Show Name text box with a title for your show.

5. From the Slides in Presentation list, select slides to include in your custom show and click the Add button to copy these slides to the Slides in Custom Show list.

TIP You can use the same slide more than once in a presentation. For example, you might want to show an Agenda slide at both the beginning and end of a presentation.

6. If you need to remove a slide from the Slides in Custom Show list, select it and click the Remove button.

 TIP Use the up and down buttons to the right of the Slides in Custom Show list to reorder a selected slide.

7. Click the OK button to save the custom show and return to the Custom Shows dialog box. From this dialog box, you can edit, remove, or copy any selected custom show.

 TIP Copying a custom slide show is useful if you want to create several similar versions of a custom show and don't want to repeat the same steps.

8. To preview what the show will look like, click the Show button. The show previews in Slide Show view.

9. Click the Close (x) button to close the Custom Shows dialog box.

To play a custom show, go to the Slide Show tab and click the Custom Slide Show button. Choose the show you want to play from the menu, and it begins automatically. You can also set up a custom show to play as the default show. Refer to section, "Setting Up a Show," earlier in this chapter for more information.

 TIP Occasionally, you might want to hide slides from view during an onscreen presentation but not delete them from the presentation itself. To do that, select the slide or slides you want to hide and click the Hide Slide button on the Slide Show tab. The slides remain in the presentation, but they don't display when you run your slide show. This is often easier than creating a custom show, particularly if you don't plan to repeat this version of your presentation.

Viewing Your Show

After you plan and set up your PowerPoint presentation, it's time to present it. To do this, press F5. Alternatively, click the From Beginning button or the From Current Slide button on the Slide Show tab (pressing Shift+F5 also accomplishes this).

TIP Before presenting your show live, you should preview it to test content, flow, and narration. After you determine that your show itself is flawless, you should work on perfecting your delivery, particularly if you don't deliver live presentations very often. By simulating live conditions as much as possible in your practice sessions, you'll increase your odds of delivering a perfect presentation.

When you present a show, PowerPoint uses the settings you entered in the Set Up Show dialog box. For example, you can view in a browser or full screen, depending on what you entered in this dialog box. Whether you need to advance each slide manually depends on your choices in this dialog box. How you navigate the presentation also depends on how you view it:

- **Full screen**—The presentation displays full screen if you choose the Presented by a Speaker or the Browsed at a Kiosk option in the Set Up Show dialog box. The major difference between the two is that when a speaker makes the presentation, you have numerous navigation options available because a person is in control of the presentation. When you browse at a kiosk, these navigation options aren't available because the show runs itself.

- **PowerPoint browser**—The show displays in the PowerPoint browser if you choose Browsed by an Individual in the Set Up Show dialog box. You can use the scrollbar to scroll through the presentation if it's available, or you can use the Page Up and Page Down keys to navigate manually. To switch to the full-screen view, right-click the screen and choose Full Screen.

TIP Displaying a scrollbar can make it easier for viewers to navigate your show. Specify whether to display a scrollbar in the Set Up Show dialog box.

Navigating a Show Full Screen

When a speaker presents a PowerPoint slide show, the presentation appears full screen. If you set up your show without automatic timing, you have to manually move among the slides during the show.

You have several ways to navigate your presentation full screen: using the invisible buttons in the lower-left corner of your screen, using the shortcut menu that displays when you right-click a slide, and using keyboard commands.

Navigating with Onscreen Buttons

To view PowerPoint's hidden navigation buttons, pause your mouse over the lower-left corner of your screen (see Figure 15.8). The following buttons display, from left to right:

- **Previous**—Return to the previous slide.

- **Next**—Move to the next slide.

- **Pen**—Display a brief menu with pen and arrow pointer options. See sections, "Setting Pointer Options" and "Using the Onscreen Pen to Mark Your Presentation," later in this chapter, for more information.

- **See All Slides**—Display thumbnails of your presentation slides. Useful for moving to a slide out of sequence.

- **Zoom**—Zoom in to an area of a slide for closer viewing.

- **Menu**—Display a menu of options. See section, "Navigating with the Slide Show Menu," later in this chapter, for more information.

FIGURE 15.8

Pause your mouse to view hidden navigation buttons.

Navigating with the Slide Show Menu

During a slide show, you can right-click anywhere on the screen to view a shortcut menu, as shown in Figure 15.9.

FIGURE 15.9

PowerPoint offers many shortcuts while you're presenting.

This menu includes the following slide show options:

- **Next**—Move to the next slide.

- **Previous**—Move to the previous slide.

- **Last Viewed**—Move to the slide last viewed.

- **See All Slides**—Display thumbnails of your presentation slides. Useful for moving to a slide out of sequence.

- **Zoom**—Zoom in to an area of a slide for closer viewing.

- **Custom Show**—Select the custom show you want to view from the list of custom shows. This option is available only if you created custom shows.

- **Show Presenter View**—Open the presentation in Presenter view.

- **Screen**—Switch to a black or white screen, show or hide ink markup, and display the Windows taskbar so that you can switch to another application.

TIP   Toggling between a black or white screen is a useful feature. For example, if you want to explain a detailed concept and want your audience to focus on what you're saying and not on the slide, you can temporarily make the screen either black or white. This is also useful during breaks for long presentations.

- **Pointer Options**—Activate the arrow pointer, pen, or highlighter; set the ink color; erase markings; and choose to hide or display the mouse cursor.

- **Help**—Open the Slide Show Help dialog box, where you can view a list of the shortcut keystrokes you can use during a slide show. See section, "Navigating with Keyboard Commands," later in this chapter, for more information.

- **Pause**—Pause a slide show that's running automatically.

- **End Show**—End the show and return to PowerPoint.

CAUTION   Although the options on this menu are useful, you'll probably want to avoid using most of these features during an actual presentation because a break in your flow can be distracting. One case in which you might want to do so during a presentation would be when you have to go back to previous slides to answer questions or clarify a point and don't want to page through numerous slides to do so.

Navigating with Keyboard Commands

Navigating your slide show with keyboard commands is a third option. Table 15.1 lists all the ways PowerPoint gives you to navigate a slide show.

 TIP Right-click anywhere on the screen and choose Help from the shortcut menu to display this list of shortcuts within your slide show.

TABLE 15.1 Slide Show Keyboard Commands

Slide Show Action	Method
Advance to next slide.	Left-click the mouse. Press the spacebar. Press the letter N. Press the right-arrow key. Press the down-arrow key. Press the Enter key. Press the Page Down key.
Return to previous slide.	Press the Backspace key. Press the letter P. Press the left-arrow key. Press the up-arrow key. Press the Page Up key.
Go to a specific slide.	Enter the number of the slide and press the Enter key.
Black/unblack the screen (toggle).	Press the letter B. Press the period key (.).
White/unwhite the screen (toggle).	Press the letter W. Press the comma (,).
Display/hide the arrow (toggle).	Press the letter A. Press the equal sign (=).
Stop/restart a timed show (toggle).	Press the letter S. Press the plus sign (+).
End the show.	Press the Esc key. Press Ctrl+Break. Press the minus (-) key.
Erase a screen drawing made with the pen.	Press the letter E.
Advance to a hidden slide.	Press the letter H.
Rehearse using a new timing.	Press the letter T.

TABLE 15.1   (continued)

Slide Show Action	Method
Rehearse using original timing.	Press the letter O.
Activate the pen.	Press Ctrl+P.
Activate the arrow pointer.	Press Ctrl+A.
Hide a pointer/button.	Press Ctrl+H.
Automatically show/hide a pointer.	Press Ctrl+U.
Zoom in.	Ctrl++.
Zoom out.	Ctrl +-.

Setting Pointer Options

You can use or hide an arrow pointer during a PowerPoint presentation. The arrow pointer can help you draw the audience's attention to objects on your slides.

To activate the arrow, move the mouse. If the arrow doesn't display, right-click and choose Pointer Options, Arrow from the menu. The arrow displays as a standard mouse pointer arrow on your screen, which you can use to point to specific areas. To change the arrow to a laser pointer, press the Ctrl key and click the left mouse button.

By default, the arrow disappears after three seconds of inactivity, and it reappears whenever you move the mouse. This setting is fine for most presentations, but you can choose to have the arrow always or never appear. To do so, right-click and choose Pointer Options, Arrow Options from the menu that appears. Then choose one of these three commands:

- **Automatic**—Display the arrow when you move your mouse and hide it after three seconds of inactivity (default).

- **Visible**—Always display the arrow in your presentation.

- **Hidden**—Never display the arrow in your presentation.

Figure 15.10 shows the standard arrow pointer with which most people are familiar.

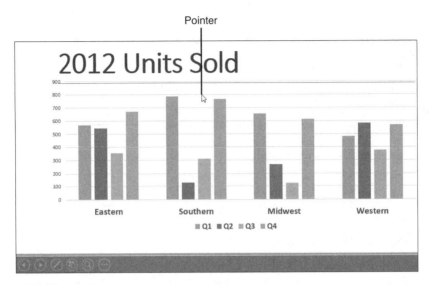

FIGURE 15.10

Use a pointer during your slide presentation.

Using the Onscreen Pen to Mark Your Presentation

Using the onscreen pen, you can actually mark right on your slides as you deliver a presentation. This feature works best if you have a pen tablet or a tablet PC, but you'll also get good value from it if all you have is a mouse.

To use the pen, right-click, choose Pointer Options, and choose the kind of ink to use (Pen or Highlighter). Your mouse cursor becomes a dot (when you choose a pen) or a colored bar (when you choose highlighter). Click and hold the mouse button and then drag the cursor to make your mark. Figure 15.11 shows some ink markings.

You can choose your pen's color by right-clicking your slide show screen and choosing Pointer Options, Ink Color. Select your preferred color on the color palette that displays. You can also preset the pen color in the Set Up Show dialog box.

When you don't need your ink markings anymore, you can erase them. To erase a specific ink marking, right-click and choose Pointer Options, Eraser from the menu that appears. The mouse cursor looks like an eraser. Click an ink marking to erase it. To erase all your ink markings, right-click and choose Pointer Options, Erase All Ink on Slide from the menu that appears or press the letter E.

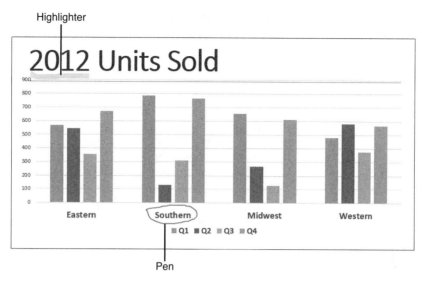

FIGURE 15.11

Use a pen or the highlighter to draw attention to elements in the presentation.

After you finish delivering your presentation, PowerPoint asks whether you want to keep your ink annotations. If you click the Keep button, the annotations become drawing objects in the presentation.

Presenting Online

PowerPoint enables you to share your presentation in high fidelity with anyone on the Web, even if they don't have PowerPoint installed on their computer.

While presenting online, you can navigate with online buttons, the slide show menu, or keyboard commands, as described in the section, "Viewing Your Show," earlier in this chapter.

 TIP Presenter view offers numerous features that enhance an online presentation. To start Presenter view manually, right-click and select Show Presenter View. Learn more in section, "Using Presenter View," later in this chapter.

To present online, follow these steps:

1. On the Slide Show tab, click the Present Online button.

2. Click the Connect button in the dialog box that displays (see Figure 15.12). If your presentation includes media files, this dialog box displays additional options.

FIGURE 15.12

View the elapsed time for each slide narration in Slide Sorter view.

 NOTE   If you aren't already logged in to your Microsoft account, PowerPoint prompts you to do so.

3. Share the link in the Present Online dialog box with remote viewers (see Figure 15.13).

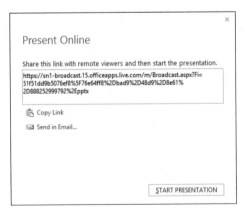

FIGURE 15.13

Share your presentation link to get started.

TIP To send your link via your default email application (such as Microsoft Outlook), click the Send in Email link. To share using instant message or web mail, click Copy Link.

4. When you're ready to present, click the Start Presentation button.

5. PowerPoint starts your slide show on the Web, where your viewers can see it.

6. When you finish your presentation, right-click and select End Show.

7. Click End Online Presentation on the Present Online tab to disconnect all your remote viewers, as shown in Figure 15.14.

FIGURE 15.14

The Present Online tab provides several tools for your online presentation.

8. Click End Online Presentation in the confirmation dialog box to confirm.

Exploring Presenter View

Presenter view enables you to display a full-screen presentation that your audience can see and another view that you, the presenter, can see with slide previews, speaker notes, a timer, and more. In PowerPoint 2013, you can use Presenter view even on computers with a single display. Figure 15.15 shows Presenter view.

To activate Presenter view, select the Use Presenter View check box on the Slide Show tab.

 NOTE Another way to activate Presenter view is to right-click an in-progress presentation and select Show Presenter View from the menu.

In Presenter view, you can perform the following tasks:

- Display the taskbar (at the bottom of the window) by clicking Show Taskbar.

- Create meeting notes in Microsoft OneNote by clicking Share Meeting Notes. This option isn't available on computers that don't have OneNote installed.

FIGURE 15.15

Presenter view simplifies giving presentations.

- View display settings (such as swapping Presenter view and slide show view and duplicating the slide show) by clicking Display Settings.

- End the presentation by clicking End Slide Show.

- View your current slide in the main window.

- Use the buttons directly below the slide to do the following:

  - Display a menu of pen and pointer tools. See section, "Viewing Your Show," for more details about these tools.

  - View all slides.

  - Black or unblack the slide show.

  - View a menu of more slide show options, such as displaying a custom show, hiding Presenter view, and accessing online help.

- Navigate your presentation using the Advance to the Next Slide button and the Return to the Previous Slide button at the bottom of the window.

- Preview the next slide and any notes on the right side of the window.

- Change font size with the Make Text Larger and Make Text smaller buttons.

Packaging a Presentation onto a CD

Sometimes a presentation needs to run on a computer other than the one on which it was created. For example, you might travel to a meeting without your laptop computer and need to give a presentation on a supplied computer. You can save your presentation as is to a CD or email it ahead—but still, you worry. Are the fonts in your presentation installed on the computer? Is this version of PowerPoint installed? Is *any* version of PowerPoint installed? Did I remember all the linked files the presentation uses?

Package for CD relieves these worries. It writes your presentation (with its fonts and linked files if you want) to a CD. It also includes the PowerPoint Viewer by default so that you always have everything you need to run your presentation. You can choose whether the presentation runs automatically when you insert the CD into a computer. You can also package more than one presentation onto a CD and choose whether they should run automatically in sequence.

 NOTE   The PowerPoint Viewer (PowerPointViewer.exe) lets people view a PowerPoint presentation when they don't have PowerPoint installed on their computers. You can freely distribute the viewer without any license fee. Although the viewer is automatically included on your presentation CD if you use Package for CD, you can also download it manually from the Microsoft Download Center (www.microsoft.com/downloads).

To package a presentation onto a CD, follow these steps:

1. Open a presentation to package.

2. Click the File tab and select Export to open the Export window in Backstage view.

3. Select Package Presentation for CD and then click the Package for CD button on the right side of the screen (see Figure 15.16).

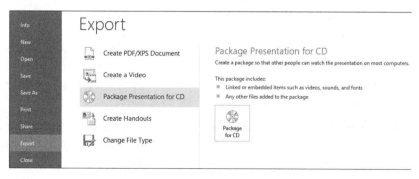

FIGURE 15.16

The Export window offers the option to package your presentation to a CD.

4. In the Package for CD dialog box, as shown in Figure 15.17, enter a name that describes the presentation you're packaging in the Name the CD field.

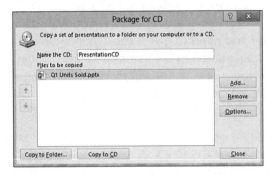

FIGURE 15.17

With Package for CD, you can deliver your presentation on another computer.

5. The current presentation's filename displays in the Files to Be Copied area. To package more presentations onto this CD, click the Add button. The Add Files dialog box opens. Select the presentations to package and click the Add button to return to the Package for CD dialog box.

6. If you are packaging more than one presentation, you can arrange the presentations in the order in which you want them to run. To move a presentation, select it and then click one of the arrow buttons on the left side of the dialog box to reposition it.

7. Click the Options button to open the Options dialog box (see Figure 15.18), where you can specify any of the following options:

- **Linked Files**—PowerPoint packages linked files by default. If you don't want to package them, click this box to remove the check mark.

- **Embedded TrueType Fonts**—If your presentation uses any fonts you're not positive are on the computer you'll use, select this check box. PowerPoint packages the fonts so that your presentation is sure to look the way you created it. You can embed other TrueType fonts that you install only if they aren't restricted by license or copyright. You'll receive an error message if you try to embed a restricted font.

- **Password to Open Each Presentation and Password to Modify Each Presentation**—If you want to prevent others from opening or changing your presentations, enter passwords in these fields.

- **Inspect Presentations for Inappropriate or Private Information**—Open the Document Inspector dialog box during the packaging process, where you can choose to inspect comments, annotations, invisible on-slide content, off-slide content, document properties, personal information, and presentation notes.

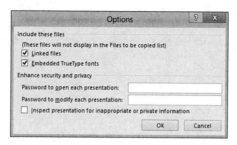

FIGURE 15.18

Specify whether to package linked files and fonts.

8. Click the OK button when you're done to return to the Package for CD dialog box.

9. If you want to create a folder on your hard drive that contains everything that will be on the CD, click the Copy to Folder button. The Copy to Folder dialog box opens (see Figure 15.19).

FIGURE 15.19

Choose where to create the folder and what to call it.

10. Type a name for the folder, choose where to add the folder, and click the OK button. PowerPoint creates the folder and copies all the files to it.

11. Place a blank writeable CD into your CD-R or CD-RW drive. If Windows asks you what to do with the CD, select Take No Action and then click the OK button. Go back to the Package for CD dialog box and click the Copy to CD button. PowerPoint writes the files to the CD.

When PowerPoint finishes creating the CD, it opens the CD drawer and asks whether you want to copy the same files to another CD. If so, place another writeable CD in the drive and click Yes. Otherwise, click No.

THE ABSOLUTE MINIMUM

Here are the key points to remember from this chapter:

- You'll find all the tools you need for managing slide shows on the Slide Show tab.

- Set up your show ahead of time in the Slide Show dialog box.

- PowerPoint can automate slide transitions, using the transition timing you set.

- You can record voiceovers to accompany any type of presentation.

- Custom shows enable you to deliver your presentation to several audiences without duplication of effort.

- You can navigate your slide show using onscreen buttons, the slide show menu, or keyword commands.

- PowerPoint enables you to share your presentation in high fidelity with anyone on the Web, even if they don't have PowerPoint installed on their computer.

- Presenter view displays a full-screen presentation that your audience can see and another view that you, the presenter, can see with slide previews, speaker notes, a timer, and more.

- The Package Presentation for CD feature makes it easy to deliver a presentation on a computer other than the one on which it was created.

16

CREATING AND PRINTING PRESENTATION MATERIALS

PowerPoint enables you to print more than just slides. You can also print notes to remind yourself of what you want to say while presenting, handouts to give to your audience, and outlines to help you proof your content. PowerPoint also includes numerous customization options for printing auxiliary materials.

Understanding PowerPoint Printing Options

PowerPoint offers several options for printing your presentation, as follows:

- **Full page slides**—Print each slide on a single page.

- **Notes pages**—Print a single slide and its accompanying notes on one page. You create notes in the Notes pane, which is visible in Normal view. Figure 16.1 shows the Notes pane, where you can create detailed speaker's notes about your presentation. Notes are a useful way to remind yourself about what you're going to present. You can also use the Notes pane to provide additional details for your audience if you plan to distribute your presentation to them.

 NOTE If you choose to print three slides per handout, PowerPoint provides lined spaces to the right of each slide where you can write notes. If you choose another number of pages, you won't have this note space.

- **Handouts**—Print a specific number of slides per page (one, two, three, four, six, or nine), either horizontally or vertically. This can greatly reduce the number of pages and amount of printer toner required to print your presentation. When you print handouts, you see only the slides, not the accompanying notes.

- **Outlines**—Print your slide content without graphic formatting.

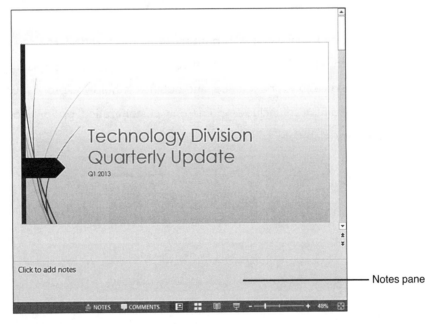

FIGURE 16.1

You can print the notes you add in the Notes pane.

To avoid wasting paper, first make sure that your PowerPoint presentation is ready to print. Set page and print options, customize headers and footers, and preview your presentation as you want it to appear when printed. Printing your presentation at least once is a good idea even if you don't plan on distributing handouts to your audience. When you proof a hard-copy version, you often notice errors that you didn't catch on the screen.

 TIP Consider a greener alternative to printing a copy of your presentation for each member of your audience. You can save your presentation as a PDF (Portable Document Format electronic document) using the same formatting options as a print presentation (slides, handouts, notes pages, and outlines). See Chapter 2, "Creating a Basic Presentation," for more information about creating PDFs. Alternatively, consider posting a public presentation on the Web at SlideShare.net or a similar presentation-sharing site.

Printing PowerPoint Presentations

The Print window in Backstage view enables you to specify print settings, preview your slides, and print your presentation. Click the File tab and select Print from the menu, as shown in Figure 16.2.

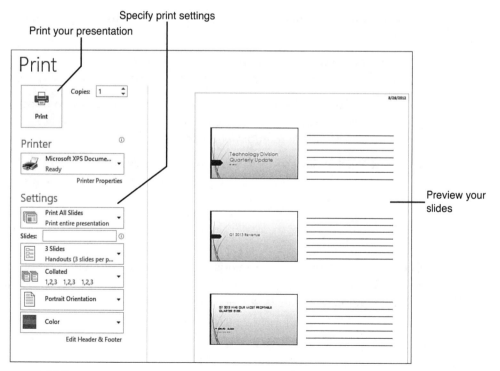

FIGURE 16.2

Prepare, preview, and print from the Print window in Backstage view.

Preparing to Print

Before you print, apply any special print settings. The Settings section includes five boxes with drop-down lists where you can specify these options (refer to Figure 16.2). The text that displays in each box varies depending on the last selection you made.

 NOTE You can customize printing defaults for the existing presentation in the PowerPoint Options dialog box. To access it, click the File tab, choose Options, and go to the Print section of the Advanced tab. See Chapter 19, "Customizing PowerPoint," for more information about these print options.

Selecting Slides to Print

Click the first box in the Settings section to select the slides you want to print. Your options include the following:

- **Print All Slides**—Print the entire presentation.

- **Print Selection**—Print slides you select in Normal view or in Slide Sorter view.

- **Print Current Slide**—Print only the current slide that displays in the Print window.

- **Custom Range**—Print the slide numbers you enter in the Slides text box. For example, you could enter **1-4, 10** to print slides 1, 2, 3, 4, and 10.

- **Custom Shows**—Select a custom show to print. This option doesn't display if you haven't created at least one custom show. See Chapter 15, "Presenting a Slide Show," for more information about custom shows.

- **Print Hidden Slides**—Print slides you've hidden. See Chapter 5, "Formatting and Organizing Objects, Slides, and Presentations," for more information about hiding slides.

Specifying a Print Layout

Click the second box in the Settings section to select the print layout you want to use. Options include Full Page Slides, Notes Pages, Outline, as well as nine different handout layouts (see Figure 16.3).

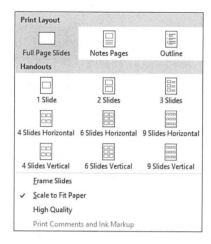

FIGURE 16.3

Your print layout options include nine different handout formats.

This menu also includes the following options:

- **Frame Slides**—Include a border around the slides.

- **Scale to Fit Paper**—Change the size of slides to fit the paper, making them either larger or smaller, as appropriate.

- **High Quality**—Print your presentation at the highest quality available with your printer.

- **Print Comments and Ink Markup**—Print comment pages and any ink markups you make onscreen with your presentation. This option is available only if your presentation contains comments or ink markups.

Collating Presentation Printouts

Click the third box in the Settings section to specify how you want to collate your printouts if you choose to print more than one copy of your presentation. Collating keeps multiple copies in sequence. If you print five copies of a presentation without collating, for example, you will print five copies of page one, five copies of page two, and so on.

Specifying Print Orientation

Click the fourth box in the Settings section to specify the orientation of your printouts: portrait or landscape. This option isn't available if you select Full Page Slides as your print layout. In this case, your slides print in landscape layout by default.

Specifying Colors Options

Click the fifth box in the Settings section to specify color options for your printed presentation. You can print in color, grayscale, or pure black and white.

If you don't have a color printer, your choice affects how your presentation prints on a black-and-white printer:

- **Color**—Your printer converts your presentation's colors to shades of gray.

- **Grayscale**—PowerPoint converts your presentation to true grayscale.

- **Pure Black and White**—PowerPoint converts your presentation to pure black and white.

 TIP Depending on the colors and shapes in your slide, the color option you select might produce different results. For example, on one slide, Color and Grayscale could produce similar results; on another slide, Grayscale and Pure Black and White could look alike. You need to experiment to see which option yields the optimal look in print.

Table 16.1 illustrates how each PowerPoint object displays when printed in grayscale or black and white.

TABLE 16.1 Grayscale and Black-and-White Objects

Object	Grayscale	Black and White
Bitmaps	Grayscale	Grayscale
Charts	Grayscale	Grayscale
Embossing	Grayscale	None
Fill	Grayscale	White
Frames	Black	Black
Lines	Black	Black
Patterns	Grayscale	White
Shadows (object)	Grayscale	Black
Shadows (text)	Grayscale	None
Slide backgrounds	White	White
Text	Black	Black

In addition to previewing colors in the Print window in Backstage view, you can also preview from the View tab. To preview in grayscale, click the Grayscale button on the View tab. The Grayscale tab displays, offering additional grayscale and black-and-white options. Click the Back to Color View button to close.

To preview the same presentation in black and white, click the Pure Black and White button on the View tab. The presentation displays in black and white and the Black and White tab displays.

Customizing Headers and Footers

You can add headers and footers to your slides, notes, and handouts when you print them. To do this, click the Edit Header & Footer link on the Print window in Backstage view. The Header and Footer dialog box opens, as shown in Figure 16.4.

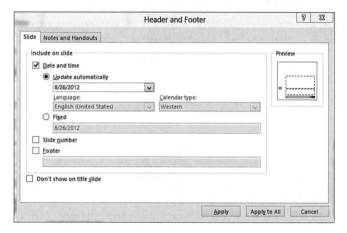

FIGURE 16.4

Indicate the headers and footers you want to print.

This dialog box includes two tabs with similar options: the Slide tab and the Notes and Handouts tab. You can add any or all of the following when you print slides, notes, handouts, or outlines:

- **Date and Time**—Select this check box and then either enter a fixed date or choose to update the date automatically. If you choose to update automatically, pick a format from the drop-down list. Options include displaying the date only, the time only, and the date and time in up to 13 different ways. You can also choose your base language and calendar type, depending on the language you choose in the Language drop-down list. If only English is enabled, the Language list isn't active. The date and time display on the upper-right corner of the page.

- **Slide Number**—Print the slide number in the lower-right corner of the page. Available only on the Slide tab.

- **Header**—Print the header text you enter in the text box on the upper-left corner of the page. Available only on the Notes and Handouts tab.

- **Page Number**—Print a page number on the lower-right corner of each page. Available only on the Notes and Handouts tab.

- **Footer**—Print the footer text you enter on the lower-left corner of the page.

- **Don't Show on Title Slide**—Don't print the selected options on the title slide. Hiding your headers and footers on the first slide of your presentation gives it a more polished look. Available only on the Slide tab.

TIP The date options you can choose from the Update Automatically drop-down list depend on your choice of language/country. For example, choosing English (UK) results in date options that display in the dd/mm/yy format rather than the mm/dd/yy format used in the United States.

Click the Apply to All button to close the dialog box.

Previewing a PowerPoint Presentation

The right side of the Print window previews the way your presentation displays when printed, as shown in Figure 16.5.

Any changes you make to your presentation settings are reflected in this view, so you can verify before printing whether the choices you make work for you.

Below the slide, you can click the left and right arrows to scroll through the presentation. You can also use the zoom control to reduce or enlarge the size of the slides.

TIP Alternatively, click the Print Preview button on the Quick Access Toolbar (or press Ctrl+P) to open the Print window and preview your presentation. See Chapter 19 for more information about adding this button to the toolbar if it isn't already available.

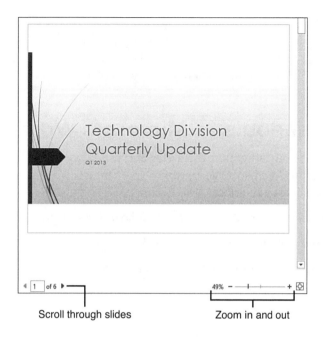

Scroll through slides   Zoom in and out

FIGURE 16.5

Preview before printing your presentation.

Printing Your Presentation

After you specify your print settings and preview the results, it's time to print.

To print your presentation, follow these steps:

1. In the Print window in Backstage view (refer to Figure 16.2), select the number of copies to print. If you want to print more than one copy, remember to specify collation options. Refer to section, "Collating Presentation Printouts," earlier in this chapter, for more information.

2. Select the printer to use from the Printer drop-down list. The list of options depends on what you connect to or install on your computer, such as printers, fax machines, PDF-creation software, and so forth.

3. Optionally, click the Printer Properties link to change the selected printer's properties and print parameters, such as page orientation (portrait or landscape).

4. Click the Print button to print your formatted presentation to the printer you selected.

TIP Alternatively, click the Quick Print button on the Quick Access Toolbar to print your presentation based on the current default settings. See Chapter 19 for more information about adding this button to the toolbar if it isn't already available.

Creating Handouts in Microsoft Word

If you prefer, you can export the slides and notes from your PowerPoint presentation to Microsoft Word, where you can use Word's formatting to create more sophisticated handouts.

To create handouts in Microsoft Word, follow these steps:

1. Click the File tab and select Export from the menu.

2. In the Export window, select Create Handouts.

3. Click the Create Handouts button. Figure 16.6 shows the Send to Microsoft Word dialog box that opens.

4. Choose one of the following page layout options:

   - Notes Next to Slides

   - Blank Lines Next to Slides

   - Notes Below Slides

   - Blank Lines Below Slides

   - Outline Only

5. Specify whether you want to paste the slides into your Word document or paste as a link. If you link the slides, they update in Word whenever you make changes in PowerPoint.

6. Click the OK button to open a Microsoft Word document in the layout you specified.

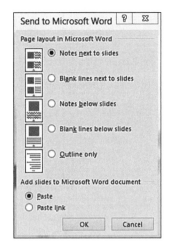

FIGURE 16.6

Create handouts in Microsoft Word from your PowerPoint presentation.

THE ABSOLUTE MINIMUM

Here are the key points to remember from this chapter:

- PowerPoint offers several options for printing your presentation: full slides, notes pages, handouts, and outlines.

- Before printing, you should specify your printing parameters, such as print layout, collation, and colors.

- If you want to create more sophisticated handouts from your PowerPoint slides, you can export to Microsoft Word for additional formatting options.

SHARING PRESENTATIONS

Sharing and collaborating with colleagues is critical to developing a successful presentation in many organizations. In this chapter, you explore the many ways to work with others on your presentations, including preparing your presentation for sharing and the many sharing options available in the Share window.

Preparing Your Presentation for Sharing

Before you share your presentation with others, you should consider doing several things: protect your presentation, inspect it for confidential information, validate its accessibility, and check for compatibility with previous versions.

Protecting Your Presentation

PowerPoint offers several options for protecting your presentation before you share it with others or post it online or in a centralized location. For example, you can apply a password, make your presentation read-only, or apply a digital signature to control presentation access. Whether you choose to protect your presentation depends on the group of people you work with, your need for security, and your audience. Obviously, if you post a presentation in a public location directed at a wide audience of viewers, you wouldn't want to protect with a password or otherwise limit access.

To protect your presentation, follow these steps:

1. Click the File tab to open Backstage view.

2. Click the Protect Presentation button.

3. Select from the following menu options (see Figure 17.1):

   - **Mark as Final**—Convert your presentation to read-only. No one can edit or make changes to a final presentation.

   - **Encrypt with Password**—Open the Encrypt Document dialog box (see Figure 17.2), where you can enter a password that others need to open your presentation in the future. PowerPoint passwords are case-sensitive. In other words, "PASSWORD" and "password" are treated as separate passwords.

      TIP If you forget your password, you can no longer open or modify your presentation, so choose a password that's easy for you to remember or write it down in a secure location.

   - **Restrict Access**—Allow others to view a presentation, but not edit, copy, or print it.

   - **Add a Digital Signature**—Open a dialog box that enables you to add a digital signature (an invisible, electronic, encrypted signature stamp that's attached in a certificate to vouch for user authenticity). Adding a digital signature to your presentation plays an authentication role similar to the signing of a paper document. The average PowerPoint user won't normally set up digital certificates; this is the domain of an organization's IT department.

FIGURE 17.1

Protecting your presentation before sharing is an optional step.

FIGURE 17.2

Apply a password to your presentation if you want to control who has access to it.

Inspecting Your Presentation

Before sharing your presentation with others, you normally review your content and run a spell check. In addition, you should also inspect your presentation for hidden data and personal information such as comments, notes, author name, or document properties. A quick check with the Document Inspector can help you avoid displaying confidential or embarrassing information with others.

  CAUTION Because you might not be able to undo changes the Document Inspector makes to your presentation, it's a good idea to run the Inspector on a copy of your original presentation.

To run the Document Inspector, follow these steps:

1. Click the File tab to open Backstage view.

2. Click the Check for Issues button.

3. From the menu that displays, select Inspect Document. The Document Inspector dialog box displays, as shown in Figure 17.3.

FIGURE 17.3

Use the Document Inspector to find and remove hidden and personal information from your presentation before sharing.

 NOTE If you don't save your presentation before running the Document Inspector, a dialog box displays, prompting you to save before continuing.

4. Select the types of content for which to search. The Document Inspector dialog box describes each content type in detail.

 CAUTION The Document Inspector doesn't search for objects with animation effects. If you're concerned about animation effects, you should search for these manually.

5. Click the Inspect button. The Document Inspector dialog box changes, displaying inspection results, as shown in Figure 17.4.

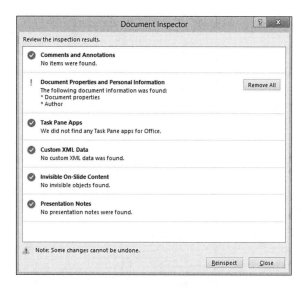

FIGURE 17.4

Specify the content you want to remove by selecting Remove All.

6. Click the Remove All button next to any items you want to remove.

7. Click the Close button to exit the dialog box.

NOTE In many cases, you inspect your presentation before sending it out for review by others and then again before finalizing to ensure that you remove all comments inserted during the review process.

Checking Your Presentation for Accessibility

If you publish your presentation to a general audience or know that people with disabilities will view it, you should check your presentation for accessibility.

To check accessibility, follow these steps:

1. Click the File tab to open Backstage view.

2. Click the Check for Issues button.

3. From the menu that displays, select Check Accessibility. The Accessibility Checker pane opens, as shown in Figure 17.5.

FIGURE 17.5

Verify that your presentation is accessible to people with disabilities.

4. Review and fix each potential issue based on the comments in the pane. For example, the Accessibility Checker might identify missing alt text or find issues with the reading order of content on your slides, problems that would cause difficulty for someone with a visual impairment who uses a screen reader.

5. Click the Close (x) button to close the pane and return to your presentation.

Running the Compatibility Checker

If you want to save your presentation as an earlier version of PowerPoint, you could lose features that weren't yet available in that previous version. See Chapter 2, "Creating a Basic Presentation," for more information about saving in a previous version of PowerPoint.

To run the Compatibility Checker, follow these steps:

1. Click the File tab to open Backstage view.

2. Click the Check for Issues button.

3. From the menu that appears, select Check Compatibility. The Microsoft PowerPoint Compatibility Checker dialog box appears, as shown in Figure 17.6.

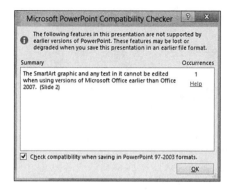

FIGURE 17.6

Verify that your presentation won't lose special effects or features if you save as a previous version of PowerPoint.

4. Review the summary results in the Compatibility Checker and decide either to revise your presentation or accept the limitations of saving in a previous version.

5. Click the OK button to close the dialog box and return to your presentation.

Sharing Your Presentation with Others

PowerPoint offers numerous ways to share your presentation with others, including several that are new to PowerPoint 2013. You'll find a wide variety of sharing options in the Share window in Backstage view.

Sharing Presentations with Others

You can save your presentations to SkyDrive directly from Microsoft PowerPoint and then invite other people to view, edit, or collaborate on them.

 TIP   See Chapter 20, "Accessing PowerPoint on the Web and Mobile Devices," for more information about SkyDrive, Microsoft's online storage and collaboration solution.

To share your presentation with others, follow these steps:

1. Click the File tab and select Share.

2. In the Share window, select Invite People to display the Invite People section on the right side of the screen (see Figure 17.7).

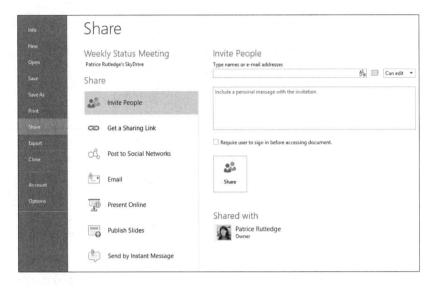

FIGURE 17.7

Sharing presentations with others is easy in PowerPoint 2013.

 NOTE If you haven't saved your presentation to SkyDrive yet, PowerPoint prompts you to click the Save to Cloud button to do so.

3. Enter the names or email addresses of the people you want to share with.

4. By default, PowerPoint enables the people you share with to edit your presentations. Select Can View from the drop-down list if you want to restrict this to viewing only.

5. Optionally, select the Require User to Sign In Before Accessing Document if you want to require a sign-in.

6. Click the Share button.

7. Click the Proceed button in the warning dialog box to confirm that you want to share. PowerPoint notifies the people about the presentation you want to share with them.

 NOTE *Co-authoring* is an Office feature that enables you to work on the same document simultaneously with other colleagues no matter where they're located. Co-authoring requires either a SkyDrive account or Microsoft SharePoint. To activate this feature, more than one person needs to open the same presentation in either SkyDrive or SharePoint. See Chapter 20 for more information.

Sharing via a Link

If you've saved your presentation online, you can share it with a link. To create a link, follow these steps:

1. Click the File tab and select Share.

2. In the Share window, select Get a Sharing Link to display the Get a Sharing Link section on the right side of the screen (see Figure 17.8).

 CAUTION The Get a Sharing Link option doesn't display if you saved your presentation only to your computer.

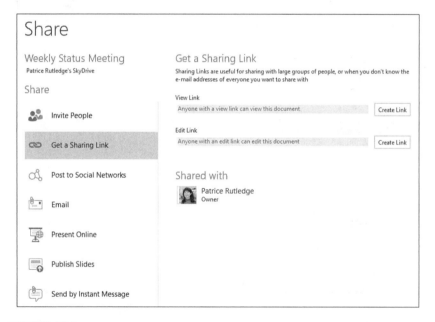

FIGURE 17.8

Share links to presentations stored online.

3. Click the Create Link button next to either View Link or Edit Link, depending on the rights you want to provide.

4. Copy the link provided and share with the appropriate people.

To disable a link, click the Disable Link button next to the link you no longer want.

Sharing on Social Networks

You can share your online PowerPoint presentations on social networks such as Facebook, Twitter, and LinkedIn. To share a presentation on a social network, follow these steps:

1. Click the File tab and select Share.

2. In the Share window, select Post to Social Networks to display the Post to Social Networks section on the right side of the screen (see Figure 17.9).

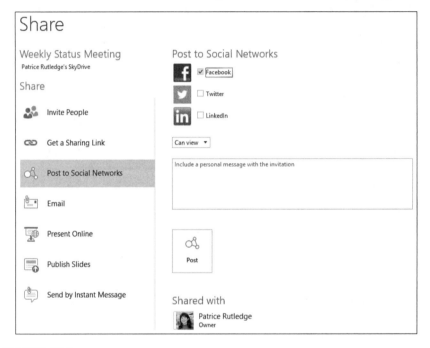

FIGURE 17.9

Get social by sharing presentations on your favorite sites.

 CAUTION The Post to Social Networks option doesn't display if you haven't saved your presentation online.

 NOTE If you haven't connected with any social networks yet, click the Click Here to Connect to Social Networks link to do so. You're prompted to log into your Microsoft account and connect with your preferred social sites.

3. Select the check box next to each social site on which you want to share.

4. By default, PowerPoint enables the people you share with to view your presentation, but you can choose Can Edit from the drop-down list if you want to provide editing functionality.

5. Optionally, add a personal message about the presentation you're sharing.

6. Click the Post button to post on your selected social sites.

 CAUTION Think carefully before sharing presentations socially and consider who could potentially view or edit your presentation by doing this.

Sharing via Email

PowerPoint provides numerous options for sharing your presentation with others via email. To do so, follow these steps:

1. Click the File tab and select Share.

2. In the Share window, select Email to display the Email section on the right side of the screen (see Figure 17.10).

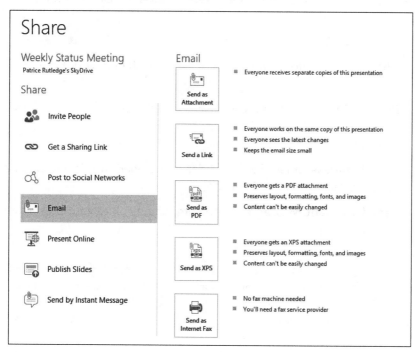

FIGURE 17.10

Choose one of several email-sharing options.

3. Choose from one of the following options:

- **Send as Attachment**—Open your default email application, such as Microsoft Outlook, and attach a copy of the open presentation.

- **Send a Link**—Open your default email application and insert a link to a presentation stored in a shared location, such as a SharePoint site or SkyDrive site. If your presentation isn't stored in a shared location, this option isn't available.

- **Send as PDF**—Save your presentation as a PDF and attach it to an email message. PowerPoint opens your default email application to send your message.

- **Send as XPS**—Save your presentation as an XPS file and attach it to an email message. PowerPoint opens your default email application to send your message.

- **Send as Internet Fax**—Send your presentation as a fax through a fax service provider. If you haven't already signed up with a provider, selecting this option opens a website with a list of potential providers.

See Chapter 2 for more information about saving in PDF or XPS format.

Other Ways to Share Your PowerPoint Presentations

The Share window offers three other options for sharing your PowerPoint presentations:

- **Present Online**—Select Present Online in the Share window to start an online presentation. See Chapter 15, "Presenting a Slide Show," for more information about presenting online.

- **Publish Slides**—Select Publish Slides in the Share window to publish slides to a slide library or a SharePoint site.

- **Send by Instant Message**—Send someone a link to your presentation by instant message.

 NOTE You must have SharePoint installed to take advantage of the slide library feature. If you don't, consider sharing your presentations on SkyDrive. You can also publish your slides to an accessible folder on your own computer or to a network share drive.

THE ABSOLUTE MINIMUM

Here are the key points to remember from this chapter:

- Before sharing your presentation, you can protect it with a password, inspect it for confidential information, validate its accessibility, and check for compatibility with previous versions.

- The PowerPoint Share window enables you to share your presentation on the Web, via email, on social sites, and via a link.

18

WORKING WITH HYPERLINKS AND ACTION BUTTONS

Interactivity can enliven any PowerPoint presentation, whether you present live or let your audience view it online. Fortunately, PowerPoint makes it easy to link to the Web, to other slides in your presentation, or to external files.

Working with Hyperlinks

Just like on the Web, you can create hyperlinks in your PowerPoint presentations. Unlike with a typical slide show, where you must proceed sequentially through your content, you can move through a hyperlinked presentation in whatever order makes sense for the audience. You can also hide information and then show it only if your audience needs or asks for it.

The first step in creating a hyperlink is to identify the object to link. You can link any object, including text, clip art, WordArt, charts, shapes, and more.

Inserting Hyperlinks

In PowerPoint, you can insert hyperlinks that go to an external website, jump to another location in your presentation, or open an external application.

Inserting Hyperlinks to an External Website

Inserting hyperlinks to external websites is a common use of PowerPoint's hyperlink feature. For example, let's say you're making a presentation to the board of directors of your company. You suspect some board members will want to know more about current promotions by a rival company. You can create a hyperlink in your slide show that opens up your web browser, connects to the Internet, and displays your competitor's website. Of course, if no one asks or if time is running short, you don't even need to use the link. But you know it's there, just in case.

 NOTE When you create a hyperlink for the first time, you use the Insert Hyperlink dialog box. If you change the hyperlink, the Edit Hyperlink dialog box displays. These dialog boxes are identical except for the Remove Link button found in the Edit Hyperlink dialog box, which enables you to remove the selected hyperlink.

To insert a hyperlink to an external website, follow these steps:

1. In Normal view, select the text or object you want to link (see Figure 18.1).

2. On the Insert tab, click the Hyperlink button. Alternatively, press Ctrl+K. The Insert Hyperlink dialog box displays (see Figure 18.2).

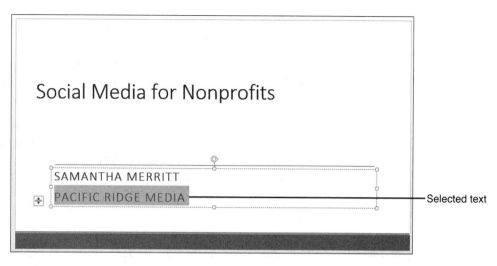

FIGURE 18.1

Select text or any other object to which you want to add a hyperlink.

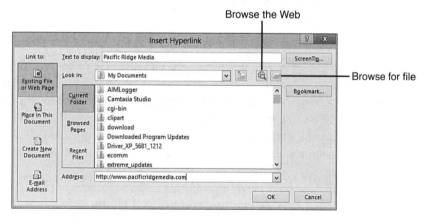

FIGURE 18.2

Use the Insert Hyperlink dialog box to specify the location you want to link to the selected text or object.

3. By default, PowerPoint selects the Existing File or Web Page button and the Current Folder button. This view lets you find the URL you want in several ways:

   - If you know the URL, type it in the Address field. Be sure to type the URL exactly as it appears, including uppercase and lowercase letters and all special characters, such as the tilde (~). If you can, go to the site, copy the URL from the Address field in your browser, and paste it in this field.

- If the link is to a location that you have visited recently, select it from the drop-down list of URLs in the Address field.

- If you don't remember the location's URL but have recently visited there, click the Browsed Pages button and choose the location from a list of places you recently visited on the Web.

- If you don't remember the URL, click the Browse the Web button (small button to the right of the Look In field) to go to your browser, enabling you to browse for the Internet location you want. When you find the location, switch back to PowerPoint (use the Windows taskbar or press Alt+Tab), and the URL from your browser appears in the dialog box.

4. Click the OK button.

If you add a link to text, that text now displays underlined and in a different color. The actual color you see depends on the PowerPoint theme you use. If you add the link to any other object, the object's appearance doesn't change, but the object is linked nonetheless.

Inserting Hyperlinks to Another Slide in Your Presentation

In addition to linking to websites, you can also link to other slides in your presentation. Creating links to other slides helps you customize your slide show so that you can move quickly to the slides you need. For example, after your opening title slide, you might want to include a table of contents slide with hyperlinks from each topic to a specific location in the slide show. On the last slide for each topic, you can include a link back to the table of contents slide.

To insert a link to another presentation slide, follow these steps:

1. In Normal view, select the text or object on the slide you want to link.

2. On the Insert tab, click the Hyperlink button to open the Insert Hyperlink dialog box.

3. Click the Place in This Document button. PowerPoint displays a list of slides in the current slide show (see Figure 18.3).

4. Select the slide to which you want to jump.

5. Click the OK button.

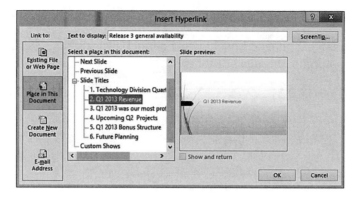

FIGURE 18.3

Quickly link to a slide in your open presentation.

Inserting Hyperlinks to Other Files

PowerPoint also enables you to create a hyperlink to another document, either on your own computer or on a network if you're connected to one. When you jump from your presentation to another file, the application displaying that file starts. For example, other PowerPoint files open in PowerPoint, Word documents open in Word, and so on.

To insert a link to another file, follow these steps:

1. In Normal view, select the text or object you want to link.

2. On the Insert tab, click the Hyperlink button to open the Insert Hyperlink dialog box (refer to Figure 18.2).

3. To specify the appropriate file to link to, you can perform one of the following actions:

   • Type the name of the file in the Address field, including its full pathname (for example, **c:\my documents\sales.xls**).

   • Select a file in your current folder.

   • Click the Recent Files button to display a list of recently accessed files.

   • Click the Browse for File button (small button to the right of the Look In field) and browse your computer or network for the file you want.

   • Click the Create New Document button to link to a new document that you can create now or later (see Figure 18.4).

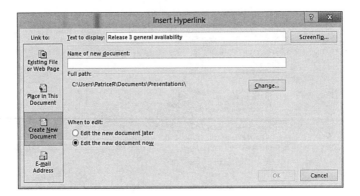

FIGURE 18.4

Insert a link to a new document such as another PowerPoint presentation, Excel spreadsheet, or Word document.

 TIP If you select another PowerPoint file, you can click the Bookmark button to choose a specific slide to open.

4. Click the OK button.

Inserting a Hyperlink to an Email Address

Finally, you can insert a link to send an email from your presentation. This is primarily useful if you plan to publish your presentation on the Web and want to let your audience contact you after viewing it.

 TIP As a shortcut, just type your email address directly on your slide (for example, type **jsmith@pearson.com**). PowerPoint recognizes common email formats and automatically creates a link for you.

To insert a link to an email address, follow these steps:

1. In Normal view, select the text or object you want to link.

2. On the Insert tab, click the Hyperlink button to open the Insert Hyperlink dialog box (refer to Figure 18.2).

3. Click the E-mail Address button.

4. Type the address in the E-mail Address field and enter a subject. You can even select the email address from a list of recently used email addresses (see Figure 18.5).

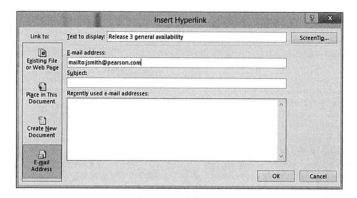

FIGURE 18.5

Create a link to an email address to enable the viewer to send a message.

5. Click the OK button.

Creating Invisible Text Hyperlinks

Linked text looks different from the nonlinked text around it—it's underlined. You might not want the text to look different, but you still want to be able to click that text and jump to the linked page or document. The solution is simple: Cover the text with a shape, link the shape, and then make it invisible.

To create an invisible hyperlinked object, follow these steps:

1. On the Insert tab, click the Shape button and insert a shape, such as a rectangle, that covers the text you want to link.

2. With the shape selected, click the Hyperlink button on the Insert tab.

3. Type the URL in the Address field.

4. Click the OK button.

5. Right-click the shape and choose Format Shape from the menu that displays. PowerPoint opens the Format Shape pane (see Figure 18.6).

6. Click Fill and select the No Fill option button.

7. Click Line and select the No Line option button.

8. Click the Close (x) button in the upper-right corner of the pane.

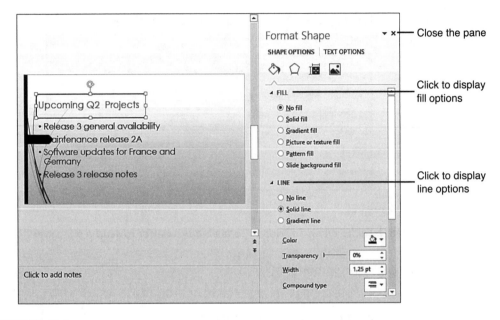

FIGURE 18.6

Use the Format Shape pane to remove fill color and line color, thus making the shape invisible.

An invisible linked object now displays over the text you want linked. When you play your slide show, move the mouse pointer to that text area and then click when the mouse pointer changes to a hand. To the audience, it looks like you are clicking on text, although you are actually clicking a linked invisible graphic shape.

An additional benefit to using an invisible link is that no one but you has to know the link is there. If you don't use it, no one will ever know. Text linked in the normal manner, on the other hand, begs to be clicked because the text looks so obviously different.

Customizing Hyperlink ScreenTips

When you point your mouse at a linked object during a presentation, a ScreenTip displays, detailing the location of the link. You can customize the ScreenTip to make it easier for you (or the audience) to know just where you will go if you click the linked object.

To customize a ScreenTip, follow these steps:

1. Right-click the linked text or object and select Edit Hyperlink from the menu that appears.

2. Click the ScreenTip button. PowerPoint displays the Set Hyperlink ScreenTip dialog box (see Figure 18.7).

FIGURE 18.7

Customize the ScreenTip that displays when you move the mouse pointer to a linked object.

3. Type the text you want to display in the ScreenTip in the ScreenTip Text field.

4. Click the OK button to return to the Edit Hyperlink dialog box.

5. Click the OK button to save your changes.

Modifying Hyperlinks

The Edit Hyperlink dialog box is a powerful tool for quickly and efficiently modifying your hyperlinks.

To modify an existing hyperlink, follow these simple steps:

1. Right-click the linked text or object, and then select Edit Hyperlink from the menu that appears to open the Edit Hyperlink dialog box, as shown in Figure 18.8.

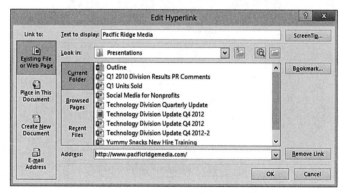

FIGURE 18.8

The Edit Hyperlink dialog box lets you update or change an existing hyperlink.

2. Make any desired changes, such as entering a new URL or selecting a different PowerPoint slide to jump to.

3. Click the OK button to save your changes.

Removing Hyperlinks

After inserting a hyperlink, you might decide that you don't want it or that you need to link a different object instead. To remove a hyperlink, right-click a selected object and select Remove Hyperlink from the menu that displays.

Using Action Settings

Action settings provide another way to add interactivity and links to your presentation. You can start an action by clicking an object with the mouse or simply by passing the mouse pointer over it. Action settings duplicate some of the functionality of a hyperlink: You can add links to the Web or to another PowerPoint slide, for example. They also offer additional interactivity options such as playing a sound file or running a macro.

To add an action to a PowerPoint object, follow these steps:

1. Select the object to which you want to add an action.

2. On the Insert tab, click the Action button to open the Action Settings dialog box, as shown in Figure 18.9.

FIGURE 18.9

Use a mouse click or mouse over to perform actions in your presentation.

3. Choose the Mouse Click tab if you want to start the action with a mouse click; choose the Mouse Over tab to start the action by passing the mouse over the object. The Mouse Click and Mouse Over tabs are nearly identical. The only real difference is the method by which you start the action.

 CAUTION Passing the mouse over an object to start an action is the easier method, but be careful not to get too close to the object too soon or you might start the action before you intend to.

4. Choose the action to take when you click or pass over the object:

   - **None**—No action occurs. Choose this option to remove a previously placed action.

   - **Hyperlink To**—Create a hyperlink to a selected slide within your presentation, another PowerPoint presentation, another file on your computer, or a web page.

   - **Run Program**—Run the program whose path you specify in the text box. Click the Browse button to open the Select a Program to Run dialog box, where you can search for the program.

    TIP You can also use this field to open a file in another program. For example, entering **c:\download\budget.xls** opens Excel and the Budget worksheet that's in the Download folder.

   - **Run Macro**—Choose from a list of PowerPoint macros you've created.

   - **Object Action**—Open, edit, or play an embedded object. This option is available only for objects that you can open, edit, or play, such as a media clip or something created with another application and embedded into your presentation.

   - **Play Sound**—Play an audio file you select from the drop-down list. You can select other sounds by choosing Other Sound from the drop-down list.

   - **Highlight Click**—Highlight the selected object when you click the mouse. (Available only on the Mouse Click tab.)

   - **Highlight When Mouse Over**—Highlight the selected object when you mouse over. (Available only on the Mouse Over tab.)

5. Click the OK button to close the Action Settings dialog box.

To modify or delete an action setting, select the object, click the Action button, and make your changes in the Action Settings dialog box. To remove the action, select None.

Using Action Buttons

Action buttons provide you with another way to use objects to perform certain actions. PowerPoint includes 12 different action buttons:

- Back or Previous
- Forward or Next
- Beginning
- End
- Home
- Information

- Return
- Movie
- Document
- Sound
- Help
- Custom

These buttons function in much the same way as applying an action setting to an existing object. When you place an action button on a slide, the Action Settings dialog box appears. You can then specify mouse actions for the action button. Many action buttons perform common tasks such as moving to a previous slide, so this action is defined by default in the Action Settings dialog box.

To place an action button on a PowerPoint slide, go to the Insert tab and click the Shapes button. Select one of the action buttons that appear at the bottom of the gallery (see Figure 18.10), and then click and drag on the slide to create the button.

FIGURE 18.10

The Shapes gallery includes several ready-made action buttons.

As soon as you finish, the Action Settings dialog box opens, in which you can accept the default action setting or specify the action to attach to this button. Enter the required information and click the OK button. The action button now displays on your PowerPoint slide, where you can resize and reposition it if you like. For a further explanation about the options in the Action Settings dialog box, refer to section, "Using Action Settings."

To modify an action button, right-click the button, choose Edit Hyperlink from the menu, and make any changes in the Action Settings dialog box. To remove an action button, select it and press the Delete key.

Testing Hyperlinks and Action Settings

Before you present to an audience, test all your hyperlinks to make sure you set them up correctly. The last thing you want during your presentation is a surprise when you click a hyperlink.

To test the hyperlinks, action settings, and action buttons in your presentation, press F5 to start the slide show at the beginning of your presentation.

 TIP If only one slide in your presentation includes a link, go to that slide and click the Slide Show button in the lower-right corner of your screen to start the presentation from the selected slide.

Scroll through your presentation, testing every hyperlink, ScreenTip, action setting, and action button. Verifying that all external links work is particularly important. If you notice any errors, fix them and retest your presentation.

THE ABSOLUTE MINIMUM

Here are the key points to remember from this chapter:

- PowerPoint enables you to create hyperlinks to websites, slides in your presentation, external documents, and email addresses.

- You can create a link from any object, including text, clip art, WordArt, charts, shapes, and more.

- You can customize the ScreenTip that displays when you pause over a hyperlink.

- **Action settings** and action buttons offer other ways to add interactivity and links to your presentation.

- Be sure to test all hyperlinks thoroughly before giving your presentation.

IN THIS CHAPTER

- Working with the Quick Access Toolbar
- Setting PowerPoint Options
- Setting Presentation Properties
- Working with Slide Masters

19

CUSTOMIZING POWERPOINT

Although many PowerPoint users create outstanding presentations without ever customizing PowerPoint, others prefer making a number of changes to suit their work style and presentation needs. Fortunately, PowerPoint offers numerous customization options. In this chapter, you find out how to customize all aspects of PowerPoint, including the Quick Access Toolbar, Ribbon tabs, and slide masters.

Working with the Quick Access Toolbar

The Quick Access Toolbar is a customizable toolbar that contains popular commands you may use regardless of which tab currently displays. By default, the Save, Undo, and Repeat buttons are available from the Quick Access Toolbar, shown in Figure 19.1.

Click to modify the toolbar

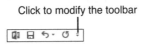

FIGURE 19.1

The Quick Access Toolbar gives you ready access to popular PowerPoint commands.

Moving the Quick Access Toolbar

The toolbar's default location is in the upper-left corner of the screen. If you prefer, you can move the toolbar to just below the Ribbon. To move the toolbar, click the down arrow to its right, next to the Repeat button, and select Show Below the Ribbon from the menu that displays.

 NOTE There are only two options for placing the Quick Access Toolbar. You can't move it to any other location on your screen.

Adding and Removing Quick Access Toolbar Commands

To quickly add the most popular commands to the toolbar, click the down arrow to its right and choose from the available options:

- New
- Open
- Save
- Email
- Quick Print
- Print Preview and Print
- Spelling
- Undo
- Redo
- Start from Beginning
- Touch Mode

A check mark is placed before each active command on the toolbar, such as the default commands Save, Undo, and Repeat. To add another command from this menu to the toolbar, click it. To remove one of these commands from the toolbar, click it again and the check mark disappears.

To add a command button from another tab to the toolbar, right-click it on the Ribbon tab and select Add to Quick Access Toolbar from the menu that displays. For example, let's say you want to add the New Slide button to the Quick Access

Toolbar. To do so, go to the Home tab, right-click the New Slide button, and select Add to Quick Access Toolbar. The New Slide button is placed on the Quick Access Toolbar to the right of the Repeat button.

To remove a button, right-click it on the toolbar and choose Remove from Quick Access Toolbar from the menu that displays.

 TIP You can perform advanced customizations to the Quick Access Toolbar in the PowerPoint Options dialog box, described in the next section of this chapter.

Setting PowerPoint Options

PowerPoint lets you change many basic options, such as how you edit, save, or print your presentations, and how you view PowerPoint. Changes you make in the PowerPoint Options dialog box (see Figure 19.2) become your new default settings until you change them again.

To access the PowerPoint Options dialog box, click the File tab and choose Options.

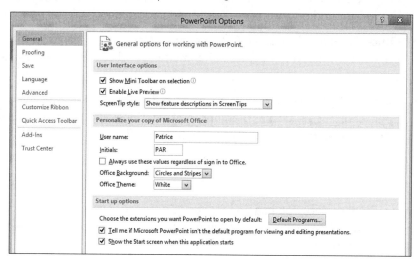

FIGURE 19.2

Use the PowerPoint Options dialog box to change many of PowerPoint's default settings.

Personalizing PowerPoint

On the General tab of the PowerPoint Options dialog box, you can change the most popular options in PowerPoint:

- **Show Mini Toolbar on Selection**—Display the mini toolbar when you select text, enabling fast access to common formatting tools, including font style, font color, bolding, and more.

- **Enable Live Preview**—Preview potential formatting changes directly in your presentation before actually applying them.

- **ScreenTip Style**—Display enhanced ScreenTips with or without feature descriptions or no ScreenTips at all.

- **User Name**—Whenever you use options that require your name, PowerPoint uses the name found here.

- **Initials**—Whenever user initials are required, PowerPoint uses the initials found here.

- **Always Use These Values Regardless of Sign in to Office**—Use the data you entered in the User Name and Initials fields to override the data in the Office account you signed in to on the Account window.

- **Office Background**—Choose between the default Circle and Stripes background, one of the alternative backgrounds, or no background. Note that this refers to the background of the program, not to the background color of your slides.

- **Office Theme**—Choose an Office theme: White (the default), Light Gray, or Dark Gray. This option controls the interface and colors of Office itself, not your slides.

- **Start Up Options**—Specify default PowerPoint extensions, the default application for viewing and editing presentations, and whether you want to display the start screen when you open PowerPoint.

Setting Proofing Options

On the Proofing tab, you can specify AutoCorrect and spelling options. Chapter 4, "Working with Text," covers spelling options. This section focuses on AutoCorrect options.

Setting AutoCorrect Options

AutoCorrect is a useful feature that can help save time and automatically correct mistakes you frequently make. By default, Office includes AutoCorrect substitutions for common misspellings, such as correcting "teh" to "the," but you can also add your own. If you need to enter a long name or term frequently, you can save yourself time and effort if you enter a shorter term and have PowerPoint fill in the longer term.

For example, say that the name of your latest product is "All-Natural, Fat-Free Chilly Cherry Sorbet." You're tired of typing that phrase over and over, so you set up an AutoCorrect entry named "CCS" and have PowerPoint automatically enter "All-Natural, Fat-Free Chilly Cherry Sorbet" any time you type the letters CCS.

 NOTE Be aware that any AutoCorrect entries you make in PowerPoint also carry over to other Microsoft Office applications, such as Word, Excel, Outlook, and so forth.

In addition, if you know that you always misspell a particular word, you can enter the word as you normally misspell it in the Replace field and then enter the correct spelling in the With field.

To open the AutoCorrect dialog box, click the AutoCorrect Options button on the Proofing tab. The AutoCorrect dialog box for your installed language opens, as shown in Figure 19.3.

FIGURE 19.3

You can view and modify automatic correction options in the AutoCorrect dialog box.

This dialog box includes four tabs: AutoCorrect, AutoFormat As You Type, Actions, and Math AutoCorrect.

Default AutoCorrect options on the AutoCorrect tab include the following:

- **Show AutoCorrect Options Buttons**—Display the AutoCorrect Options button after an automatic correction occurs. Pause the mouse over the small blue box beneath the correction and click the down arrow to view a menu of options (see Figure 19.4). From here, you can revert back to your original entry, stop automatically correcting this type of entry, or open the AutoCorrect dialog box.

FIGURE 19.4

Choose from several options when you automatically correct text entries in PowerPoint.

- **Correct TWo INitial CApitals**—Automatically correct instances in which you accidentally type two initial capital letters in a row. You can enter exceptions to this rule if you like (such as ID).

- **Capitalize First Letter of Sentences**—Automatically capitalize the first letter of all sentences.

- **Capitalize First Letter of Table Cells**—Automatically capitalize the first letter of text in a table cell.

- **Capitalize Names of Days**—Automatically capitalize days of the week, such as Monday, Tuesday, and so forth.

- **Correct Accidental Use of cAPS LOCK Key**—When the caps lock feature is on and you type regular sentences, AutoCorrect turns off caps lock and fixes the capitalization of whatever you typed.

- **Replace Text As You Type**—Automatically replace AutoCorrect entries as you type them.

Customizing AutoCorrect Entries

You can customize AutoCorrect entries. The lower portion of the AutoCorrect dialog box includes a list of existing automatic corrections, where you can do the following:

- Add an AutoCorrect entry by typing the term to replace in the Replace field and its replacement in the With field. Then click the Add button.

- Delete an existing entry by selecting it and clicking the Delete button.

- Change an existing entry by selecting it and entering the new data in the Replace and/or With fields, as needed. Then click the Replace button.

Specifying AutoCorrect Exceptions

To specify AutoCorrect exceptions to these rules, follow these steps:

1. In the AutoCorrect dialog box, click the Exceptions button. Figure 19.5 illustrates the AutoCorrect Exceptions dialog box.

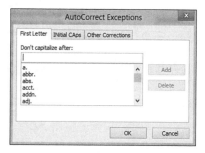

FIGURE 19.5

Make exceptions to AutoCorrect functionality.

2. On the First Letter tab, you can specify abbreviations that end with a period that you don't want to treat as the end of a sentence. PowerPoint ignores standard rules of capitalization here and doesn't capitalize the next letter after the period. Terms such as *etc.* and *abbr.* are already included, but you can also add your own or delete any existing entries.

3. On the INitial CAps tab, shown in Figure 19.6, you can enter any capitalized terms that you don't want PowerPoint to convert to lowercase. For example, to avoid having the term *ID* converted to *Id* based on the normal rules of capitalization, add it to this list.

FIGURE 19.6

Automatically resolve capitalization problems on this tab.

4. On the Other Corrections tab, you can list words you don't want to correct.

5. Click the OK button to return to the AutoCorrect dialog box.

AutoFormatting As You Type

The AutoFormat As You Type tab of the AutoCorrect dialog box enables you to replace and apply a number of formatting options as you type. You save time because you don't need to format manually. Figure 19.7 shows this tab.

 NOTE These options are all selected by default, but you can remove the check marks if you want to deactivate them for any reason.

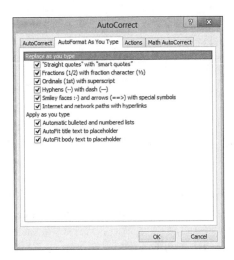

FIGURE 19.7

You can see and change automatic correction options in this dialog box.

Options include:

- **"Straight Quotes" with "Smart Quotes"**—Insert a "curly" quotation mark when you type a quotation mark. If this check box is not selected, you get "straight" quotation marks, a throwback to typewriter days.

- **Fractions (1/2) with Fraction Character (½)**—Replace 1/4, 1/2, and 3/4 with formatted fractions such as ¼, ½, and ¾.

- **Ordinals (1st) with Superscript**—Replace manually entered ordinals with superscript ordinals.

- **Hyphens (--) with Dash (—)**—Replace manually entered hyphens with an em dash. Using two hyphens is a holdover from typewriter days when there was no way to type a proper em dash.

- **Smiley Faces :-) and Arrows (==>) with Special Symbols**—Replace typed representations of faces and arrows with face and arrow characters. For example, you can replace :-) with ☺.

- **Internet and Network Paths with Hyperlinks**—Apply a hyperlink to an Internet address so that it opens a browser when you click it.

- **Automatic Bulleted and Numbered Lists**—Apply automatic bulleting or numbering when PowerPoint detects that you're creating a list (when you use an asterisk for a bullet, for example).

- **AutoFit Title Text to Placeholder**—Resize text if it won't fit in a title placeholder. For example, if your theme's title text is 44 points by default, you can have the font size reduced if your title is too long to fit. When PowerPoint fits title text to the placeholder, the AutoFit Options button appears. Click the down arrow on the right side of the button to display a menu from which you can accept or reject automatic fitting and open the AutoCorrect dialog box.

- **AutoFit Body Text to Placeholder**—Resize text if it won't fit in a body text placeholder. This option works in much the same way as the AutoFit Title Text to Placeholder option.

Setting Up Additional Actions

On the Actions tab, you can set up additional options for specific words or phrases, such as dates and measurements, in your presentations. As an example, let's say that you enable the Date action. When you right-click a date on a PowerPoint slide, you can select Additional Actions from the menu that displays to show your calendar in Outlook.

Setting Math AutoCorrect Options

If you include mathematical equations in your presentation, use the Math AutoCorrect tab to enter specific text that PowerPoint converts to the correct symbol. For example, you can type **\Delta** to enter Δ on your slide.

Setting Save Options

Click the Save tab to view and change Save options (see Figure 19.8).

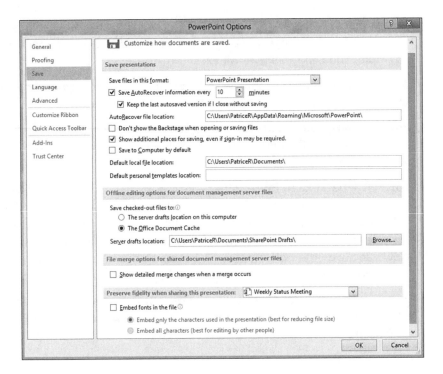

FIGURE 19.8

The Save tab of the PowerPoint Options dialog box helps change default file-saving options.

Save options include the following:

- **Save Files in This Format**—By default, PowerPoint saves its files in the PowerPoint presentation format (*.pptx). If you work in an environment in which some people use older versions of PowerPoint, you might need to agree on a common format for everyone to use. Alternatively, you might want to save your presentation in a web format. Other options include PowerPoint Macro-Enabled Presentation, PowerPoint 97–2003 Presentation, Strict Open XML Presentation, and OpenDocument Presentation.

 CAUTION Saving a PowerPoint presentation in an earlier format might result in the loss of certain features available only in PowerPoint 2013.

- **Save AutoRecover Information Every *NN* Minutes**—This automatic backup provision saves a temporary copy of your presentation (typically in the \Windows\Temp folder) as frequently as you specify with this option. If you exit your document properly, the automatic backup file is erased. If you don't exit properly (for example, because of a power failure), PowerPoint opens this file the next time you use PowerPoint so that you can determine whether it contains changes you didn't save.

- **Keep the Last Autosaved Version if I Close Without Saving**—Saves your latest autosaved version if you forgot to save when closing or your computer crashes.

- **AutoRecover File Location**—Specify the location to place your autosaved files.

- **Don't Show the Backstage When Opening or Saving Files**—Backstage view displays by default during these actions, but you can disable this if you prefer.

- **Show Additional Places for Saving, Even if Sign-in May Be Required**—By default, PowerPoint displays this notification, but you can disable this feature.

- **Save to Computer by Default**—Saves files to your computer by default. Otherwise, you have to do this manually.

- **Default Local File Location**—PowerPoint saves your presentations in the folder you specify. Initially this is usually your Documents folder, but that can vary depending on your operating system and how PowerPoint was installed.

- **Default Personal Templates Location**—If you have your own templates, you can specify where you store them.

- **Save Checked-Out Files To**—Save checked-out files either to the server drafts location you specify or to the Office document cache.

- **Show Detailed Merge Changes When a Merge Occurs**—If you compare and merge different versions of your presentation during a review process, you can display detailed changes.

- **Preserve Fidelity When Sharing This Presentation**—Select a presentation to preserve from the drop-down list. The list displays only presentations currently open.

- **Embed Fonts in the File**—Select this option if you want to embed fonts in the current document. Options include embedding only characters in use to reduce file size and embedding all characters so that others can edit the presentation.

Setting Language Options

The Language tab enables you to select languages for editing, display, help, and ScreenTips. These options are most useful if you plan to create presentations in a language other than English or want to enable a different version of English, such as English for the UK or Canada if your default is the United States.

Setting Advanced Options

Click the Advanced tab (see Figure 19.9) to display advanced options for editing, printing, and formatting a presentation.

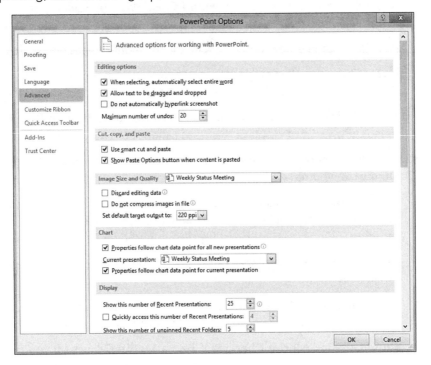

FIGURE 19.9

The Advanced tab of the PowerPoint Options dialog box offers advanced editing, printing, and slide show options.

This page includes the following sections:

- **Editing Options**—Specify text selection, drag-and-drop, and undo options. Be aware that increasing the number of undos enlarges your document and also increases the risk of file corruption. Unless you need more, stay with the default number, or fewer.

- **Cut, Copy, and Paste**—Enable Smart Cut and Paste, which verifies that there's one space before and after the text and that there are no spaces before the end punctuation if you paste the text at the end of a sentence. Also, you can choose to show the Paste Options button, which enables you to make choices about how you want to paste a copied object or text, such as whether to keep source or target design template formatting.

- **Image Size and Quality**—Select options that affect image size and quality, such as discarding editing data, not compressing images in the file, and setting default target output. Remember that uncompressed images increase file size, which makes your presentation more prone to corruption.

- **Chart**—Specify whether you want the data label to follow data points as they move in your charts.

- **Display**—Display a specific number of recent documents, shortcut keys in ScreenTips (such as Ctrl+S when you pause the mouse over the Save button), or a vertical ruler for better object positioning. You can also disable hardware graphics acceleration, which can improve video quality during recording. Optionally, specify the default view for opening documents, such as the view saved in the file, Normal view, Slide Sorter view, and so on.

- **Slide Show**—Specify whether you want to display a menu upon a right mouse click or a pop-up toolbar during a slide show. You can also choose to end your show with a black slide, which makes for a cleaner ending.

- **Print**—Specify general print options such as background printing (which enables you to continue working on your presentation while you print), printing TrueType fonts as graphics (if your printer has trouble recognizing your fonts), and printing at the highest quality your printer enables. See Chapter 16, "Creating and Printing Presentation Materials," for more information about printing.

- **When Printing This Document**—When you print your current document, by default you use the most recently used PowerPoint print settings. Modify this by specifying exact print settings for the open document such as the print format (full slides, handouts, notes, and so forth) and color (full color, grayscale, or black and white).

- **General**—Add sound effects for screen elements such as menus and buttons or show add-in user interface errors.

Customizing the Ribbon

The PowerPoint Ribbon shown in Figure 19.10 is command central for your presentation design activity and offers an easy way to perform common tasks. Although many users are happy to use the Ribbon as it is, PowerPoint also enables you to customize the Ribbon to your exact specifications.

On the Customize Ribbon tab in the PowerPoint Options dialog box (see Figure 19.11), you can control which tabs display on the Ribbon and which buttons and groups display on each tab.

Click to hide (unpin) the Ribbon

FIGURE 19.10

Customize the Ribbon or even hide it from view.

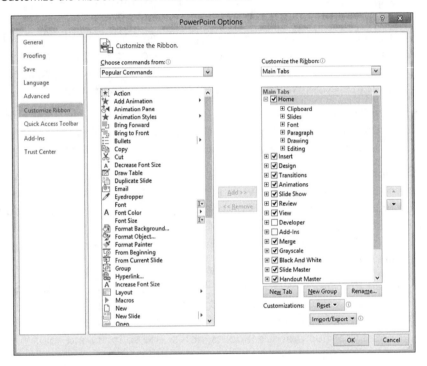

FIGURE 19.11

Customize the Ribbon by adding and removing command buttons.

 TIP You can also access the Customize Ribbon tab by right-clicking the Ribbon and choosing Customize the Ribbon from the menu.

The left side of the tab lists commands that you can add and remove from the Ribbon. These commands usually display as buttons, such as the New Slide button on the Home tab. The right side of the Customize Ribbon tab lists Ribbon tabs and the commands on each tab.

On the Customize Ribbon tab, you can take the following actions:

- Select or deselect the check box next to any tab to show or hide it on the Ribbon.

- Select a command on the right side of the screen (currently visible on the Ribbon) and click the Remove button to remove it from the tab. You can always restore this later.

- Use the Move Up and Move Down buttons to reposition the placement of any tab or command.

- Rename a tab or command by selecting it and clicking the Rename button.

- Reset the Ribbon to its default by clicking the Reset button. You have the option to reset only a selected Ribbon tab or all Ribbon customizations.

- Export your customizations to an exported Office UI file or import a file you've already exported.

- Create new groups on a Ribbon tab and add new commands to it. Note that you must create a new group to add a command to a Ribbon. You can't add a single command without specifying a custom group for it nor can you add a command to one of the default PowerPoint groups.

- Create a new Ribbon tab and add groups and commands to it.

Adding Commands to a Ribbon Tab

To create a new group with commands on an existing tab, follow these steps:

1. On the Customize Ribbon tab, select the type of tab you want to add a command to from the Customize the Ribbon list. Options include All Tabs, Main Tabs, and Tools Tabs. The list of tabs below populates based on the category you choose.

 NOTE Main tabs are the tabs that display on the PowerPoint Ribbon. Tools tabs are the contextual tabs that display when you select an object such as a shape or chart.

2. Select the tab to which you want to add the command.

3. Click the New Group button. PowerPoint inserts a new group at the end of the tab list.

4. Click the Rename button, change the default name to something more meaningful, and click the OK button to close the dialog box.

5. Select the command category you want from the Choose Commands From list. The list of commands below populates based on the command category you choose.

6. Select the command you want to add to the Ribbon.

7. Click the Add button to add it to the selected group. Be sure that you've selected your new group on the right side of the screen. PowerPoint won't allow you to add a command to a default PowerPoint group.

8. Use the Move Up and Move Down buttons on the far right of the dialog box to adjust the location of your new button on the Ribbon.

9. Click the OK button to save your changes and close the dialog box. The Ribbon now displays the new command.

Adding a new tab is similar to adding a new group. Just click the New Tab button instead of the New Group button.

Customizing the Quick Access Toolbar

The Quick Access Toolbar tab of the PowerPoint Options dialog box (see Figure 19.12) enables you to perform advanced customizations to the Quick Access Toolbar, such as adding commands not accessible from the toolbar and rearranging the order of toolbar buttons.

On the Quick Access Toolbar tab, you can do the following:

- Select a command on the right side of the screen (currently visible on the toolbar) and click the Remove button to remove it. You can always restore this later.

- Use the Move Up and Move Down buttons to reposition the placement of any command.

- Reset the toolbar to its default by clicking the Reset button. You have the option to reset only the Quick Access Toolbar or all customizations.

- Export your customizations to an exported Office UI file or import a file you've already exported.

- Add a new command to the Quick Access Toolbar.

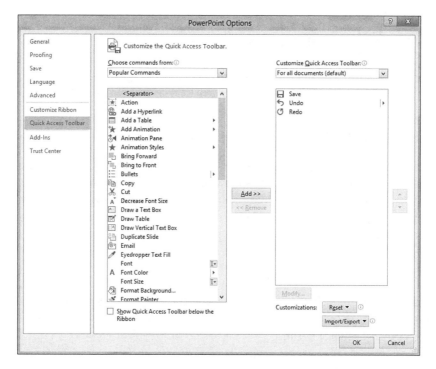

FIGURE 19.12

Perform advanced customizations to the Quick Access Toolbar.

To add a new command to the Quick Access Toolbar, follow these steps:

1. Select the command category you want from the Choose Commands From list. Some options match tab names and others reflect the category. The list of commands below populates based on the command category you choose.

2. Select the command you want to add to the toolbar, and click the Add button to add it to the right side of the dialog box.

3. Use the Move Up and Move Down buttons on the far right of the screen to adjust the location of your new button on the toolbar.

4. By default, the toolbar appears the same for all presentations. If you want to specify that the changes you just made should apply to only the current presentation, click the down arrow next to the Customize Quick Access Toolbar list and choose your presentation name from the list.

5. Click the OK button to save your changes and close the dialog box.

TIP   Hate the Quick Access Toolbar and want to get rid of it entirely? Remove all buttons and click OK. The toolbar buttons and icons disappear from your screen. If you change your mind, click the File tab, select Options, and go back to the Quick Access Toolbar tab, where clicking Reset restores everything again.

Setting Add-In Options

On the Add-Ins tab, you can view and manage PowerPoint add-ins, which offer supplemental features that enhance your PowerPoint experience. You can also download add-ins from the Microsoft Download Center (www.microsoft.com/downloads). Go to the Add-Ins tab on the Ribbon to access the features of the add-ins you've activated.

Setting Trust Center Options

The Trust Center tab describes security and privacy issues. Click the Trust Center Settings button to open the Trust Center dialog box, where you can specify security and privacy settings.

Setting Presentation Properties

As you create and modify your presentation, you automatically change many of the presentation's properties. To view and modify presentation properties, click the File tab and then select Info to open Backstage view. On the right side of the screen, you can view basic details about your presentation properties. To view more information or edit properties, click the Properties button (it's just below the thumbnail image) and select Show Document Panel from the menu. PowerPoint opens the Document Properties dialog box, as shown in Figure 19.13.

FIGURE 19.13

Enter data to identify your presentation in the Properties dialog box.

In this dialog box, the name of the presentation author displays by default. (Change this by clicking the File tab, selecting Options, and entering a new user name.) You can also optionally enter a title, subject, keywords, category, status, and comments.

TIP To remove this data from a presentation before sharing, use the Document Inspector (File tab, Info, Check for Issues). See Chapter 17, "Sharing Presentations," for more information.

For more options, click the down arrow to the right of Properties and choose Advanced Properties from the menu. A dialog box with the name of your presentation appears. This dialog box enables you to specify file details, enter a custom summary, display detailed presentation statistics, and create custom properties.

Working with Slide Masters

PowerPoint helps you achieve a consistent look in your slide presentations. You want your audience to focus on the message and not be distracted by poor and inconsistent design from one slide to the next.

Slide masters help you achieve this uniformity by storing data about a presentation's theme and slide layouts—such as colors, fonts, effects, background, placeholders, and positioning—and applying it consistently throughout your presentation. Each presentation contains at least one slide master. In most cases, you won't need to do anything to the slide master but you can customize it if you choose. For example, you can change the default fonts, placeholders, background design, color scheme, or bullets, you can reposition placeholders, and you can add a logo. You can also create additional slide masters.

A template file (*.potx) can contain one or more slide masters. Each slide master can contain one or more sets of slide layouts, including custom layouts.

See Chapter 2, "Creating a Basic Presentation," and Chapter 3, "Customizing Themes and Backgrounds," for more information about themes and layouts.

Modifying the Slide Master

To modify your slide master, go to the View tab and click the Slide Master button. PowerPoint displays the slide master layout and editing screen (see Figure 19.14).

You can modify either the slide master, which affects the entire presentation's design, or the master for a specific slide layout, such as the title master or the title and content master.

 NOTE All changes you make to the title or other text while in the slide master editing screen apply to all slides in your slide presentation except those based on a specific layout master that overrides the slide master, thus helping you achieve consistency from slide to slide.

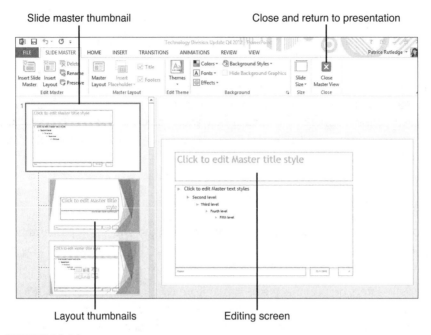

FIGURE 19.14

The slide master editing screen helps you change the overall look and layout of your custom design templates.

Place the mouse pointer over the thumbnails on the left side of the screen to display which thumbnail is for the overall slide master and which is for each layout master. Select the thumbnail to make formatting changes to the desired master. The master includes several areas you can modify: Title, Subtitle, Text, Date, Footer, and Number.

 NOTE In the Date, Footer, and Number areas, you normally don't add text but instead format the <date/time>, <footer>, and <#> placeholders. This information is added when you edit the header and footer. An exception might be the page numbering, where you can add and format "Page" before the <#> placeholder.

To modify an area, select it and apply the desired formatting changes from the Slide Master tab or the Format tab, which offers formatting options that should already be familiar to you. The Format tab appears when you click in the editing screen. Click the Close Master View button to exit and return to your presentation.

If you modify the slide master first, perhaps little needs to be changed for the title slide. However, you might make the title font larger, position it differently, or add a graphic object to the screen. Furthermore, you can delete the Date, Footer, and Number area boxes and create a different date or footer for the title slide.

 CAUTION Be sure that you have modified the slide master before changing the title layout. Initially the title master uses the same fonts and other attributes as the slide master.

Adding a Slide Master

In PowerPoint, a template file (*.potx) can have one or more slide masters. To add a slide master, follow these steps:

1. On the View tab, click the Slide Master button to open the slide master editing screen.

2. Click the Insert Slide Master button in the Edit Master group on the Slide Master tab. A custom slide master displays. The thumbnails for the slide master and its related layouts appear below the thumbnails for your existing slide master. If you previously had only a single slide master, your new slide master will be numbered as Slide Master 2, as shown in Figure 19.15.

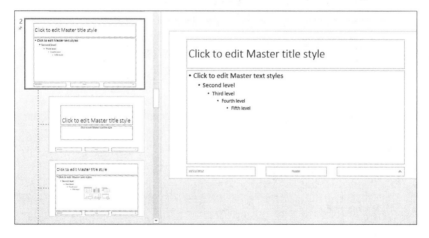

FIGURE 19.15

Easily identify multiple slide masters in PowerPoint.

3. Make any desired changes to the slide master and layouts just as you would with your original slide master. The Slide Master and Format tabs offer many formatting options.

4. Click the Save button on the Quick Access Toolbar to open the Save As dialog box.

5. Accept the default filename or enter a new name.

6. From the Save As Type drop-down list, choose PowerPoint Template and click the Save button. Your new slide master is now available in the template you saved.

Creating a Custom Layout

PowerPoint offers numerous predefined layouts—such as Title Slide, Title and Text, and Title and Content—that you can select by clicking the Layout button on the Home tab. These predefined layouts should be sufficient for most presentations, but sometimes you might need something a little different.

To create a custom layout, follow these steps:

1. Go to the View tab and click the Slide Master button. PowerPoint displays the slide master layout and editing screen.

2. Go to the Slide Master tab, select the thumbnail of the layout before which you want to add the custom layout, and click the Insert Layout button in the Edit Master group. A custom layout appears, as shown in Figure 19.16, whose thumbnail is just below the selected layout.

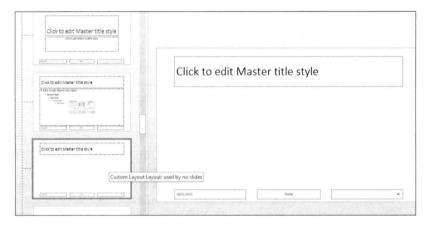

FIGURE 19.16

Create a custom layout if none of the standard layouts meets your needs.

3. By default, the custom layout contains a title placeholder and three footer placeholders for the date/time, generic footer, and slide number. To remove these placeholders, deselect the Title and Footers check boxes in the Master Layout group.

4. To add other placeholders, click the Insert Placeholder button in the Master Layout group. Options include the following placeholders: content, text, pictures, charts, tables, SmartArt, media, and online images.

5. Select a placeholder from the list, click a location on the slide layout, and drag the mouse to create an appropriately sized placeholder.

6. Continue adding placeholders and formatting your layout with the options on the Slide Master and Format tabs.

7. When you finish, select the thumbnail of the custom layout and click the Rename button in the Edit Master group on the Slide Master tab. The Rename Layout dialog box displays.

8. Enter a new name for your layout and click the Rename button.

9. Click the Save button on the Quick Access Toolbar to open the Save As dialog box.

10. Accept the default filename or enter a new name.

11. From the Save as Type drop-down list, choose PowerPoint Template and click the Save button. Your custom layout is now available when you click the New Slide button on the Home tab.

Renaming a Slide Master or Layout

If you create a new slide master or layout, you'll probably want to rename it. To rename a slide master or layout, follow these steps:

1. On the View tab, click the Slide Master button to open the Slide Master editing screen.

2. Select the thumbnail of the slide master or layout you want to rename on the left side of the screen.

3. Click the Rename button in the Edit Master group on the Slide Master tab. The Rename dialog box opens.

 NOTE If you're renaming a slide master, the name of this dialog box is Rename Master. If you're renaming a layout, the name is Rename Layout.

4. Enter the new name for the slide master or layout and then click the Rename button.

Duplicating a Slide Master or Layout

Sometimes you want to create a slide master or layout that is similar to something that currently exists, yet requires a few small changes. Rather than starting from scratch, you can duplicate the existing master or layout and make your changes from there.

To duplicate a slide master or layout, follow these steps:

1. On the View tab, click the Slide Master button to open the slide master editing screen.

2. Select the thumbnail of the slide master or layout you want to duplicate on the left side of the screen.

3. Right-click the thumbnail and choose either Duplicate Slide Master or Duplicate Layout from the menu. Alternatively, press Ctrl+D on the keyboard to duplicate. A duplicate of your slide master or layout displays, which you can then customize.

Deleting a Slide Master or Layout

If you make a mistake or no longer need a slide master or layout, you can delete it. To delete a slide master or layout, follow these steps:

1. On the View tab, click the Slide Master button to open the slide master editing screen.

2. Select the thumbnail of the slide master or layout you want to delete on the left side of the screen.

3. Click the Delete button in the Edit Master group on the Slide Master tab. The slide master or layout is deleted.

Preserving a Slide Master

If you want to retain a slide master with your presentation even though you haven't applied it to any slides, you can choose to preserve it.

To preserve a slide master, follow these steps:

1. On the View tab, click the Slide Master button to open the slide master editing screen.

2. Select the thumbnail of the slide master you want to preserve on the left side of the screen.

3. Click the Preserve button in the Edit Master group on the Slide Master tab. The slide master is preserved.

Applying a Theme to a Slide Master

If you want to apply a new theme to a slide master, you can easily do so. When you apply a new theme to a master, the theme also applies to the layouts that comprise the master. Keep in mind that if you have only one slide master, applying a theme creates a second slide master with the chosen theme. If you apply a new theme to a slide master other than your original slide master, the master's theme changes to your new selection.

To apply a theme to a slide master, follow these steps:

1. On the View tab, click the Slide Master button to open the slide master editing screen.

2. Select the thumbnail of the slide master whose theme you want to change on the left side of the screen.

3. Click the Themes button in the Edit Theme group on the Slide Master tab.

4. Choose a new theme to apply from the gallery. If you selected a slide master other than the original master, the theme is applied to the master. Otherwise, PowerPoint creates a new slide master with the chosen theme.

See Chapter 3 for more information about PowerPoint themes.

Modifying the Handout and Notes Masters

In addition to the presentation itself, PowerPoint lets you modify the handout and notes masters. To modify the handout master, go to the View tab and click the Handout Master button. PowerPoint displays the Handout Master editing screen and Handout Master tab (see Figure 19.17).

On the handout master, you can perform the following tasks:

- Choose the number of slides you intend to include on each handout page by clicking the Slides Per Page button on the Handout Master tab. Choices include one, two, three, four, six, and nine handouts per page.

- Modify, reposition, or delete the Header, Footer, Date, and Page Area text boxes.

- Access the Format tab by selecting an object, where you can make edits to the text on the handout master.

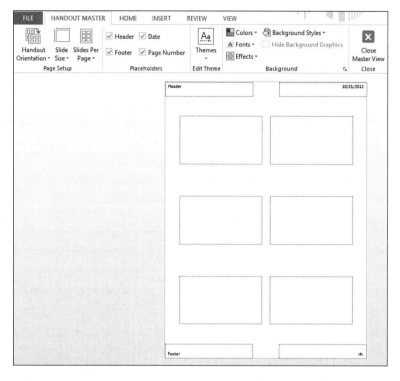

FIGURE 19.17

The handout master defines the default layout for your template's printed handouts.

 TIP You can easily change the number of slides to be included in the handouts in the Print dialog box when you actually print the handouts, without customizing the handout master.

To modify the notes master, go to the View tab and click the Notes Master button. PowerPoint displays the Notes Master editing screen (see Figure 19.18).

On the notes master, you can perform the following tasks:

- Reposition or resize the slide area, depending on how much area you want for the text (notes).

- Reposition or resize the notes area.

- Modify, reposition, or delete the Header, Footer, Date, and Page Area text boxes.

- Change the notes page orientation to either portrait or landscape.

- Access the Format tab by selecting an object, where you can make edits to the text on the handout master.

FIGURE 19.18

The notes master defines the default layout for your template's printed notes.

 CAUTION   Although you can change the background colors and color schemes for the handout and notes masters, you probably won't want to do so. Handouts and notes are usually printed, and background colors aren't necessary or wanted. You can, however, add a graphic element, such as a company logo, which then displays on each printed page.

THE ABSOLUTE MINIMUM

Here are the key points to remember from this chapter:

- The Quick Access Toolbar is a customizable toolbar that contains popular commands you may use regardless of which tab currently displays.

- PowerPoint lets you customize many basic options, such as how you edit, save, and print your presentations and how you view PowerPoint. You can also customize the Ribbon and the Quick Access Toolbar.

- You can view, modify, and delete presentation properties such as the author name, title, subject, keywords, and more.

- Customizable slide masters help you achieve a consistent look in your presentation slides.

ACCESSING POWERPOINT ON THE WEB AND MOBILE DEVICES

Even if you're away from the computer where you installed PowerPoint 2013—or away from any computer, for that matter—you can access your PowerPoint presentations. In this chapter, you find out how to access PowerPoint on the Web and from mobile devices. You also discover how to make the most of PowerPoint's integration with SkyDrive as well as the PowerPoint web app.

Using SkyDrive

By default, you can store and share your presentations on SkyDrive, Microsoft's online storage solution. SkyDrive offers several gigabytes of free online storage that you can use to collaborate with colleagues anywhere in the world using a PC, Mac, or mobile device (such as smartphone, iPad, or other tablet). SkyDrive requires a free Microsoft account to access. If you have an existing account with another Microsoft application such as Hotmail or Messenger, you already have an account. If you don't, you can sign up for a free account when you access SkyDrive.

 CAUTION Be aware that SkyDrive could change or include new features in the future.

 NOTE You can also share presentations on SharePoint. Because installing and deploying SharePoint is normally the domain of a corporate IT department, it's beyond the scope of this book. To learn more about SharePoint, go to http://sharepoint.microsoft.com.

Getting Started with SkyDrive

To log in to SkyDrive, go to http://skydrive.com (see Figure 20.1) and enter the username and password for your Microsoft account. If you don't have a Microsoft account, sign up for a free account by clicking the Sign Up Now link.

FIGURE 20.1

Getting started with SkyDrive takes only a few minutes.

On SkyDrive, shown in Figure 20.2, you can perform the following tasks:

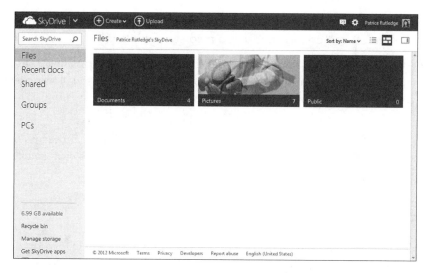

FIGURE 20.2

Store, share, and collaborate on presentations on SkyDrive.

- Create new folders by clicking the Create button and selecting Folder from the menu. You can share folders with everyone (a public folder), only people in your network, or select people you have provided access to. Alternatively, you can make your folder private so that only you can access it.

- Add files to your folders by clicking the Upload button. From here, you can browse your computer and select the files you want to upload. You can upload files with sizes up to 300MB on SkyDrive.com or up to 2GB from the SkyDrive app that you install on your computer. See section, "Adding Files to SkyDrive," later in this chapter, for more information.

- Open individual files by clicking a folder icon and then clicking the file's icon.

- Create a new PowerPoint presentation by clicking the Create button and selecting PowerPoint Presentation from the menu. You can also choose to create a new Word, Excel, or OneNote file.

- Share folders and files by right-clicking them and selecting Share from the menu. From here, you can send a link by email, share on social sites such as Facebook and Twitter, and share a link that enables others to view or edit your content.

- Create groups of people to share and collaborate with by clicking the Groups link.

- Increase your storage capacity by clicking the Manage Storage link in the lower-left corner and choosing a paid storage plan.

- Get free SkyDrive apps by clicking the Get SkyDrive Apps link in the lower-left corner. Options include a Windows desktop app as well as apps for the Windows phone, iPhone, iPad, or an Android device.

 TIP This chapter covers just a subset of what you can do on SkyDrive. For more details, go to http://windows.microsoft.com/ en-US/skydrive/help-center.

Adding Files to SkyDrive

Although you can save your PowerPoint presentations to SkyDrive by default, you can also do so manually.

 TIP Adding files to SkyDrive isn't limited to PowerPoint presentations. You can also store any other files on SkyDrive, such as other Office documents, photos, PDFs, and so forth.

To add an existing file to SkyDrive, follow these steps:

1. In the SkyDrive main window (refer to Figure 20.2), select the folder where you want to store your file.

2. Click the Upload button.

3. Navigate to the file you want to upload and then click the Open button to return to SkyDrive. PowerPoint uploads the file to the selected folder.

Creating a New Presentation in SkyDrive

Another option is to create a new PowerPoint presentation directly in SkyDrive. You can edit this presentation in the web app or download it later for use in the desktop version of PowerPoint.

To create a new PowerPoint presentation in SkyDrive, follow these steps:

1. In the SkyDrive main window (refer to Figure 20.2), select the folder where you want to store the presentation you create.

2. Click the Create button and select PowerPoint Presentation.

3. Enter a presentation name and then click the Create button, as shown in Figure 20.3.

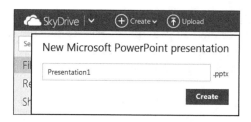

FIGURE 20.3

Create a PowerPoint presentation directly in SkyDrive.

4. Select a theme to apply to your presentation, select an optional variant, and then click the Apply button (see Figure 20.4).

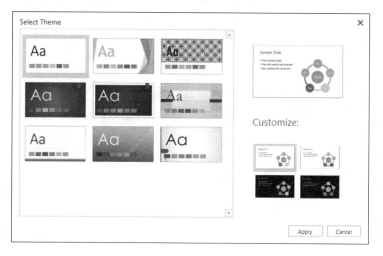

FIGURE 20.4

Themes and variants are also available in the web app.

The Microsoft PowerPoint web app opens in edit mode, where you can add content to your presentation. See section, "Editing a Presentation in the PowerPoint Web App," later in this chapter, for more information.

Using the Microsoft PowerPoint Web App

Microsoft Office offers web-based versions of its most popular applications, including PowerPoint, Word, Excel, and OneNote. To use the PowerPoint web app, you need either Microsoft SharePoint (primarily for use in large organizations) or a SkyDrive account (for use by anyone with web access).

With the web app, you can view and edit PowerPoint presentations from any computer. It's important to note, however, that the web app's editing features comprise a subset of the features available in the desktop version of PowerPoint. You should plan to perform only basic edits in the web app.

 NOTE This section focuses on accessing the web app on SkyDrive. Installing and deploying SharePoint is normally the domain of a corporate IT department, and someone from that department would set up your access rights to the web app via SharePoint.

Exploring the PowerPoint Web App

You can access the web app by creating a new presentation (refer to section, "Creating a New Presentation in SkyDrive") or by opening an existing presentation (see section, "Editing Presentations in the PowerPoint Web App").

Figure 20.5 displays the PowerPoint web app.

FIGURE 20.5

Access PowerPoint on the Web with the PowerPoint web app.

The menu options include the following:

- **File**—Open Backstage View.

- **Edit Presentation**—Edit your presentation in either the web app or the desktop version of PowerPoint.

- **Share**—Share your presentation by email or on social sites.

- **Start Slide Show**—Display your presentation in slide show view.

- **Comments**—Add or view comments.

To return to SkyDrive, click the SkyDrive link in the upper-left corner of the screen.

Editing Presentations in the PowerPoint Web App

You can edit any presentation that you create or store in SkyDrive. To edit a presentation, follow these steps:

1. Right-click the presentation you want to edit and select Open in PowerPoint Web App from the menu. If you haven't activated the web app, you're prompted to do so.

2. From the Edit Presentation menu, select Edit in PowerPoint Web App (see Figure 20.6).

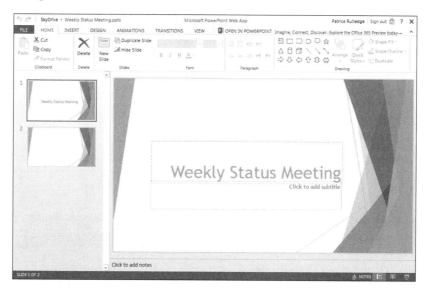

FIGURE 20.6

Edit directly in the Web App.

3. Edit your presentation. The commands and buttons on these tabs function in much the same way as they do in the desktop version of PowerPoint. The main difference is that you can perform the commands online on a computer that doesn't have PowerPoint installed.

NOTE The PowerPoint web app doesn't have a Save button because it saves your changes automatically.

THE ABSOLUTE MINIMUM

Here are the key points to remember from this chapter:

- PowerPoint works directly with SkyDrive, Microsoft's online storage and collaboration solution.

- The PowerPoint web app enables you to view, edit, and collaborate on presentations on the Web.

IN THIS CHAPTER

- Extending PowerPoint with Third-Party Software
- Getting Creative with Third-Party Templates, Backgrounds, and Clip Art
- Enhancing Your PowerPoint Experience with External Hardware
- Integrating PowerPoint with Twitter

EXTENDING POWERPOINT WITH THIRD-PARTY TOOLS

PowerPoint offers a vast array of advanced features, but even the most comprehensive application can't be all things to all people. Fortunately, a number of third-party developers have created unique and useful tools with the PowerPoint user in mind.

In this chapter, you learn about third-party software and tools that make PowerPoint even more useful, creative, and powerful.

Extending PowerPoint with Third-Party Software

With its numerous features, PowerPoint 2013 lessens the need for many third-party applications. However, there are still times when you might want to take advantage of the advanced functionality of specialty software. This section covers a trio of options worth considering.

Camtasia Studio

Camtasia Studio 8 (www.techsmith.com/camtasia.html) is a complete video recording, editing, and publishing solution. With Camtasia, you can record your presentation directly in PowerPoint and then enhance it with Camtasia's many powerful features before publishing. Options include editing audio and video, inserting title clips, applying visual effects such as zoom-and-pan, adding callouts and hotspots, and creating picture-in-picture recordings with video.

If you want to create e-learning tutorials, Camtasia Studio also offers interactive quizzes and SCORM (Sharable Content Object Reference Model) compliance. Using PowerPoint with Camtasia is a popular way to create e-learning programs quickly, in an environment that's familiar to any Microsoft Office user.

 NOTE If you're new to e-learning, some of its terminology might be unfamiliar to you. Most e-learning solutions are SCORM-compliant. This means that they meet the standards specified by SCORM for web-based e-learning systems. Many e-learning solutions, particularly those run by larger organizations, use a learning management system (LMS) to manage their e-learning content and delivery.

Articulate Studio

Articulate Studio '09 (www.articulate.com) offers the following suite of e-learning applications that integrate with PowerPoint, each of which you can also purchase separately:

- **Articulate Presenter**—Create e-learning courses in PowerPoint and convert them to Flash. Advanced features include animation support, voice synchronization, presenter videos, learning game and quiz integration, SCORM-compliance, LMS support, and more.

- **Articulate Quizmaker**—Create custom Flash quizzes and surveys that integrate with Articulate Presenter and offer more than 20 different question types.

- **Engage**—Engage your audience with interactive content, including timelines, media tours, pyramids, guided images, glossaries, labeled graphics, and tabs.

- **Video Encoder**—Convert videos to Flash video format and edit, crop, and format videos.

Another option is Articulate Online, an alternative to a complex LMS system, which provides online reporting and quiz/survey tracking.

 NOTE Articulate is currently developing a new version of its software, Articulate Studio '13, which will offer publishing to the iPad and HTML.

Adobe Presenter

Adobe Presenter 8 (www.adobe.com/products/presenter.html) enables you to create multimedia presentations and on-demand and real-time e-learning courses from within the familiar PowerPoint environment. Then, you can extend your presentation with quizzes, surveys, interactivity, and more. With the Presenter mobile app, you can also publish your videos to tablet devices, including the iPad.

Presenter integrates with Adobe Captivate (for software simulations and branched scenarios) and Adobe Connect (for web conferencing) to design a complete solution. You can purchase Adobe Presenter on its own or as part of the Adobe eLearning Suite of applications.

Getting Creative with Third-Party Templates, Backgrounds, and Clip Art

Even though Office.com (http://office.microsoft.com) offers an array of templates, backgrounds, clip art, photos, videos, and animations to use in your presentations, sometimes you just want something different.

The good news is that numerous third-party providers offer collections of templates, clip art, and more. You're sure to find the exact match for your presentation needs. Here are some interesting places to start:

- **CrystalGraphics** (www.crystalgraphics.com) provides a solid collection of PowerPlugs, tools that enhance the quality of any PowerPoint presentation. Options include video backgrounds, transitions, charts, pictures, animations, templates, TV-style 3-D titles, 3-D characters, shapes, presentation shells, photo animations, map slides, and music.

- **Ppted.com** (www.ppted.com) offers another extensive collection of PowerPoint templates, textures, and backgrounds. You can also purchase many third-party PowerPoint products and related hardware from this site.

- **Clipart.com** (www.clipart.com) is a solid resource for images, offering a vast collection of more than 10 million objects, including clip art, photos, fonts, and sounds. Clipart.com is available by subscription, with timeframes ranging from one week to one year.

- **Presentation Pro** (www.presentationpro.com) offers PowerPoint templates, graphics, icons, animations, video clips, layouts, and map slides, many of which are bundled into cost-saving packages. Presentation Pro also sells a variety of PowerPoint plug-ins, including HTML iSpring Converter, Flip PowerPoint (to create flipbooks), Demo Creator, and PDF to PowerPoint.

Enhancing Your PowerPoint Experience with External Hardware

Software isn't the only option for third-party PowerPoint tools. Several unique hardware solutions are available that solve common problems and make delivering PowerPoint presentations a more productive experience.

Impatica ShowMate

The Impatica ShowMate (www.impatica.com) is a small device that connects your smartphone to a projector, enabling you to deliver a PowerPoint presentation without the need for a bulky computer. This plug-and-present solution works with BlackBerry, Palm, Sony Ericsson, and Windows Mobile smartphones.

Impatica also offers Impatica for PowerPoint 5, an application that enables you to create e-Learning for computers, tablets, and smartphones.

TurningPoint

TurningPoint (www.turningtechnologies.com) is a PowerPoint add-in that works with wireless keypads to form an audience response system you can use in real time during your presentations. Members of your audience receive a credit card–sized ResponseCard keypad that they click in response to an interactive polling slide in your PowerPoint presentation. The results are submitted to a wireless receiver, which you can then share with your audience or analyze for reporting purposes.

NOTE Audience response systems such as TurningPoint are popular in both the corporate and education markets. TurningPoint offers several additional features specifically for use in schools and universities, including the ability to integrate special ExamView questions into your PowerPoint presentation.

Papershow

Papershow (www.papershow.com) contains a Bluetooth digital pen, USB key loaded with software, and interactive paper that transmits to your screen, all bundled in a case that fits in your pocket. You can import your PowerPoint presentation into Papershow, print it on the interactive paper, and then annotate your presentations on a screen.

Laser Mouse

The Laser Mouse (www.lasermouse.com) is a long-range wireless remote mouse with a built-in laser pointer. It's designed specifically with the delivery of PowerPoint presentations in mind, with a navigation disk and slide advance button.

Integrating PowerPoint with Twitter

The use of Twitter during conference and other large presentations is on the rise. Rather than having your audience's commentary take place solely on this backchannel, you can become part of it and integrate Twitter into your presentation. This section introduces you to two innovative ways to do just that.

Poll Everywhere

Poll Everywhere (www.polleverywhere.com) enables you to maximize the use of Twitter during a live presentation by polling your audience.

To start, you ask your audience a question—either a multiple-choice question or an open-ended question. They respond via Twitter, SMS text message, a smartphone's web browser, or a computer's web browser. You can display the real-time poll results directly in your PowerPoint presentation.

SAP PowerPoint Twitter Tools

SAP (http://timoelliott.com/blog/powerpoint-twitter-tools) has released a series of free PowerPoint Twitter tools that increase audience interactivity during your presentations. These include the following:

- PowerPoint Twitter feedback slides, which display tweets on PowerPoint slides during your presentation, with the capability to filter spam or any content you don't want to share

- PowerPoint AutoTweet, which enables you to tweet key points during your presentation

- PowerPoint Twitter voting, with real-time results displayed in bar charts and pie charts

- PowerPoint Twitter ticker bar, which displays the last ten tweets at the bottom of your presentation slides

- PowerPoint mood meter, which enables your audience to communicate their agreement or disagreement with key presentation points

- PowerPoint crowd meter, used to monitor and display the crowd noise in your room

- PowerPoint zoom text, which zooms text on your screen

- PowerPoint Twitter update bar

THE ABSOLUTE MINIMUM

Here are the key points to remember from this chapter:

- You can expand on the power of PowerPoint with third-party software, tools, and hardware.

- If you want to create e-learning with PowerPoint, consider an application such as Camtasia Studio, Articulate Studio, or Adobe Presenter.

- Although PowerPoint and Office.com offer numerous design options, third-party vendors can give you access to even more themes, templates, backgrounds, clip art, photos, videos, and animations.

- External hardware can often solve common problems and make delivering PowerPoint presentations a more productive experience.

- You can integrate PowerPoint with Twitter during a conference presentation using tools that help you engage your audience, take a poll, and manage the backchannel.

Index

MAKE THE MOST OF YOUR SMARTPHONE, TABLET, COMPUTER, AND MORE!

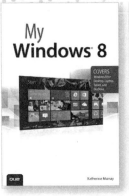

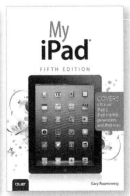

ISBN 13: 9780789749482   ISBN 13: 9780789749635   ISBN 13: 9780789748515   ISBN 13: 9780789750334

Full-Color, Step-by-Step Guides

The "My..." series is a visually rich, task-based series to help you get up and running with your new device and technology and tap into some of the hidden, or less obvious features. The organized, task-based format allows you to quickly and easily find exactly the task you want to accomplish, and then shows you how to achieve it with minimal text and plenty of visual cues.

Visit quepublishing.com/mybooks to learn more about the My... book series from Que.

quepublishing.com

Try Safari Books Online FREE for 15 days

Get online access to Thousands of Books and Videos

Safari Books Online

FREE 15-DAY TRIAL + 15% OFF*
informit.com/safaritrial

Feed your brain

Gain unlimited access to thousands of books and videos about technology, digital media and professional development from O'Reilly Media, Addison-Wesley, Microsoft Press, Cisco Press, McGraw Hill, Wiley, WROX, Prentice Hall, Que, Sams, Apress, Adobe Press and other top publishers.

See it, believe it

Watch hundreds of expert-led instructional videos on today's hottest topics.

WAIT, THERE'S MORE!

Gain a competitive edge

Be first to learn about the newest technologies and subjects with Rough Cuts pre-published manuscripts and new technology overviews in Short Cuts.

Accelerate your project

Copy and paste code, create smart searches that let you know when new books about your favorite topics are available, and customize your library with favorites, highlights, tags, notes, mash-ups and more.

* Available to new subscribers only. Discount applies to the Safari Library and is valid for first 12 consecutive monthly billing cycles. Safari Library is not available in all countries.

que®   quepublishing.com

| Browse by Topic ▾ | Browse by Format ▾ | USING | More ▾ |

Store | Safari Books Online

QUEPUBLISHING.COM
Your Publisher for Home & Office Computing

Quepublishing.com includes all your favorite—
and some new—Que series and authors to help you
learn about computers and technology for the home,
office, and business.

Looking for tips and tricks, video tutorials, articles and
interviews, podcasts, and resources to make your life
easier? Visit **quepublishing.com**.

- **Read the latest articles and sample chapters**
  by Que's expert authors

- **Free podcasts** provide information on the
  hottest tech topics

- **Register your Que products** and receive updates,
  supplemental content, and a coupon to be used
  on your next purchase

- **Check out promotions and special offers**
  available from Que and our retail partners

- **Join the site** and receive members-only offers
  and benefits

Business Management
Finance and Investing
Graphics, Pictures & Video
Gadgets & Hardware
General Computing
Entertainment & Gaming
Internet & Web Apps
Computer Software
Operating Systems
Web Design & Development

QUE NEWSLETTER
quepublishing.com/newsletter

 twitter.com/
quepublishing

 facebook.com/
quepublishing

 youtube.com/
quepublishing

 quepublishing.com/
rss

®   Que Publishing is a publishing imprint of Pearson

CHECK OUT THESE OTHER
ABSOLUTE BEGINNER'S GUIDES
FROM QUE PUBLISHING

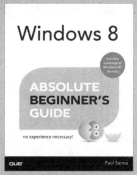

Windows 8

ABSOLUTE BEGINNER'S GUIDE

no experience necessary!

Paul Sanna

ISBN: 9780789749932

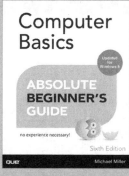

Computer Basics

ABSOLUTE BEGINNER'S GUIDE

no experience necessary!

Sixth Edition

Michael Miller

ISBN: 9780789750013

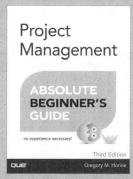

Project Management

ABSOLUTE BEGINNER'S GUIDE

no experience necessary!

Third Edition

Gregory M. Horine

ISBN: 9780789750105

No experience necessary!

Coming in 2013

Project 2013 Absolute Beginner's Guide, ISBN: 9780789750556

SharePoint 2013 Absolute Beginner's Guide, ISBN: 9780789748553

Access 2013 Absolute Beginner's Guide, ISBN: 9780789748713

quepublishing.com

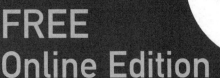

FREE
Online Edition

Safari
Books Online

Your purchase of *PowerPoint 2013 Absolute Beginner's Guide* includes access to a free online edition for 45 days through the **Safari Books Online** subscription service. Nearly every Que book is available online through **Safari Books Online**, along with thousands of books and videos from publishers such as Addison-Wesley Professional, Cisco Press, Exam Cram, IBM Press, O'Reilly Media, Prentice Hall, Sams, and VMware Press.

Safari Books Online is a digital library providing searchable, on-demand access to thousands of technology, digital media, and professional development books and videos from leading publishers. With one monthly or yearly subscription price, you get unlimited access to learning tools and information on topics including mobile app and software development, tips and tricks on using your favorite gadgets, networking, project management, graphic design, and much more.

Activate your FREE Online Edition at
informit.com/safarifree

STEP 1:   Enter the coupon code: FWJUHFH.

STEP 2:   New Safari users, complete the brief registration form.
           Safari subscribers, just log in.

If you have difficulty registering on Safari or accessing the online edition,
please e-mail customer-service@safaribooksonline.com